Integration of Developmentally Disabled Individuals into the Community
---

Integration of Developmentally Disabled Individuals into the Community

Edited by
Angela R. Novak and **Laird W. Heal, Ph.D.**
Department of Special Education
University of Illinois, Urbana

Foreword by **Philip Roos**
Executive Director
National Association for Retarded Citizens

Baltimore · London

Paul H. Brookes, Publishers
Post Office Box 10624
Baltimore, Maryland 21204

Copyright 1980 by Paul H. Brookes Publishing Co., Inc.
All rights reserved.

Typeset by The Composing Room of Michigan, Grand Rapids.
Manufactured in the United States of America by Universal
  Lithographers, Inc., Cockeysville, Maryland.

Library of Congress Cataloging in Publication Data

Main entry under title:

Integration of developmentally disabled individuals
  into the community.

  Bibliography: p. 209
  Includes index.
  1. Mentally handicapped—United States—Addresses, essays, lectures. 2. Developmentally disabled—United States—Addresses, essays, lectures. I. Novak, Angela R., 1951–   II. Heal, Laird W., 1933–
HV3006.A4I57   362.3   80-21082
ISBN 0-933716-10-9 (pbk.)

Contents

Contributors vii
Foreword/*Philip Roos* ix
Preface xiii
Acknowledgments xvii
Dedication... xix

Part I	UNDERLYING CONCEPTS OF DEINSTITUTIONALIZATION
Chapter 1	Deinstitutionalization and Mentally Retarded Persons / *Barry Willer, Richard C. Scheerenberger, and James Intagliata* ...3
Chapter 2	Empirical Support for Deinstitutionalization / *Mary E. Pilewski and Laird W. Heal* 21
Chapter 3	Ideological Responses of Society to its Handicapped Citizens / *Laird W. Heal* 35

Part II	THE DEINSTITUTIONALIZED PERSON IN THE COMMUNITY
Chapter 4	Characteristics of Community Residential Facilities / *Laird W. Heal, Angela R. Novak, Carol K. Sigelman, and Harvey N. Switzky* 45
Chapter 5	Factors That Affect the Success of Community Placement / *Carol K. Sigelman, Angela R. Novak, Laird W. Heal, and Harvey N. Switzky* 57
Chapter 6	Generic Services for Developmentally Disabled Citizens / *Vernon T. Savage, Angela R. Novak, and Laird W. Heal* ..75
Chapter 7	Physical and Social Integration of Developmentally Disabled Individuals into the Community / *Francis A. Moreau, Angela R. Novak, and Carol K. Sigelman* 91

Part III TRAINING FOR INTEGRATION

Chapter 8 A Behavioral Approach to Integrating Individuals into the Community / *Richard P. Schutz, R. Timm Vogelsberg, and Frank R. Rusch* 107

Chapter 9 Issues in Communication Research Related to Integration of Developmentally Disabled Individuals / *George R. Karlan* 121

Part IV ADDITIONAL PERSPECTIVES TO DEINSTITUTIONALIZATION

Chapter 10 Evaluation of Residential Alternatives / *Laird W. Heal and Thomas J. Laidlaw* 141

Chapter 11 Legislative Constraints and Facilitations for Community Integration / *Cheryl Hanley-Maxwell and Laird W. Heal* .. 163

Chapter 12 Litigation Concerning Community Integration / *Nancy Emmel* 173

Chapter 13 Backlash to the Deinstitutionalization Movement / *Angela R. Novak* 181

Part V CONCLUSIONS

Chapter 14 Implications for Direct Service Planning, Delivery, and Policy / *James E. Martin and Thomas J. Laidlaw* 193

Epilogue: A Perspective on the Present and Notes for New Directions / *Angela R. Novak* 203

References 209

Index 235

Contributors

Nancy Emmel
Law School
St. Louis University
St. Louis, MO 63108

Laird W. Heal
Department of Special Education
University of Illinois
288 Education
Urbana, IL 61801

James Intagliata
Division of Community Psychiatry
State University of New York
Buffalo, NY 14215

George Karlan
Department of Special Education
University of Illinois
288 Education
Urbana, IL 61801

Thomas Laidlaw
Developmental Services Center
1304 W. Bradley
Champaign, IL 61820

James Martin
Department of Special Education
University of Illinois
288 Education
Urbana, IL 61820

Cheryl Hanley-Maxwell
Regional Educational Services Agency
407 W. Nevada
Urbana, IL 61801

Francis A. Moreau
Department of Vocational and
 Technical Education
340 Education Building
University of Illinois
Urbana, IL 61801

Angela Novak
Department of Special Education
University of Illinois
288 Education
Urbana, IL 61801

Mary E. Pilewski
Developmental Services Center
1304 W. Bradley
Champaign, IL 61820

Philip Roos
Executive Director
National Association for
 Retarded Citizens
Arlington, TX 76011

Frank R. Rusch
Department of Special Education
University of Illinois
288 Education
Urbana, IL 61801

Vernon T. Savage
Psychological Services
Oberlin College
Room 208 Peters Hall
Oberlin, OH 44014

Richard Scheerenberger
Central Wisconsin Center for the
  Developmentally Disabled
317 Knutson Dr.
Madison, WI 53704

Richard Schutz
Department of Special Education
University of Illinois
288 Education
Urbana, IL 61801

Carol K. Sigelman
Department of Psychology
Eastern Kentucky University
Richmond, KY 40475

Harvey N. Switzky
Department of Special Education
Northern Illinois University
DeKalb, IL 60115

R. Timm Vogelsberg
Center for Developmental Disabilities
University of Vermont
499 C Waterman Bldg.
Burlington, VT 05405

Barry Willer
Division of Community Psychiatry
State University of New York
Buffalo, NY 14215

Foreword

Philip Roos

Approaches to mental retardation and related developmental disabilities have undergone extraordinary changes during the past two decades. No longer is "humane custodial care" considered an appropriate option, even for severely handicapped persons. The pall of hopelessness that dominated the field of mental retardation for centuries has finally been replaced by a new optimism, based in part on technological innovations and in part on sociological and legal developments. The dramatic improvement in services for mentally retarded people reflects underlying ideologies that have redirected professional thinking.

Perhaps the most fundamental of these concepts is the principle of individualization, which holds that every mentally retarded or developmentally disabled person should be considered as a unique person, with individual needs and goals. Thus, individualized planning of services and programs has become a cornerstone of accreditation standards and laws.

This concept developed, at least in part, as a reaction against regimentation and supersimplistic solutions predicated on labeling. The principle of self-actualization, another important concept, holds that all retarded and developmentally disabled persons should be provided the maximum opportunity to make their own decisions and to shape their own destinies. This principle requires designing conditions for these people that will offer them choices among desirable alternatives. It has also been incorporated in laws and standards that require retarded individuals or their representatives to actively participate in the design and evaluation of their own programs.

Another key principle that underlies many of the recent changes in the field of mental retardation and developmental disability is the so-called developmental model. This concept advocates approaching every developmentally disabled person with positive expectations that he or she has the capacity to grow, learn, and develop. This model emphasizes the potency of environmental conditions and the malleability of the human organism. Program goals are identified as fostering individuals' capacity to cope with their environment, increasing the complexity of their behavior, and enhancing their human qualities, as culturally defined.

Perhaps the most influential of these current concepts is the principle of normalization. When first developed in the Scandinavian countries in the 1960s, this principle was the result of concern with practices that fostered deviancy by dealing with handicapped people in denormalized ways. Thus, normalization was designed to remedy the effects of denormalization. When imported to the United States in the late 1960s, normalization was defined as providing retarded people with conditions that approximate the normal conditions of life to the greatest degree possible. The goal of normalization was to normalize environments and not people. The implicit assumption was often made, however, that normalizing environments would result in more normalized behavior.

It was not until 1972, however, that Wolfensberger redefined normalization to include the goal of generating and/or maintaining normative behavior. This interpretation of normalization is quite different from the earlier model, in that the intent is to normalize both environments and people. Yet normalization has been widely used as the rationale for all kinds of changes without stipulating which of the two common interpretations of the principle is intended. Indeed, many of those using the concept may be unaware that it has at least two different interpretations, which may lead to divergent consequences.

One of the major concerns in the area of mental retardation and developmental disability has been the provision of residential services. This emphasis can be related in part to the importance that we place on our home as a major source of security and emotional gratification. It is also related to the concern that a significant number of retarded people may be incapable of living independently, so that some form of supervised living situations is an essential component of any comprehensive service system. The emphasis placed on residential services can also be traced to the preeminence that multipurpose institutions have achieved since their inception over one hundred years ago. Indeed, for decades the institution was the only clearly defined service for mentally retarded persons.

As carefully documented in this book, recent years have witnessed a major shift in orientation toward institutions. The term "deinstitutionalization" has been generally adopted to refer to a three-pronged approach to decentralize residential services and improve their quality. These three elements consist of: (1) preventing institutional placements and minimizing length of placements; (2) development of community-based residential alternatives; and (3) improving institutions so as to better meet the needs of those who can allegedly benefit from institutional placement.

Unfortunately, deinstitutionalization has become the focus of controversy, polarization, and intense emotionality. This is due in part to supersimplistic misinterpretation of the concept as implying the total elimination of institutions. The term itself has acquired connotations suggesting that it refers to an "anti"-institutional movement. As a result, it may have lost its value as an objective description of a complex process, and might best be replaced by a term that has not yet acquired strong affective valence.

Great gains have been made in improving the quality and diversity of residential services for mentally retarded and other developmentally disabled people. These gains have been primarily the result of the new ideologies noted above, translated into social and legal action. It has become increasingly apparent, however, that these ideologies rest on ethical and philosophical premises rather than on empirical evidence. Many of the assertions supporting changes in services for mentally retarded and developmentally disabled people have been advanced with strong conviction, but often with minimal research support. It is not surprising that, as the conflict surrounding deinstitutionalization has intensified, decision makers and courts have increasingly insisted on empirical data to substantiate the validity of claims regarding the merits of various residential options.

This book now provides a detailed compilation of research findings on a wide spectrum of subjects related to the integration of mentally retarded and other developmentally disabled people into the community. The authors have carefully presented a wealth of data and systematically interpreted their significance regarding current ideologies and controversial issues. They have also attempted to assess the limitations of the evidence, and they have skillfully identified important unanswered questions. One of the major contributions of the book is that it contains concrete proposals for further studies designed to clarify important unresolved issues.

This scholarly analysis of the movement toward residential decentralization reveals that a great deal of relevant research has already been completed. Much of the evidence clearly supports current ideology regarding the value of integrating mentally retarded and other developmentally disabled people into community settings, but not all of the research is unequivocal on this issue. It is becoming clearer that many of the issues are highly complex. Obviously, a great deal more research is needed to provide meaningful answers to important questions, many of which are identified in this book. We now have a firm empirical foundation on which to build the scientific investigations that will help to resolve some of the important questions that remain unanswered.

Preface

The process of social change affects the planners of the change, those to whom the change is directed, and the members of the social system directly and indirectly affected by the change. Seldom has a social reform moved as swiftly from conceptualization to implementation as the movement called deinstitutionalization. Stimulated primarily by the report of the President's Panel on Mental Retardation in 1962, it was a brief five years before the growth of institutions for persons who were mentally retarded was arrested and reversed. The replacement of public residential facilities by various community-based residential alternatives for the nation's developmentally disabled citizens is one of the most remarkable social changes in this century, ranking with the desegregation of the public schools in its ideological and political impact.

Because of the deinstitutionalization movement, human service professionals are facing important changes in policies, decision making, and in the philosophy of what and how residential, vocational, medical, social, educational, recreational, and community services shall be provided to formerly institutionalized and other developmentally disabled individuals. Handicapped persons are experiencing environmental and psychological change as they are moved to smaller facilities, homes, and apartments in the world outside the institution. The community that is receiving these deinstitutionalized individuals is changing its stance toward who its neighbors are and should be, its perception of deviancy, and its conception of its own homogeneity.

As social scientists, we are interested in monitoring the events of this important reform, and in noting the facts and interpretations that will facilitate society's understanding of its past, present, and future. Thus, the core of this manuscript is a summary of current knowledge about the phenomenon called "deinstitutionalization." This is a book for those interested in how mentally retarded and other developmentally disabled persons who have been released from institutions are succeeding in living in the community, and how the community is reacting to its new neighbors. It is a statement about the *process* of deinstitutionalization.

The first section of the book deals with the underlying concepts involved in deinstitutionalization. Chapter 1 presents an overview of the deinstitutionalization process from the perspective of the community mental health movement that directly anticipated it. It analyzes the deinstitutionalization movement in terms of three components: prevention of institutionalization of candidates who can be assimilated into the community; normalization of institutional conditions for those whose current least restrictive residential alternative is a public institution; and discharge of those who are currently institutionalized. Two of these premises—the historical commingling of developmental disabilities with mental health, and the position that improved institutions are a valid alternative in the continuum of residential alternatives—are offered here for historical comprehensiveness only; after Chapter 1, the philosophy and focus of this text is integration and the components of successful life in the community. Chapters 2 and 3, respectively, set out empirical and ideological rationales for community integration of handicapped individuals, and conclude the background information section of the book.

The deinstitutionalized person functioning in the community is the subject of the second section. Chapter 4 describes the types and characteristics of existing community residential alternatives. Research about those individuals who live successfully in these facilities, what environments facilitate successful placement, and which community settings bode success for which types of individuals, is summarized in Chapter 5. Chapter 6 describes generic community services available to developmentally disabled citizens and stresses their importance for the success of the individuals involved. Chapter 7 assesses various aspects of the extent and quality of physical and social integration of developmentally disabled persons into the community, including attitudes of community members toward residents in their neighborhoods.

The actual experience of deinstitutionalization begins with handicapped persons learning to live in the community, as is discussed in the third section, which covers training for integration. A behavioral approach to this training and preparation is elaborated in Chapter 8. Chapter 9 extends the general discussion from Chapter 8 to describe approaches to training language and communication, skills essential to the integration of developmentally disabled individuals into the community.

Ancillary issues to the process of deinstitutionalization are elaborated in the fourth section of the book. Chapter 10 describes instruments and techniques for evaluating the success of the placement of individuals in the community. Chapter 11 describes legislative avenues and restrictions used either to facilitate or to resist deinstitutionalization, and Chapter 12 focuses on judicial decisions in these areas. Chapter 13 discusses various counterreactions toward the movement, bringing to light the precariousness of this social change.

In conclusion, Chapter 14 draws on the information featured throughout the rest of the book in order to present practical implications for the planner, the policy maker, and the practitioner involved in direct service delivery. Finally, the Epilogue delineates a critical perspective toward present practices in community integration, and offers commentary for new directions.

We have written for persons in several areas, including direct service personnel and university educators in regular and special education, psychology, social work, rehabilitation, guidance and counseling, vocational education—everyone working with or training others to work with handicapped individuals in their residential environments and in adjustment to the community. This research should be useful for evaluating and implementing change in these environments. It should also be useful for developing and planning in-service and preservice education for those who work in institutions, group homes, foster homes, intermediate care facilities, supervised apartments, and generic and specialized service agencies that have developmentally disabled clients. Local, state, and federal department administrators involved in planning and policy making should also find this book a valuable resource. Those involved in research concerning residential alternatives will find an up-to-date summary of what we know and what we don't know about deinstitutionalization, with delineations of research directions for the future included.

This book is also intended for those who are indirectly affected by the deinstitutionalization movement—parents, cabdrivers, storekeepers, employers, neighborhood residents—those coming into contact with disabled individuals on the street or at work, reading about them in newspapers and magazines, and watching television programs that have a "handicapped" theme. Individuals with curiosity for discovering more about this social phenomenon will find explanations and answers that are as accurate and meaningful as we can produce at this time.

To those who are "making it" in the community right now, we have attempted to explain, describe, justify, incite, explicate, and—most of all—promote acceptance.

A.R.N.
L.W.H.
September, 1980.

Acknowledgments

We are grateful to many people for their aid and support in this effort. First, thanks go to our colleagues who shared their prepublication data with us: Elinor Gollay, Robert Bruininks, Marsha and Gary Seltzer, Barry Willer, Jim Intagliata, Marty Wyngaarden, and Ruth Freedman. Our gratitude goes to Bob Flynn, Marc Gold, Ed Seidman, Greig Siedor, and Bob York for reading and suggesting ideas for certain portions of the manuscript. We salute the word-processing typing pool at the University of Illinois College of Education, especially Shirley Burton, Terry Piazza, Judy McClughen, Debbie Foertsch, and June Chambliss, for their patience through our seemingly infinite changes and for their highly professional work.

A.R.N.
L.W.H.

I would personally like to thank my friends at NARC who first interested me in this area of research: Elizabeth Boggs, Frank Menolascino, Franklin Smith, Philip Roos, Richard Rothmund, Webb Spraetz, Ron Neman, and especially Gene Patterson. Thanks is reserved also for Elio Pascutti for his support during the Heal and Daniels study, which is featured in Chapter 10. And finally, special recognition goes to my wife, Marcia Heal, for her editing and continual support.

L.W.H.

Special thanks to my colleagues for their constant encouragement during the hectic time of preparation of the manuscript: Bill Bursuck, Barbara Kammerlohr, Steve Rock, and Bill Schofield (p.s.: did it help at all on Special Fields I?) My thanks to David Cohen for constantly challenging my ideas. And thank you for the typing, the comments, and the shoulder, David Stone.

A.R.N.

Dedication

To Our Parents

Through their dedication to their children, they nurtured the forces that allowed this book to be written. Although our fathers won't see this volume, we particularly dedicate our efforts here to their memory.

Integration of Developmentally Disabled Individuals into the Community

Part I
UNDERLYING CONCEPTS OF DEINSTITUTIONALIZATION

Chapter 1
Deinstitutionalization and Mentally Retarded Persons

Barry Willer, Richard C. Scheerenberger, and James Intagliata

---

The community mental health movement has been described as a revolution in psychiatry (Bellak, 1964) that, according to Baker and Schulberg (1967), was part of the cultural revolution of the 1960s, characterized by the "open society" concept and a concern for human rights. Community mental health not only represented a change in mental health service delivery, it represented a major shift in ideology (Baker & Schulberg, 1967). Bloom (1977) described the principal ideological shifts in terms of the emphasis placed on community-based services, the total community, prevention, a "system" of services with effective planning involving community participation, provision of indirect (consultation and education) rather than direct services, short-term therapeutic approaches, and the expanded use of nonphysicians and nonprofessionals in the provision of services.

To most persons the principles of community mental health have become highly familiar; however, to those in other fields, it is often viewed as a singular concept, whereas it is in fact a complex belief system calling for major change in the manner in which mental health services are delivered. Deinstitutionalization, the term used to describe the changes that are occurring in mental retardation services, similarly involves much more radical change than first impressions would imply. In fact, many of the concepts of deinstitutionalization, although stated differently, are highly similar to those of the community mental health movement.

Stedman (1977) pointed out that deinstitutionalization means to most people the physical removal of handicapped persons from state institutions and their placement at home or in a replacement home. Certainly this is the meaning the term has in most of the mental health literature. However, to the President's Committee on Mental Retardation (1976) and to most persons associated with

---

Reprinted from *Community Mental Health Review,* August, 1978, by permission of the authors and The Hayworth Press.

mental retardation, it means reduction in admissions to public institutions through the development of alternative community methods of care and more effective methods of selection and screening. It also means return to the community for those residents who are prepared for and capable of functioning in an appropriate community setting. Finally, it means reform of institutions, the "establishment and maintenance of a responsive residential environment which protects human and civil rights and which contributes to the expeditious return of the individual to normal community living, whenever possible" (National Association of Superintendents of Public Residential Facilities for the Mentally Retarded, 1974, p. 4).

Deinstitutionalization and community mental health are rooted in the civil rights movement of the 1960s. As Scheerenberger (1976a) pointed out, "the genuine goal of both deinstitutionalization and normalization is the increased independence and quality of life for the mentally retarded" (p. 177). The principle of normalization was developed in the Scandinavian countries and formulated to provide handicapped persons with the same rights and benefits of all citizens (Nirje, 1969). It is the keystone of deinstitutionalization, and applies to all services to handicapped persons: community, community residential, and institutional. "Normalization means that deviant persons should be exposed to experiences that are likely to elicit or maintain normative (accepted) behavior" (Wolfensberger, 1970, p. 292). More specifically, it means that handicapped persons should be helped to become less handicapped, and should be presented to society in such a way as to emphasize their similarities rather than their differences, and that the attitudes of society should be shaped to be more accepting of handicaps and handicapped persons (Wolfensberger, 1970).

There can be little argument, at least at the present, with the notion that each mentally retarded person has the right to, and will benefit from, the most normalized social and physical environment possible. The problem arises in attempting to define normalization for a specific individual who may be severely handicapped (Rosen & Kivitz, 1973). Frequently this problem has been dealt with by examination of the qualities of the environment, with perhaps insufficient attention paid to the capabilities and needs of the individual (Throne, 1975). For example, a frequently used concept now is that of the "least restrictive environment," an expression derived from a court decision (Scheerenberger, 1977) and used to describe the rights of mentally retarded persons to an environment that provides the minimum supervision and the smallest living unit necessary, and the highest possible integration of the individual within the mainstream of the community. The concern is for normalized environments, but what is actually desired is an environment most suited to the needs, capabilities, and rights of the individual.

Deinstitutionalization and the field of mental retardation may incorporate slightly different concepts and language from community mental health, but the similarities between the two fields far outweigh the differences. One major exception, however, is the rate at which the populations of public institutions have declined. Conroy (1977) reported that in the United States the number of persons in mental institutions has declined from a peak of 559,000 in 1955 to 193,000 in 1975. This represents a decline of 65 percent. In contrast, the peak for public institutions for the mentally retarded was reached as recently as 1970 (189,549) and by 1976 had only declined by 18 percent to 154,856 (Scheerenberger, 1976b). It should be noted, however, that recent observations suggest that institutional depopulation of the mentally ill was carried out too rapidly, with insufficient attention given to developing an adequate system of follow-up care (Bassuk & Gerson, 1978).

There are a number of reasons why the depopulation of institutions has occurred more slowly for retarded persons than it has for psychiatric patients. One is the difference in legal background. The impetus for deinstitutionalizing psychiatric patients was the community mental health movement, which was mainly the result of federal legislation. Deinstitutionalization of mentally retarded persons, on the other hand, has been spurred on more by litigation and specific court decisions. For this reason it is important to review the legislation and legal proceedings that have served as background to deinstitutionalization.

Another important reason why the rate of release from institutions has been more conservative for mentally retarded persons than it has for psychiatric patients is the fact that the two populations are very different. Because of the nature of their handicap, a much larger proportion of the mentally retarded require supervised residential care in the community than do patients released from psychiatric institutions. Also, in the field of mental retardation it is thought that severely and profoundly retarded persons should, in fact, be served in an institution (Miller, 1975), and that for some the institution may allow for more humane treatment than would a community residence (Butterfield, 1977). Thus, much more than the community mental health movement, the deinstitutionalization movement in mental retardation has called for the reform and normalization of institutions rather than their replacement. To illustrate this, whereas federal and state monies continue to be used to improve the facilities and staffing of public institutions for the mentally retarded, the National Institute for Mental Health has just phased out two programs for upgrading mental hospitals (Hospital Improvement Program [HIP] and Hospital Staff Development Program [HSD]) and transferred their funds to pilot the new Community Support Program (*APA Monitor,* 1977). Hence, the reform of institutions and the nature of their role in a comprehensive service delivery system must be carefully reviewed for a more complete understanding of deinstitutionalization in mental retardation.

Another major reason for the progress made in mental health is the development of the community mental health center as the focal point and primary alternative to the mental hospital. It is intended to provide all of the basic clinical services, both inpatient and outpatient, as well as emergency treatment, partial hospitalization, and consultation and education. No such model for a comprehensive service center exists as an alternative to the institution for mentally retarded persons living in the community. One reason may be that proportionately more mentally retarded persons require supervised living arrangements than do the mentally ill, and thus much more attention has been paid to development of residential alternatives such as group residences and foster family care. Although mentally retarded persons also require support services, such as day activity centers, medical care, and family support services, much less attention has been paid to their development and expansion to meet the needs of the formerly institutionalized (General Accounting Office, 1977). Development of residential alternatives and community support programs for mentally retarded persons also need to be reviewed.

One further difference between deinstitutionalization and community mental health is the emphasis placed by the latter on planning, coordination, and continuity of services. Although there is still some concern about the relationship between various components of the service system (Gottesfeld, 1976) and the effectiveness with which they have actually functioned (Bassuk & Gerson, 1978), at least a model for coordination of services through the community mental health center has been developed. Models of service delivery and coordination in mental retardation still center on the institution and even rely on the institution to provide many of the community services. Service delivery models are important to the discussion of community based services and deinstitutionalization.

LITIGATION AND LEGAL ACTION

As indicated previously, various forms of litigation and specific court decisions have played major roles in facilitating both deinstitutionalization and institutional reform. Underlying most of these court decisions is the all-important Fourteenth Amendment, which provides for "due process" and "equal protection." According to Schwindler (1974), an authority on constitutional law, the fundamental objective of the due process of law clause

> is to safeguard the individual and his well-being—i.e., his life, his independence of action, and his possessions. It is the basic standard of conduct in governments dealing with individuals requiring that government abide by the required limits and procedures which the people have set up as guidelines to its actions. In the twentieth century it has been distinguished both as a procedural and a substantive right. (p. 201)

The procedural dimension of the due process clause requires that safeguards be established and followed to ensure each person a fair and equitable hearing. This includes such aspects as prior notice, adequate legal representation or counsel, and trial by jury.

The substantive right (or principles of liberty) associated with the due process clause was well defined by Amos in 1938:

> ... not only has the citizen the right to be free from the mere physical restraint of the person as by incarceration, but the term is deemed to embrace the right of the citizen to be free in the enjoyment of all his faculties; to be free to enjoy them in all lawful ways; to work and live where he will; to earn his livelihood by

any lawful calling; to pursue any livelihood or avocation; and for that purpose to enter into all contracts which may be proper, necessary, and essential to his carrying out to a successful conclusion the purposes mentioned above. (Boggs, 1966)

In other words, no individual may have any of his civil rights denied without the full sanction of the courts, and then only when all procedural safeguards have been assured. This clause also has been interpreted to mean that any mentally retarded person involuntarily committed to a residential facility must receive a full treatment program, not simply custodial care.

Although it is impossible to discuss in detail all significant court decisions, their major implications with regard to deinstitutionalization and institutional reform are reviewed briefly.

Litigation and Deinstitutionalization

Court decisions pertaining to deinstitutionalization have emphasized three critical aspects. First, they have placed marked restrictions on who should be considered eligible for admission:

> No borderline or mildly retarded person shall be a resident of the institution. (*Wyatt v. Stickney*, 1972)

> No person classified as borderline, mildly or moderately retarded according to the standards of classification at Cambridge shall be admitted unless that person suffers from psychiatric or emotional disorders in addition to his retardation. . . . (*Welsch v. Likens*, 1974)

> No person shall be admitted unless he is "dangerous to himself or others." (*Lessard v. Schmidt*, 1972)

Second, retarded persons, even those considered eligible under the court orders, should not be admitted to a residential facility until all other community resources have been explored:

> No person shall be admitted to the institution unless a prior determination shall have been made that residence in the institution is the least restrictive habilitation setting. (*Wyatt v. Stickney*, 1972)

> No mentally retarded person shall be admitted to Cambridge State Hospital on civil commitment if services and programs are available in the community. (*Welsch v. Likens*, 1974)

Third, no retarded person should remain in a residential facility longer than necessary:

> Residents shall have a right to the least restrictive conditions necessary to achieve the purposes of habilitation. To this end, the institution shall make every attempt to move residents from: a) more to less structured living; b) larger to smaller facilities; c) larger to smaller living units; d) group to individual residence; e) segregated from the community to integrated living. (*Wyatt v. Stickney*, 1972)

On the other hand, neither shall the retarded be returned to the community indiscriminately:

> No resident may be transferred to a community residential facility or foster home unless it has been duly licensed; and the defendants are to make a written determination of the eligibility of each resident at Cambridge for community placement and review such determination at least yearly. The defendants are to provide the court with a written plan to develop alternative residential care for all residents. (*Welsch v. Likens,* 1974)

The intent of these decisions is clear. A residential facility shall be used only as a last resort and only if the retarded person's needs can be met.

Perhaps the most condemning judgment by a Federal district court concerning the utilization of public residential facilities for the mentally retarded was issued in a *Memorandum of the United States Upon Relief, Halderman et al. v. Pennhurst State School et al.*, dated January 24, 1978. In this memorandum, the United States District Court for the Eastern District of Pennsylvania declared:

> Further, the court found that principles of equal protection prohibit segregation of the retarded in an isolation of clearly separate and not equal facilities such as Pennhurst where habilitation does not measure up to minimally adequate standards. Moreover the court found that under Section 504 of the Rehabilitation Act of 1973, unnecessarily separate services are discriminatory and unlawful. Pennhurst, as an institution for the retarded, is a monumental example of unconstitutionality with respect to the habilitation of the retarded. As such it must be expeditiously replaced with appropriate community-based mental retardation programs and facilities designed to meet the individual needs of each class member.

This Federal court decision seriously challenges the appropriateness of residential programs under any circumstances. It will be interesting to see whether this judgment will be upheld by a higher court.*

Litigation and Residential Reform

The celebrated landmark case related to residential reform and right to treatment was *Wyatt v. Stickney* (1972). This class action suit was brought against the Alabama Department of Mental Hygiene in 1970, alleging failure of the state to provide proper treatment for the mentally retarded in a public residential facility.

In 1971, Judge Johnson of the District Court of the United States for the Middle District of Alabama, North Division, heard testimony from persons directly involved with the Partlow State School and from representatives of various professional organizations concerned with the mentally retarded. His final judgment was precedent setting not only because it declared that the constitutional rights of the retarded were being violated, but also because the final document included a 20-page appendix that defined minimum treatment standards for the state school to meet. These standards were specific, and encompassed such areas as admission policies, resident rights to treatment and habilitation, staffing patterns, records and review, physical plant and environment, medication, and resident labor.

---

*Editor's Note: In December, 1979, the Third Circuit Court of Appeals upheld 38 of the original 41 paragraphs of the *Pennhurst* decision. As of June, 1980, the U.S. Supreme Court has agreed to review the decision.

Federal court judgments of this nature have emphasized five broad aspects of institutional reform. First, all retarded persons have basic rights that must be recognized. Second, as previously discussed, residential facilities should serve a very select population and prepare as many residents as possible for return to their home communities. Third, each resident is to have his/her total needs met on an individual basis. "Almost all of the residents, no matter the degree of severity of their retardation, are capable of some growth and development if given adequate care and suitable treatment" (*Welsch v. Likens,* 1974).

Fourth, restraints, certain aversive stimuli, and other possible negative treatment procedures were restrictively circumscribed:

> Residents shall have a right to be free from unnecessary or excessive medication. Medication shall not be used as punishment, for the convenience of staff, as a substitute for program, or in quantities that interfere with the resident's rehabilitation program. (*Wyatt v. Stickney,* 1972)

Finally, the residential facility must provide a humane physical and psychological environment. Standards under this category identified a broad array of resident rights such as the rights to privacy and to appropriate physical surroundings.

Although the preceding comments were relatively few, they illustrate the fact that Federal courts are unequivocally committed to precluding the necessity of residential care whenever possible, and are equally dedicated to the assurance that persons in residential facilities receive due service. The rights and needs of the mentally retarded must be recognized and satisfied.

INSTITUTIONAL REFORM

As evidenced by the preceding discussion of litigation, the Federal courts, as well as other organizations, agencies, and individuals, are highly concerned with improving the quality of life in a residential facility. Federal regulations associated with Title XIX of the Social Security Act as well as the standards of the Joint Commission on Accreditation of Mental Retardation Facilities demand major revisions in philosophy, management, and programming.

Change of Role within the Total Service System

Institutions are no longer viewed as isolated, independent facilities. Today, they represent but one element in a broad spectrum of comprehensive services offered through community delivery systems.

Institutions in the future will provide extended services for only a limited number of residents, those who are severely and profoundly retarded with major multiple handicapping conditions requiring constant medical supervision and the most sophisticated behavioral programs. The needs of these persons will be met in an environment as normal as possible, and each resident undoubtedly will have a legally recognized guardian.

A second population to be served, at least on an interim basis, will be the extremely difficult-to-manage mentally retarded individual who cannot be coped with successfully in the community. It is hoped that, as community services become better defined and more versatile, even this type of problem will be resolved within the local setting.

Residential facilities of the future, however, will continue to provide a series of vital services to mentally retarded persons and their families living in the community, including intensive diagnostic services, highly specialized treatment services for youngsters with severe motor, behavioral, or dental problems, respite care, genetic counseling, and community technical assistance.

Changes in Programming and Physical Plant

In the future, programs for mentally retarded persons in residential facilities will not only emphasize each individual's total developmental needs, but also foster increased levels of independence. Regardless of level of retardation or accompanying handicapping conditions, independence, be it in terms of activities of daily living (ADL) skills or decision making, will be the priority goal. Simple conformity to institutional policies of convenience will no longer be tolerated.

One very critical dimension of providing appropriate developmental programs in as normalized an environment as possible is the need to "deinstitutionalize" the physical plant. The mass living circumstances that all too often typify the institutional setting have historically adversely affected the residents' developmental progress, individual initiative, and desirable mental health. It is of extreme importance that the privacy of each individual be respected, that s/he have a place to which s/he can retreat, a place to store and use his/her personal possessions, and a place to call his/her own. Everyone needs his/her own territory, a territory free from constant disruption and possible harm. Newer residential facilities have, in most instances, taken into consideration the humane aspects of the living environment, and older ones are being remodeled.

Changes in Relations with Families

As the rights of mentally retarded persons, regardless of age or ability, become more fully recognized, corresponding parental rights and prerogatives decrease. This is most evident in a number of recently revised state statutes dealing with admission and discharge practices as well as with the definition of who will make what decisions under what circumstances. In Wisconsin, for example, as soon as an individual, mentally ill or mentally retarded, reaches age 14, s/he is to play an important role in decisions affecting his/her life, including admission, treatment, program, and discharge. In most states, the old law and tradition that parents automatically remain guardians of their mentally retarded offspring throughout their lives is no longer valid. In most cases, a guardianship hearing has to be held at the age of majority, and the parents may or may not be appointed guardians. Furthermore, it has become common for guardianship to be limited to those areas in which the mentally retarded person actually needs guidance or assistance. No longer does guardianship of the person imply that all his/her civil rights have been suspended. In many respects, parental authority over mentally retarded children has diminished; nevertheless, the parents remain very important in the lives of their mentally retarded children.

RESIDENTIAL ALTERNATIVES TO INSTITUTIONS

Deinstitutionalization has created a tremendous need for establishment of residential alternatives to institutions. Because of the variation in individual needs for training and supervision, institutional alternatives vary greatly on restrictiveness. The most ideal, most normalized, and least restrictive alternative in most instances is the individual's natural home (Stedman & Eichorn, 1964). In situations where the individual is capable of enjoying and benefitting from the environment of a homelike setting, but for one reason or other cannot return to his/her own home, the next best alternative is (foster) family care (Adams, 1970). A third alternative, broadly classed as community care facilities, varies a great deal in terms of restrictiveness across settings. Community care facilities are also known as group homes, hostels, boarding houses, or halfway houses, and differ from family care homes in terms of the organization of services and method of reimbursement (O'Connor, 1976). A final residential alternative, the health-related facility, which includes nursing homes, represents the most restrictive community-based environment, both because of the nature of the facility and because of the needs of the individual. Individuals placed in health-related facilities are usually more severely retarded and generally have specific medical needs requiring frequent attention. Because of the dearth of literature on health-related facilities, only family care, community care facilities, and natural homes are reviewed here.

Family Care

Most alternatives to institutions for mentally retarded persons have been with us since the early part of this century. It is only today's social climate that has served to support the huge expansion in availability and use of these alternatives (Rosen, Clark, & Kivitz, 1976). Family care, for example, was first introduced to the United States as an alternative for the mentally ill in 1885 (Doll, 1962). It was first recommended for use with the mentally retarded during the 1930s, on the basis that it represented a more "normal" alternative to institutions, was less expensive, and provided meaningful employment in the community (Pollock, 1936). However, family care for the mentally retarded was never as popular as it is today.

In New York State, in 1975, two out of three placements from public institutions went to family care, with little variation as a result of age or level of disability (Willer, Atkinson, & Intagliata, 1977). It is also the most popular placement type in California (Justice, Bradley, & O'Connor, 1971). Nationally, however, only 17 percent of all placements are to family care, reflecting the large variation that exists across the United States (Wyngaarden & Gollay, 1976).

Despite the popularity of family care, we know surprisingly little about how effective it is, or what factors are important to success. On the surface, because the retarded person is being placed with an already functioning family, we feel that s/he is being offered the closest approximation to normal family living, and that this represents the best opportunity to maximize the social and emotional development of the person (Adams, 1970). However, we also know that family care has the highest rate of return to the institution (Willer et al., 1977; Wyngaarden, Freedman, & Gollay, 1976). Reinstitutionalization rates from family care placements have been reported as 31 percent (Bishop, 1957), 30 percent (Wyngaarden et al., 1976), and 48 percent (Willer et al., 1977).

In spite of these high return rates, studies searching for factors predictive of outcome in family care have generally been unsuccessful. With respect to characteristics of retarded persons, including level of retardation, Bishop (1957) and Carhill, Rader, and Schonfeld (1967) were unable to identify any that were related to success. With respect to the characteristics of family care providers, Fanshel (1960) reported that the strong nurturing and protective characteristics that make foster mothers good for infants are usually not good predictive clues for the care of older children. Furthermore, Murphy (1964) reported that the characteristics of family care providers that led to success with female clients were different from those that led to success with males. It should be noted, however, that these two studies dealt with generic foster care rather than family care for retarded persons in particular. In one of the few studies dealing specifically with family care for retarded persons, Windle, Stewart, and Brown (1961) were unable to identify any characteristics of providers that were related to success. With respect to characteristics of the community in which a family care home is located, however, two studies have reported identifying characteristics related to success. Bishop (1959) reported that rural areas and small towns, as opposed to larger cities, had proved to best meet the needs of family care clients in his sample. Similarly, Murphy (1964) reported that suburban homes were found to achieve significantly poorer results with family care than were homes in rural settings, regardless of the characteristics of the child or of the individual home. Murphy suggested that the key factor that might explain these findings could be the different degrees of community integration and social support available in the different settings.

The generally unsuccessful results of studies to identify factors predictive of success in family care suggest two conclusions. First, if success can be predicted at all, the predictor is unlikely to be one simple factor. Rather, it seems more reasonable that success results from some sort of complex interaction involving characteristics of the client, the care provider, and the residential location. Second, it may be more profitable to attempt to predict success in specific rather than general terms. Factors of success for young children in family care may be quite different from factors of success for older adults.

In spite of the fact that no empirical evidence has linked characteristics of family care providers to success, family care providers continue to be recruited and selected in large numbers. Wolins (1968) warned that, the greater the demand for such homes, the less predictable become the decisions of licensing workers. In generic foster care there has been so much concern raised about rapidly rising costs and possible abuses that judicial review procedures have been made mandatory in some states (Festinger, 1976). These facts, along with the high recidivism rates previously described, suggest that states that use family care as the primary placement may not be choosing the best alternative, unless stringent review procedures are employed.

The difficulties of finding high quality family care providers for mentally retarded persons should not be minimized. Garrett (1970) suggested that foster parents for mentally retarded children need the same qualities as foster parents for nonretarded children, but to a much greater degree. Rich (1965) reported that foster parents boarding retarded children had altered their family routines to meet the needs of the children far more than had the foster parents of nonretarded children. Finally, Adams (1970) warned that a severely retarded child can impose a severe burden of care even on a relatively stable family.

Given these demands, where can qualified family care providers be found? Justice et al. (1971) reported that, in California, half of the care providers had previous experience with the retarded, frequently because they had worked in a state institution for the retarded. The question then becomes, is this the kind of background experience desired for placements serving as institutional alternatives? Other authors have suggested that family care providers cannot simply be found, but rather must be trained. Mamula (1971) suggested that care providers be assisted in developing plans with specific objectives for client progress, and Garrett (1970) discussed the need to provide family care providers with sequential educational opportunities for increasing their competence in serving the client. It should be noted, however, that family care providers are reimbursed for services by the state and therefore have essentially no more responsibility than any other state employee, even though there is clearly more responsibility when one provides 24-hour care (Adams, 1970).

It is interesting to note that, when family care providers were asked what they saw as the main problems of caring for retarded children, they did not list behavior problems of the children or difficulties in relating to natural parents of the children, as frequently as they listed problems related to the general public. In their study of family care providers, Justice et al. (1971) found that the main problem for care providers was public misconceptions about mental retardation, leading to antagonism of neighbors and friends, exclusion of the retarded person from community activities, problems with zoning regulations, and so forth. The second most frequent problem related to interactions with the school system (for children) and the lack of other kinds of support services. Similarly, Garrett (1970) noted the importance to family care providers of feeling accepted by their neighbors and others important to them, as well as having the necessary community resources and supports available. As is discussed below, the lack of available support services is a serious problem for all placements.

Community Care Facilities

Community care facilities, as we know them today, have changed somewhat from their predecessors, called "colonies" when they were introduced to the United States in the early 1900s. At that time the colony plan called for a number of formerly institutionalized retarded persons to be living in a large house or group of homes, and to work either on a farm or in a small, controlled factory (Adams, 1971). Bernstein (1927), an early supporter, argued for the colony plan because it offered fewer restrictions, more humane care, and was less humiliating. Perhaps more importantly, however, during this period of time it was also economically beneficial (Davies, 1959). When it became less feasible economically (for example, during the depression years), it became less popular. Since then, the economical feasibility has improved, not because of the availability of simple manual labor jobs as in the 1920s, but because of the comparatively high costs of institutional care (MacMillan, 1977).

Since the early days of the colony, the community care facility has evolved into a broad spectrum of group living arrangements ranging from unstructured, unsupervised apartments with independent living units to highly structured, well-staffed group homes for the severely and profoundly retarded. Also, it has become a popular form of placement in the United States. A national survey of institutions for the mentally retarded (Wyngaarden & Gollay, 1976) indicates that approximately 30 percent of persons are placed there. In New York State the figure is less, about 6 percent in 1975, but this figure is expected to rise rapidly since more residences are being set up (Willer et al., 1977).

The success rate of community care facilities is much better than that for family care, and in some cases appears better than all other placements. Wyngaarden et al. (1976) reported a reinstitutionalization rate of 10 percent for persons placed initially in a community care facility. This compared favorably with family care (30 percent) and is similar to natural family placements (11 percent). In the New York State study, Willer et al. (1977) reported reinstitutionalization rates (within 6 months of release, excluding returns for respite) of 7 percent for community care facilities, 48 percent for family care, and 36 percent for natural family placements.

The most common community care facility is a larger home, located near a business area or large grocery store, with around 12 fairly high-functioning clients, half of whom are drawn from an institution and half from their own homes (O'Connor, 1976). There are two types of staffing patterns: in the first the home has live-in houseparents, and in the second there are a full-time administrator and a number of direct care staff. Staffing ratios generally average one staff person for every two residents (O'Connor, 1976). It is the opportunity to select better-functioning residents that may account for the lower reinstitutionalization rate in community care facilities. Another factor may be the lesser adjustment required of the individual relative to his/her institutional experience.

Despite the high success rate, community care facilities suffer from a number of problems that may serve in the future to reduce their effectiveness. In some regions of the United States, community care facilities have been developed as private, profit-making enterprises in the manner of family care programs, where care providers are provided a fee for service. Segal and Aviram (1976) described this new and largely ungoverned system of facilities as a large social experiment that is likely to suffer from the inherent danger of no planning and low accountability. Bjaanes and Butler (1974) described some community care facilities as custodial, doing little to facilitate normalization, providing little supervision, and having few available daytime activities. Because of the custodial nature of these facilities, there is little need for the individual to return to the institution—all of the qualities of institutional environment are already available.

One major difficulty with community care facilities, especially when they are being initially set up, is site selection and community reaction. Ames and Levy (1973) discussed the problems of choosing a site that has easy accessibility to transportation and to community facilities, has appropriate bylaws allowing unrelated persons to live in the same dwelling, and still provides a suitable normalized household environment. Community reaction plays a role in site selection when there is a need to change existing local bylaws or if local bylaws are being ignored (Horejsi, 1975). After the site has been selected, the most serious problems for those who operate community care facilities appear to be related to funding, staffing, and gaining access to needed community support services for residents (O'Connor, 1976). In all, successful operation of a community care facility appears to be a highly difficult task, and it is not surprising that there is high variation in quality and in environmental conditions (Butterfield, 1977).

Natural Home

One rather curious phenomenon regarding placement of retarded persons from institutions is the variation across regions and states in the proportion of persons placed in community care facilities, family care, or the natural home. Nationally, about 40 percent of placements are to natural family homes, but this ranges from 62 percent in the Southern states to 29 percent for institutions located in north central states (Wyngaarden & Gollay, 1976). Willer et al. (1977) reported that placements to natural families from institutions in New York State was only approximately 11 percent.

Despite the fact that the natural home represents the most normalized placement for retarded persons (Stedman & Eichorn, 1964) and is the most preferred placement for the individuals themselves (Wyngaarden et al., 1976), it is obviously not the preferred placement in some regions. There are a number of possible reasons why home placement does not occur. One reason why institutionalization was frequently recommended not long ago was that many persons believed that a retarded person's presence in the home would have deleterious effects on the family, especially on the retarded person's siblings. Despite evidence to the contrary, many may still believe this to be the case and advise against or at least do not pursue having the retarded person placed in his/her own home.

Another reason why placement with family or relatives might not be popular from the family's perspective is that the family probably became accustomed to living without the retarded individual and, having discharged the responsibility for care and nurturance to the state, is not likely to be willing to have this responsibility returned (Stedman, 1977). In some ways this might suggest that they were mistaken in having him/her institutionalized in the first place (Willer et al., 1977). Mercer (1966) pointed out that families who have the most difficulty accepting their relative home again are those who originally decided to institutionalize because the burden of caring for the child had simply become too great.

One further inhibitor to more fully utilizing the natural home for placement is ease of placement for institutional staff. There is no doubt that parents' first reactions to discharge of their son or daughter are tantamount to regarding it as a crisis (Stedman, 1977). Very few families initiate the discharge (Wyngaarden et al., 1976), and few want their son or daughter to return home even though, in the end, this may be the result of the discharge process (Mercer, 1966). However, within a fairly short period of time after placement, many families change their minds and decide that home is where s/he should be, and that the last place they want to see their son or daughter living is back in the institution (Willer et al., 1977). Because of the initial lack of interest, it would obviously take more energy and time on the part of the placement staff to place a person with their own family than to place the person in family care or a community care facility where placement is attached to fiscal reimbursement. Wolfensberger (1971) pointed out that it is only sociopolitical attitudes that prevent us from arranging to pay natural parents as family care providers for their own children. Clearly payment of natural parents is an idea of merit and deserves experimentation. In fact, parents of retarded persons in New York can now qualify as family care providers and be reimbursed as such, given that their son or daughter is 18 years of age or older.

As the deinstitutionalization movement proceeds, more and more retarded persons will be living in alternative residential settings, requiring the development of more community residential facilities and the location of more family care homes. However, the inherent problems of staffing, siting, and funding community residential facilities is likely to limit this particular option for many persons. Also, the literature on generic foster family care suggests that there may be limits to the number of quality foster families available, especially for handicapped individuals (Adams, 1970). In short, deinstitutionalization programs, to be successful, will have to develop the natural family placement option more fully. Clearly, this is the least expensive and most readily available alternative to institutions, but to be fully utilized much more effort must be given to community support services (Scheerenberger, 1976a).

COMMUNITY SUPPORT SERVICES

The development of viable residential alternatives to institutions is essential to the success of deinstitutionalization programs in the United States. However, because deinstitutionalization also involves prevention of institutionalization, there are many retarded individuals who will thus remain in their own homes, and for these people and their families success will more likely be determined by the availability of community support services. Moreover, a follow-up study of discharges from public institutions (Wyngaarden et al., 1976) indicated that, regardless of residential placement, the amount of community support for mentally retarded persons was directly related to the community adjustment of the individual. More specifically, this study found that, the more support available, the more likely is the mentally retarded person to remain out of the institution, to have more independence, and to have fewer needs unmet by generic community agencies (Gollay, 1976).

For the purposes of this paper, the term "community support services" is used to refer to services to individuals that support them in their adjustment in the community, and services to care providers or natural family members that support them in their attempts to provide necessary care and nurturance for mentally retarded individuals. According to Gelman (1974), the purpose of individual support services is to integrate the individual into the mainstream of community life as much as possible. The services necessary to accomplish this goal fall into several broad categories: education and training, day activity, leisure, medical care, psychological counseling, and specialized therapies.

There is not always agreement among service providers, care providers, institutional personnel, and so forth as to what services are most needed for successful integration of the mentally retarded individual. Mamula and Newman (1973) argued that the overwhelming problem leading to unsuccessful placements is the behavior of the individual, and therefore stress the need for psychological counseling and behavior management training of care providers. Scheerenberger (1976a) described a study in which parents of children on a waiting list for institutionalization were asked what community services were most needed. Naturally, the most frequently mentioned service was community-based residential care, but second was day activity programs, such as public school programs and day care. Family care providers have also indicated a high need for recreation and day activity programs, but in addition suggest the need for expanded medical services (Justice et al., 1971).

The follow-up study of Wyngaarden et al. (1976) revealed that need for services varied greatly according to the level of adjustment of the individual. Well-adjusted individuals, as measured by community tenure, were less frequently seen by their care providers as needing services, and the service most frequently seen as needed but not used was speech therapy. For unsuccessful placements the services most frequently seen as needed were day activity and recreational programs, although psychological services also were mentioned as highly needed. Thus, there appears to be some disagreement regarding need for individual services in the community. Certainly more research is required in order to properly prioritize service need, but in all likelihood the apparent differences in perceived need for services can be explained by the regional disparity of available services, and the general need for *all* kinds of support services because of the heterogeneity of the population being served (Tarjan, 1976).

Another way to assess service need is to examine service use. Unfortunately, this is another area of research that is incomplete. For example, we know very little about service use by persons who are mentally retarded but have never been institutionalized. For formerly institutionalized persons, most attend school or some other day activity program, workshop, and so forth (91 percent). They are involved in organized recreational programs (80 percent), receive counseling (32 percent), have speech therapy (28 percent), have physical therapy (8 percent), see a physician (19 percent), and visit a dentist (5 percent) at least once a month (Wyngaarden et al., 1976). All of these services except counseling were used less frequently by persons who ultimately returned to the institution. Interestingly, the institution was much more likely to be the provider of these services for returnees than for persons who adjusted to the community setting and did not return to the institution.

A second form of community support services includes all services rendered to care providers that are intended to benefit the retarded individual in an indirect fashion (Kadushin, 1967). Such services as home management programs, family/parental counseling (Beck, 1962), family education, homemaker services (Arnold & Goodman, 1966; Holt, 1975), and respite programs are all types of support services. Therefore, we are primarily talking about services to the natural family and to family care providers. For persons discharged from public institutions, the most frequently used support services included preparatory training, ongoing counseling, consultation on specific problems, and respite (Wyngaarden et al., 1976). Fewer of these services were used by natural families as compared with family care providers, although natural family members expressed a greater unmet need for these services.

There is little argument that direct services for individuals and support services for care providers are essential to successful deinstitutionalization, both for persons discharged from institutions and for persons who will never be placed in an institution. However, as deinstitutionalization programs reduce the number of persons in institutions, they will necessarily increase the demand for community services, which in turn will lead to direct or indirect competition for services among these two groups of retarded citizens. Horejsi (1975) further suggested that, because the present system of services was generally established by parent groups, representatives of parents of the noninstitutionalized mentally retarded are not likely to adapt the services to the special needs of the formerly institutionalized. Thus, the creation of new services, regardless of their appropriateness to the needs of persons leaving institutions, does not guarantee that these persons will have an opportunity to make use of them. What is required is not only new services, but a careful look at how services are organized and how depopulation of institutions has been planned.

There are a number of other problems that have argued for review and revision of the organization of services. Segal (1977) provided a long list of problems in service delivery: adequate transportation, distribution of services, lack of trained professionals, lack of agency coordination, lack of community awareness, and the unresponsive nature of generic services. In a study specific to use of generic services, Scheerenberger (1970) found that staff of these services rarely refused to serve mentally retarded persons, but poor publicity, prohibitive cost, and unequal distribution of services reduced accessibility. Gelman (1974) also suggested the need for expanded use of generic services, as well as the need for increased accountability through program evaluation and citizen participation in evaluation and planning for services. For these and other reasons, the interest in the way services are organized has become a central issue in deinstitutionalization programs in the United States.

Wolfensberger (1970) outlined the implications of the normalization principle for service delivery. On the basis of those implications, major revision was made to services in Nebraska (Wolfensberger & Menolascino, 1970), and the resulting service system has been used as a model in other states (Horejsi, 1975). Scheerenberger (1974) outlined the five essential components of a model for deinstitutionalization that served to expand some of the major aspects of the Nebraska plan. First is the need for local or regional boards to plan and coordinate services. Second, there should be an independent monitoring agency that is separate from the local planning board. Third, quality technical assistance must be made available to planning boards and agencies. Fourth, there must be adequate financial support. Finally, retarded persons should be represented in interactions with the service delivery system by responsible advocates.

Service delivery models that aim to provide comprehensive community services, with continuity of care suitable for the heterogeneous population of mentally retarded persons, have become major aspects of the deinstitutionalization ideology. Also important are accountability, program evaluation, citizen advocacy, citizen/consumer participation, and so forth. All of these components, added to the development of new services, establishment of residential alternatives to institutions, and reform of the institutions, form the essence of deinstitutionalization. Thus, deinstitutionalization, like community mental health, involves considerably more than simply the depopulation of state institutions.

DISCUSSION

A close examination of the ideology of deinstitutionalization in mental retardation reveals strong similarities to community mental health. Emphasis is placed on community-based services, and there is similar emphasis on prevention and the need for a "system" of services. However, there are also major differences from community mental health. First, depopulation has occurred at a much slower pace. Second, much more emphasis has been placed on institutional reform, partly because of a different legal history and partly because there is general acceptance in the mental retardation field of the notion that institutions are still necessary for certain members of the mentally retarded population. Finally, much more emphasis has been placed on development of community-based residential alternatives to institutions, including community care facilities and family care homes.

Deinstitutionalization in mental retardation, regardless of differences from and similarities to community mental health, is likely to be affected by the growing criticisms of community mental health. The major criticisms have been concerned with "dumping," that is, removing persons, especially the severely disabled, from public institutions and placing them into the community without adequate social support (Kirk & Therrien, 1975; Zusman & Lamb, 1977). Other criticisms generally reflect on the failure of community mental health centers to coordinate community-based services and to assure continuity of care (Bassuk & Gerson, 1978). The backlash of criticism and reduced community support is likely to be undifferentiated and will probably affect future services for the mentally retarded.

The future of deinstitutionalization for mentally retarded persons is an uncertain one. A primary factor will be whether or not there is continued public and political support for deinstitutionalization in general. This support is likely to depend on the ability of community mental health to survive its present period of criticism, and to develop effective models for delivery of service. Unfortunately, the ability of mental retardation services to be responsive to the needs of their particular client group is unlikely to be the major factor affecting support for deinstitutionalization of mentally retarded persons.

Chapter 2
Empirical Support for Deinstitutionalization

Mary E. Pilewski and Laird W. Heal

Although humanitarian reasons alone require that alternatives be developed to replace the type of institutional care documented by Blatt and Kaplan (1966) in *Christmas in Purgatory,* research on the effects of institutionalization and other forms of environmental deprivation provides empirical basis for selecting environmentally enriched residential alternatives for developmentally disabled infants, children, adolescents, and adults.

Research on the effects of environmental deprivation and enrichment is constrained by a commonly held value that the social scientist should not submit a human subject to an intervention that may be harmful and, furthermore, should not withhold an intervention that may be beneficial. Illogical and perverse as this value might seem, it very often places the scientist at the mercy of the "natural experiment," the accidental intervention that occurs to one group but misses another. The natural experiment is always open to the criticism that the groups differ in some way that is completely independent of the putative intervention. For example, it is logically impossible to find a noninstitutionalized control group with whom to compare a group of institutionalized subjects. The two groups might be matched on age, IQ, sex, parents' marital status and income, and social status, but one can never logically conclude that the two groups are identical in every respect except for their place of residence. Selection biases are inevitable. There could be many reasons why one group of parents retained their children at home while the other group did not.

Given the constraint of the comparison of intact groups in a natural experiment, this chapter attempts to interpret the findings of research into environmental deprivation and enrichment in order to provide a better understanding of what environmental features appear to be essential for normal development. The entire developmental period is reviewed. First, the effects of infant deprivation are studied, and the ameliorative results of subsequent environmental enrichment are examined. This is followed by a review of the research on the effects of environmental deprivation and enrichment on children, adolescents, and adults.

ENVIRONMENTAL DEPRIVATION IN INFANCY

A number of research studies have reported varying degrees of deprivation, neglect, and abuse of human infants. This deprivation has generally been associated with depressed physical and intellectual development.

Intellectual Development in Environmentally Deprived Infants

There is a large (and growing) body of literature dealing with early experiences and subsequent effects in infants. Although not all of these studies have concerned children who are mentally retarded, intellectual development (i.e., IQ) is one of the usual measurements considered, and it seems reasonable to draw conclusions based on some of this material.

One of the earliest of these studies (Spitz, 1945, 1946) focused on infants in two institutions from two different Western hemisphere nations. Spitz reported a dramatic decrease in the developmental quotients of 19 infants after separation from their mothers; he then reported an equally dramatic increase after the reunion of the infants with their mothers. Other observations indicated that the infants in one of the institutions were not only separated from their mothers, but lacked any kind of stimulation; they were completely isolated from the other babies by having sheets draped over the sides of their cribs, and their fingers and toes were their only "toys." The measured intelligence of these babies dropped an average of 52 IQ points by the end of their first year of life. Furthermore, Spitz describes a form of depression (anaclitic depression) observed in some, but not all, of the children who experienced 3 months or more of separation from their mothers. Numerous criticisms have been directed at Spitz's study (e.g., Pinneau, 1955a, 1955b); these were summarized by Clarke and Clarke (1976), who enumerated omissions (e.g., Spitz's failure to report why the mothers mysteriously reappeared in their children's lives) and errors (e.g., considering separation as the sole cause of mental retardation with no mention of other possibilities).

On the other hand, Bronfenbrenner (1972), while acknowledging the criticisms, supported Spitz's hypothesis that the combination of simultaneous maternal and environmental deprivation results in severe mental retardation with serious psychological withdrawal. In his support he cites not only the work of Spitz himself, but also Harlow's (Harlow, Schiltz, & Harlow, 1969) study of maternal deprivation with monkeys. Similarly, the studies of Dennis and his associates (Dennis, 1960, 1973; Dennis & Najarian, 1957; Dennis & Sayegh, 1965) indicated marked developmental retardation in infants who were seriously neglected in orphanages. Spitz's studies as well as similar investigations by Goldfarb (1943, 1945, 1947) were the bases for Bowlby's (1951) monograph for the World Health Organization, which concluded that maternal deprivation was extremely detrimental to normal child development.

Mortality in Institutionalized Infants

The ultimate index of arrested development is death. If depressed social and intellectual development can be attributed to institutions' neglect of their residents, then this neglect should also be reflected in the mortality rates of infants who are admitted to these facilities. High mortality rates among infants would indicate the need to raise the age of admission to public residential facilities (PRFs) for mentally retarded individuals.

There is evidence that the mortality rates of children who are institutionalized before the age of 5 increase as age at admission decreases. Pense, Patton, Camp, and Kebalo (1961) did a 4-year study on children admitted to five New York State institutions during a 12-month period ending March 31, 1956. All of the children had been admitted before the age of 5. Of these children, 32 percent had died by the end of the fourth year after admission. Of the 91 children under 1 year of age at admission, 66 percent had died. These figures closely replicate those of Dayton (1931) and Kramer, Person, Tarjan, Morgan, and Wright (1957). By contrast, Pense et al.'s estimate of the mortality rate of those awaiting admission to the institution was from 10 to 20 percent.

Kurtz and Wolfensberger (1969) studied mortality in all residents admitted to Beatrice State Hospital in Nebraska from 1910 to 1959. They found the same age trend as that of Pense et al. (more deaths in younger children) and, furthermore, they found that 24 percent of the children under 2 died during the first 3 months after admission. Unfortunately, for most of these studies there was not an adequate control group, either from institution waiting lists or from the general population. (Only a group from the admissions list that was refused admission on a random basis could be considered truly appropriate). One study by Dayton (1931; Dayton et al. 1932) found that the death rates of the 2- to 9-year-old population in three Massachusetts state institutions was 8 to 11 times higher than that in the general population.

The studies cited here offer little explanation for admission-related mortality, although Lind and Kirman (1958) suggested that the overcrowded state of the institutions, coupled with their large size, was a major factor. According to Kurtz and Wolfensberger (1969), there is more stress and less resistance to disease in large, overcrowded institutions for mentally retarded persons. They further suggested that this information be used in programmatic planning, perhaps by increasing medical care and awareness to help each individual survive and develop through those crucial first months.

REVERSIBILITY AND PREVENTION
OF DEPRESSED INFANT DEVELOPMENT

The preceding sections leave a pessimistic impression of the opportunities for the institutionalized or environmentally deprived infant to develop normally. However, notwithstanding this evidence of the devastating effects of infant neglect, a considerable body of research indicates that early deprivation does not necessarily result in irreversible developmental delays. For instance, a recent volume by Clarke and Clarke (1976) presents an impressive group of studies on formerly isolated children: case studies of isolated children by Davis (1947) and Koluchova (1972, 1976); a previously unpublished chapter by Kagan, including data on his studies of impoverished Guatemalan children; Dennis's (1973) conclusions and implications from his longitudinal studies of institutionalized Lebanese children; an excellent study of British residential nurseries by Tizard and Rees (1974), which documents normal cognitive development in a group of 4-year-olds who had been institutionalized from birth; and others. All support the position that deficits associated with early deprivation can be reversed.

Amelioration of Early Deprivation Effects

Some research suggests that the effects of early environmental deprivation can be completely ameliorated by subsequent environmental enrichment. Dennis (1973), in his unique longitudinal study of Lebanese orphanages, supported both the conclusion that environmental deprivation results in striking retardation of intellectual development, and the conclusion that subsequent environmental enrichment, in the form of adoption, reverses infant retardation.

Dennis's studies are especially impressive because of a natural experiment that occurred as he gathered his data. The Crèche, the Lebanese agency whose children he studied beginning in 1928, retained its foundlings from birth to age 16 until 1956, when it began a policy of adoption. Until 1956, the agency had had a long history of fostering intellectually retarded children; their IQs averaged about 50 at adulthood. Before the adoption policy, it was ambiguous whether the retardation was the result of the depriving environment of the institution or of the admission of infants whose inherited endowments were subnormal. However, adoption reversed their retardation. Children who had been adopted before they were 2 years old subsequently attained an average IQ very near 100. This accelerated development of toddlers after adoption indicates that the infants' mental retardation was occasioned by environmental deprivation, not subnormal endowment.

Very similar results were reported in this country in the classic but controversial study by Skeels and his students (Skeels, 1966; Skeels & Dye, 1939; Skodak & Skeels, 1945). Skeels followed a group of 25 children through their developing years until they were about 30 years of age. When the study began, 13 children were transferred from an orphanage to an institution for the mentally retarded. Although they were less than 3 years of age, the retarded development was already apparent. The challenge that Skeels assumed was to enrich the lives of these 13 children and observe the results of this enrichment on their development. As a contrast group he selected 12 children who had personal histories that were very similar to those of the 13 retarded children, but who themselves were not mentally retarded and who remained at the original orphanage.

The children in the "experimental" group, those considered to be mentally retarded, were placed with older, brighter female residents of Glenwood State School in Iowa. These older girls, whose mental ages ranged from 5 to 12, showered affection, attention, and stimulation on their new babies, and after 2 years in their new environments the toddlers' average IQ had risen from 63.4 to 91.8. During approximately the same period of time the contrast group had slipped from an original mean IQ of 86.7 to a mean of 60.5. After approximately 21 years the two groups were compared again. At that time all 13 children in the experimental group were self-supporting. None was a ward of any institution, public or private. In the contrast group, one had died in adolescence following continued residence in a state institution for the mentally retarded, and four were still wards of institutions. Only one had achieved a stable, self-supporting lifestyle. Although a skeptic could question the sampling procedure by which control and experimental subjects were selected, these results were so dramatic that it is difficult to attribute them to some artifact of experimental procedure.

A second natural experiment is reported by Kagan (1976). The Guatemalan Indian village that he studied was characterized by extremely neglectful traditions of infant rearing. Until they became mobile, infants in this village were confined to their cribs and had very little interaction with their parents and siblings. Their infancy was characterized by "frequent illness, lack of experiential variety, and mild malnutrition," so that at 1 year they were "quiet, nonsmiling, minimally alert, motorically flaccid, and temperamentally passive" (p. 105). However, at 13 to 16 months, when the babies became mobile, they encountered the rich environment of the village, and psychomotor development accelerated. Thus, although these children were about a year behind in their psychomotor development at age 2, their scores were remarkably similar to Guatemalan city children and American children on a variety of cognitive and perceptual tasks by the time they reached the age of 5.

Using Environmental Enrichment to Prevent Mental Retardation

The research cited in the previous section, although imperfect in design, provides persuasive evidence that developmental retardation in infancy can be reversed by subsequent enrichment. It is not surprising, then, to find evidence that environmental enrichment promotes normal development in infants and children whose backgrounds made mental retardation likely.

The Milwaukee Project (e.g., Garber & Heber, 1977) was an exception to the dependence on the natural experiment to evaluate environmental enrichment for developing infants and toddlers. Having established with epidemiological data that children of mothers whose IQs measured below 80 were 16 times more likely to become mentally retarded than the population at large, Heber and his associates randomly (with trivial constraints) assigned newborn infants of low-IQ mothers to either an enrichment preschool training program or to a nonintervention control situation. All mothers were Black, to control for ethnic factors. The program involved a multifaceted effort to provide the "best" possible medical, social, family, and preacademic enrichment for these children during their preschool years. The mothers as well as the infants themselves were trained. At 1 year of age, both groups of infants averaged a Cattell IQ score of about 115, not unusual for American Blacks. By age 4, the Wechsler Intelligence Scale for Children IQ scores had diverged, so that the experimental group had an average of about 125, and the control group had an average of about 95. The IQ scores of both groups drifted downward after age 4, so that by age 9 the average of the intervention group was about 105 and the control about 80. Although the intervention was so multifaceted that it is impossible to determine what elements were critical, there can be little doubt that early environmental enrichment can account for massive increases in cognitive functioning, and that these increases can be maintained for several years after the formal intervention has stopped.

A study by Tizard and Rees (1974, with an update in Clarke & Clarke, 1976) suggests that normal intellectual development can also occur in institutions. Tizard and Rees compared IQ and reading scores from several groups of children, all but one of which had been institutionalized in British residential nurseries during the first 2 years of their lives. Although the institutionalized groups were found to have significantly lower IQ scores than the noninstitutionalized and deinstitutionalized groups (adopted after age 2), their scores were in the normal range (105 at age $4\frac{1}{2}$; 97 at age 8). Furthermore, there were ample opportunities for selection biases in this study, making it reasonable to attribute group differences to selection, and leaving the conclusion that these residential nurseries, with many toys, books, activities, and adults, were sufficiently enriching to promote normal intellectual development throughout the preschool and early elementary school years.

Effects of Persistent Deprivation

Although infants whose environment is enriched before the age of 2 appear to develop normally, there may be progressively greater permanent retardation as environmental deprivation continues beyond that age. Dennis (1973), for example, reported that those children who were over 2 at the time of adoption increased 1 year in mental age for each year in their adopted homes, but they retained the mental age delay that existed at the time of their adoption. Indeed, no group adopted after age 2 achieved an IQ mean of 100. Further evidence for the idea that irreversible retardation can result from deprivation beyond age 2 is drawn from a second natural experiment in the Crèche. Before the adoption policy was instituted, girls and boys were segregated at age 6, girls going to an institution that was judged by Dennis to be as stark as the one from which they had come, but boys going to one that was judged much more enriched. While assignment to different environments on the basis of sex does not allow the interpretive power that accompanies random assignment, assignment of these children by sex did presumably assure that Dennis's two groups were balanced for general intellectual endowment, since there is no reason to believe that abandoned male and female infants should have different intellectual potential. Nevertheless, Dennis found that the boys at the enriched institution made intellectual gains that were indistinguishable from those of their adopted peers, despite the bias that undoubtedly operated in the selection of boys for adoption. Both groups of boys made a year's growth in mental age for each year of chronological age, but both groups were developmentally delayed in proportion to the delay in their enrichment intervention beyond the critical age of 2. Severe retardation persisted in the institutionalized girls. Dennis concluded from these lines of evidence that there is irreversible retardation in cognitive growth when interpersonal and environmental stimulation is withheld after an infant reaches 2 years of age.

Dennis's conclusion is supported only in part by the studies of neglected, isolated children (e.g., Davis, 1947; Koluchova, 1972, 1976). Koluchova's case study is especially inspiring: after 2 years in an orphanage and a subsequent $5\frac{1}{2}$ years of battering and neglect at the hands of their father and stepmother, a pair of identical twin boys was taken from their home by a Czechoslovakian court in 1967 and placed in a residential school. At the time of their discovery the 7-year-old boys had no speech, could not recognize two-dimensional pictures, and were malnourished, frightened, and severely if not profoundly mentally retarded. After spending 2 years in a residential preschool, where they progressed remarkably, the twins were adopted by a woman who lived with her sister and her sister's adopted daughter. With this very supportive and enriched home environment, the twins began school. They outpaced their younger classmates and were promoted until they were only $1\frac{1}{2}$ years older than their classmates. Their IQs, measured by the Wechsler Intelligence Scale for Children, increased steadily from 72 and 80 at age 8 to 101 and 100 at age 14. Their social development had no perceptible scars. There are, of course, many possible explanations for the remarkable progress made by these boys despite more than 7 years of severe social, environmental, and nutritional deprivation: they had adequate, if not stimulating care as infants; they had companionship in their misery and in their recovery placements; they had an extremely enriching and stable adoptive placement; and they very likely had natural endowments that were above average.

ENVIRONMENTAL DEPRIVATION EFFECTS
IN CHILD AND ADOLESCENT DEVELOPMENT

Despite the fact that they depend primarily on natural experiments, the results of research on the role of environmental deprivation in infant intellectual development are surprisingly clear. A remarkable amount of deprivation can apparently be tolerated in the first 2 years of life, provided that compensatory enrichment follows, but what of environmental deprivation, such as that which occurs in institutions for the mentally retarded, which continues throughout childhood, adolescence, and adulthood? Dennis's results suggest that institutionalization beyond infancy has effects that are more permanent than those that occur earlier. This section examines these effects; as with early deprivation, there is evidence that institutional behaviors are subject to subsequent modification.

The Methodological Dilemma

The study of the role of institutionalization in development necessarily involves an imperfect research design, since it is logically impossible to establish groups that are equivalent in every way except that one is institutionalized and the other is not. Several studies have documented the differences between these two groups. For instance, Zigler, Butterfield, and Goff (1966) developed a "Social Deprivation Scale" for the purpose of retrospectively rating social histories of persons who had been institutionalized for mental retardation. Their ratings showed that the numbers of preinstitutional residences, the proportion of time spent with the biological parents prior to institutionalization, the parents' attitudes toward institutionalization, the intellectual levels of the parents, the economic levels and job classifications of the parents, and the father's mental health, were all factors that influenced the likelihood that a mentally retarded child would be institutionalized. In another study Eyman, O'Connor, Tarjan, and Justice (1972) reported on a prospective study of institutionalized and noninstitutionalized individuals. Like Zigler et al., they attempted to identify the variables that would predict whether or not an individual would be institutionalized. Five factors proved to be significant predictors of the commitment decision: IQ, age, physical disability, adaptive behavior failures, and Anglo-American as opposed to minority ethnic background. Factors that did not discriminate were physical problems (as opposed to disabilities), ethnic origin within the minority classification (i.e., Black versus Chicano), learning problems, behavior problems, sex, or family income. Hobbs (1964) also compared differences between two groups who were mentally retarded. Both groups were between the ages of 13 and 25. The reported IQ range of the institutionalized group was 46 to 78, and that of the noninstitutionalized group was 34 to 77. She found the institutionalized group to have more antisocial or immoral behavior, to have fewer opportunities for education or professional help, to be less socially conforming, to be more often from broken homes, and to have parents with poor educational backgrounds. Hobbs cautioned against drawing hard and fast conclusions from these results, however, because parents or advocates routinely exaggerated the individuals' deficiencies in order to build a case for institutionalization.

Again, this research comparing institutionalized and noninstitutionalized groups, in which group assignment has been uncontrolled, must be interpreted with reservation. Older residents are even more subject to selection biases than infants, because it can often be argued that the institutionalized infants are no different from noninstitutionalized infants of similar parentage. Similarly, effects of experience prior to institutionalization are minimized in studies of infants. However, regardless of the care taken to identify similar institutional and noninstitutional groups, selection bias can be logically eliminated only by random assignments.

Intelligence (IQ)

IQ in and by itself does not determine the ability of an individual to function in society, but it does offer a standardized measure; therefore, it has been a useful index of institutional effects. The above-mentioned research of Dennis and of

Skeels would lead to the expectation of a direct correlation between the number of years spent in an institutionalized environment and intelligence quotient. Several studies have investigated this relationship and have generally found that it does indeed exist (Crissey, 1937; Kaplan, 1943; Kephart & Strauss, 1940; Sloane & Harmon, 1947). Additional studies (Chapanis & Williams, 1945; Hirsch, 1928; Wheeler, 1932) have indicated that IQ declines spontaneously with age in mountain children of Tennessee and Kentucky. This decline has been attributed to culturally "deprived" environments, which are evidently not restricted to institutions.

Zigler's Motivational Interpretation of IQ Test Results in Institutionalized Subjects

Zigler, who stands out as the most active social scientist to examine the behavioral effects of institutionalization, has proposed that IQ changes that occur following institutionalization result mainly from motivational rather than cognitive changes in institutionalized individuals. Although his work is to be otherwise commended for its generally competent design and systematic organization, it has been limited almost exclusively to a single index of social motivation, the marble-in-the-hole task. In this task the subject is given marbles of two colors and a box with two holes, and is instructed by the experimenter to drop the marbles of one color into one hole and the marbles of the other color into the other hole. The subject is told that s/he may play as long as s/he likes. When the subject indicates that s/he is ready to stop, the experimenter gives him/her a second task, which consists of reversing the holes into which the marbles are dropped. Again, the subject continues as long as s/he pleases. The amount of time spent on these two tasks is taken by Zigler and his associates to be an index of the reinforcing properties of this novel experimental situation, especially of the opportunity to interact with a stranger. Ordinarily this stranger, the experimenter, compliments the subject for his/her performance after the drop of every tenth marble. Zigler's research has indicated that the institutionalized subjects who are more persistent on the marble-in-the-hole task are also the subjects whose IQs have decreased the most since institutionalization. His interpretation is that this apparent decrease in their IQ scores following institutionalization results from their desire to interact with the person administering the IQ test, which distracts them from the test, and not from a depression in their cognitive functioning per se. Zigler, Balla, and Butterfield (1968) failed to replicate this relationship between IQ drop and "responsiveness to social reinforcement." However, this second study was conducted in an institution whose environment was judged by experimenters to be much less depriving. In support of their interpretation they noted that the IQs of their subjects actually rose during the course of this 3-year longitudinal study. Nevertheless, continued follow-up studies of the original sample (Zigler, Butterfield, & Capobianco, 1970) as well as replications of the basic strategy on other samples (Balla, Butterfield, &

Zigler, 1974; Zigler, Balla, & Butterfield, 1968) have been only marginal in their support of the hypothesis that it is social responsiveness, not intelligence, that changes with environmental deprivation or enrichment.

Learning Differences in Institutionalized and Noninstitutionalized Individuals

Learning differences between institutionalized and noninstitutionalized mentally retarded persons appear to parallel IQ differences. Kaufman (1963) compared institutionalized and noninstitutionalized subjects (chronological age about 13 and mean IQ about 55) with regard to their learning during a series of discrimination problems. In this type of problem, the subject is presented with two objects, one of which is associated with a reward; the task is to select the rewarded object on every trial. Subjects who are given a number of successive discrimination problems tend to improve their performance with practice. This improvement of performance over problems has been called "learning to learn" or "learning set." In Kaufman's study every subject was given 96 three-trial problems. Whereas the institutionalized and noninstitutionalized children did not differ on the number of correct responses during their first 48 problems, the nonstutitionalized children made significantly more correct responses on the last half of their problems. These results were replicated by Harter (1967) using a series of 25 four-trial discrimination problems. Harter's selection of subjects was much more comprehensive, using two mental age (MA) levels ($5\frac{1}{2}$ and $8\frac{1}{2}$) and three IQ levels (65, 100, and 130) at each MA level. However, Harter, Brown, and Zigler (1971), who matched institutionalized and noninstitutionalized subjects with MAs of about 8 years and IQs of about 62, found that the noninstitutionalized learners surpassed the institutionalized learners only when the experimenter was visible to the subjects and was interacting with them. No differences between institutionalized and noninstutionalized learners were found when the experimenter was hidden behind a one-way screen, which had been the learning arrangement in the Kaufman (1963) and Harter (1967) studies. In view of the greater responsiveness of institutionalized subjects to the experimenter in the marble-in-the-hole task, and the deterioration of learning set performance in the presence of an experimenter in a learning set task, the authors concluded that social responsiveness interferes with cognitive functioning (i.e., problem solving) and impairs learning set performance. This argument is similar to the one proposed by Zigler to account for depressed apparent IQ scores in those subjects who have a high degree of social responsiveness.

Other Measures of Motivation and Attention

In addition to social responsiveness, the construct of outer-directedness has been developed by Zigler to account for certain differences between instutionalized and noninstitutionalized subjects on his marble-in-the-hole task. Green and Zigler (1962) were surprised to find that institutionalized retarded subjects and their normal MA peers would continue to play the marble-in-the-hole game even after they had been told by the experimenter that they were free to stop anytime. In contrast, noninstutionalized retarded individuals were much more likely to conform to the suggestion of the experimenter that they stop. Green and Zigler proposed that the noninstutionalized retarded individuals had experienced much more failure from their own decisions and had adaptively come to rely on the cues and suggestions of others in determining their actions. The institutionalized subjects, they reasoned, were protected from excessive failure by the paternalism of their settings. The nonretarded subjects were protected by their history of adaptive decisions. To test this hypothesis, Achenbach and Zigler (1968) compared retarded subjects at two mental age levels on their disposition to use a light signal as a cue to select the correct object in a three-choice discrimination learning task. Consistent with their hypothesis, the noninstitutionalized retarded subjects relied much more on this cue (than the institutionalized subjects) even though they had to wait several seconds for it to appear. If noninstitutionalized subjects are disposed to rely on external signals, then one would expect that they would imitate the behavior of a model that has been rewarded in their presence. However, such imitation appears to be more prevalent in institutionalized than in noninstitutionalized subjects (e.g., Zigler & Balla, 1978). Therefore, more research is required to elaborate the relationship between institutionalization and "outer-directedness."

In another area of motivation, Rosen, Diggory, and Werlinsky (1966) investigated the level of aspiration of their mentally retarded subjects, whose average chronological age was about 17 and whose average IQ was about 75. After practicing on a nut and bolt assembly task, subjects were asked how many they thought they could do on the next try. The institutionalized subjects set higher goals and performed better than the noninstitutionalized subjects. Thus, in terms of both level of aspiration and outer-directedness, the institution seems to have a desirable impact on the motivation of mentally retarded subjects.

Crosby (1972) investigated attention and distractibility in five groups of 24 subjects each. Three of the groups were mentally retarded individuals with an average mental age of about 10 years and an average IQ of about 65: one group was persons who were institutionalized and diagnosed as brain-damaged; the second was persons who were institutionalized and diagnosed as not brain-damaged; and the third was persons from special classes in the public schools. Two nonretarded comparison groups were used: a mental age comparison group whose mean chronological age was 9 years and a chronological age (CA) comparison group whose mean CA was 15 years. The subjects' task was to watch a panel and press a button every time an X was flashed onto it. A second task required the subject to press the button whenever the X was immediately followed by an A. There were four conditions of distraction: no distraction, distraction by extraneous letters presented visually, distraction by extraneous letters presented through earphones, and distraction by both the visual and auditory conditions. Distraction signals coincided with task signals. Although the groups differed in total performance over all four distraction conditions, their differences were parallel from one distraction condition to the next. Noninstitutionalized retarded subjects tended to do better than their mental age peers, although they did more poorly than their chronological age peers. In part, then, distractibility may be reduced by the experiences of normal living in a noninstitutional environment, or distractibility may forebode institutionalization.

Speech and Language Development

Impaired speech often characterizes persons who are institutionalized for mental retardation. A survey by Sirken and Lyons (1941) determined that 60 percent of the residents at a single state school had speech defects, and 17 percent of the total institutionalized population had no speech. This was consistent with Schlanger's (1953) report that 69 percent of an institutionalized population had speech difficulties. Sievers and Essa (1961) compared 74 institutionalized and 74 noninstitutionalized mentally retarded children on the Differential Language Facility Test (DLFT) and on a speech and language evaluation. The noninstitutionalized group performed better than the institutionalized group on the total score and five of the DLFT subtests; the institutionalized group also had a higher mean verbal output and was more repetitious. McGunigle (1967) studied the relationship between age of admission, length of institutionalization, and communication. When she examined two groups of 249 residents each at Pacific State Hospital—one group whose speech was understandable by a stranger and one having no speech—she found that residents belonging to the latter group were more likely to have been admitted before the age of 5. The groups did not differ significantly in length of stay. It is, of course, unclear whether speech defects were present because of selection, deficient training programs, or institutionalized regression.

Differences in Self-Image

Zigler has also pointed out the difference in self-image between institutionalized and noninstitutionalized mentally retarded and normal children (Zigler, Balla, & Watson, 1972). Adolescents who were institutionalized were found to have greater disparity between real and ideal self-image, as well as lower self-image on both counts. This information suggests that deinstitutionalization programming should include resident success experiences, especially if the individual is preparing to move into a less restricted setting in the community.

Exceptions to Depressed Development in Institutionalized Individuals

The preceding sections have presented considerable evidence for the depressing effect of institutionalization on intellectual development and productive motivation. These findings, however, are not universal. For example, Holowinsky (1962) found no statistically significant changes in IQs over a 30-year institutionalization period in one state institution. In a semi-longitudinal study of a different state institution, Fisher and Zeaman (1970) also indicated that the IQs of institutionalized individuals are remarkably stable throughout their adult lives.

Clarke and his associates (Clarke & Clarke, 1953, 1954; Clarke, Clarke, & Reiman, 1958) have found that the psychometric intelligence of some individuals actually increases after they have been placed in an institution. They resolved this apparent paradox by investigating the preinstitutional experiences of their subjects; they found that those individuals whose IQs increased subsequent to institutionalization had come from extremely deprived environments. For these individuals, then, institutionalization actually represented an enriching intervention.

The Social Responsiveness Interpretation of IQ Changes in Institutionalized Individuals

Zigler and his associates (Zigler & Williams, 1963; Zigler et al., 1970) have provided a motivational interpretation of the relationship between preinstitutionalization experience and institutional IQ change. As noted above, this longitudinal study reported a substantial decline in IQ, especially during the first 5 years of institutionalization. Furthermore, the decline was greatest for those individuals who had normal or enriched preinstitutional family lives; i.e., the IQ decrease was greatest in those subjects for whom the institution represented the greatest negative contrast to their prior setting. Zigler and his colleagues concluded that, when an institution is more sterile than a preinstitutional setting, individuals have greater motivation to socialize with adults, which, in turn adversely affects their performance on IQ tests. However, subsequent research (Balla et al., 1974; Zigler & Balla, 1972; Zigler et al., 1968) has provided only modest support for this notion.

Effects of Length of Institutionalization and Age at Admission on Placement Success

If institutionalization forestalls development, then the longer an individual spends in an institution or the younger s/he is at admission, the more difficult it should be to make an adjustment to the demands of the community when s/he is discharged. McCarver and Craig (1974) reviewed the research concerning community adjustment of persons who had been institutionalized for mental retardation at different ages. These studies tend to contradict one another. For example, MacMillan (1962) and Wolfson (1956) examined recidivism of discharged institution residents and found that the younger the age of admission the less likely the chance of returning to the institution, although Wolfson found this to be true only for females. Like so many other issues pertaining to the benefits or deficiencies of institutionalization, however, evidence exists to support the opposite view: that persons admitted at older ages have a greater likelihood of success (Hartzler, 1951; Tavris, 1964).

Kraus (1972) and Song and Song (1969) found that length of residence favorably correlates with success on community jobs. However, McCarver and Craig (1974) were not convinced that longer institutionalization is better than shorter, since they also presented a number of studies that either found no significant correlates of length of stay or found that the shorter the stay, the better the community adjustment. Wyngaarden, Freedman, & Gollay (1976) found that age and length of institutionalization did not correlate with permanence of placement, but that tenure at the discharging institution did. The individuals who were successful in their current community living were those who had had long stays at a single institution and had few interinstitution transfers or prior community placements.

Classification of Institutional Climate

It is extremely difficult to interpret studies that compare different institutions because of the complexity of the dimensions along which institutions vary. Recognizing the necessity to quantify institutional climates, several investigators (King & Raynes, 1968a, 1968b; King, Raynes, & Tizard, 1971; McCormick, Balla, & Zigler, 1975) have developed instruments with which to classify the resident management system of an institution. These instruments have four dimensions, which are presumably correlated: the rigidity of the program, the regimentation of group activities, the depersonalization or dehumanization of institutional practices, and the social distance between residents and staff. The measurement of several institutions in an unnamed New England state, in England, and in an unnamed Scandinavian country indicates that institutions differ greatly on these dimensions. For instance, McCormick et al. (1975) reported that management practices are generally more resident oriented in Scandinavia than in New England, that larger institutions are more institution oriented in their resident care practices than smaller institutions, and that management is more resident oriented in facilities where the residents are mildly retarded than where they are severely and profoundly retarded. This final effect was especially pronounced in the United States.

CONCLUSIONS

In his paper entitled "A Provocative Case of Over-achievement by a Mongoloid," Butterfield (1961) described a 36-year-old man with Down's syndrome (Stanford-Binet IQ of 28) who could read, write legibly, and play the piano. He further described the symbiotic relationship of the youth with his mother after she became bedridden from illness. The son kept house for his invalid mother, doing the shopping, the housecleaning, and all errands that were required. It is hard to imagine these skills developing in an institution, but it is easy to imagine their developing when two people are placed into the community, where they must depend on each other. The literature reviewed in this chapter mirrors the story of this man and his mother. The home environment provides both the enrichment and the necessity for development; both of these are deficient in most institutional settings.

Chapter 3
Ideological Responses of Society to its Handicapped Citizens

Laird W. Heal

Society's responses to persons with handicaps have been characterized by astounding variability. As Wolfensberger (1969, 1972, 1976) has noted, such individuals have been deified by some and exterminated by others. This chapter summarizes the dominant ideologies (i.e., systems of values and human service models) that underly these diverse responses, and develops a logical analysis of the appropriate ideological posture of a democratic society toward its handicapped citizens.

"Handicap" is used here in its broadest sense. Any individual whose physical or behavioral characteristics fall "below" those that are culturally normal is seen to be handicapped. The absence of some body part, the subnormal ability to read or cypher, and the disposition to respond abnormally during social interaction are all handicaps. Furthermore, many cultural minorities (racial, sexual, ethnic), although probably not considered handicapped by most, are subject to similar responses from the larger society. Indeed, it is difficult to tell which response is more generic, discrimination against cultural minorities or discrimination against handicapped minorities. This definition exposes the relative nature of handicapping conditions. Everyone is handicapped given a social setting in which they deviate from the norm. A woman in a male gay bar and an American tourist in China are examples. The sighted man who drifted into H. G. Well's "Country of the Blind" was unbearably persecuted despite the benign, peaceful culture that he found there. He was eventually required to choose between an operation to remove his eyes and banishment from the valley. This allegory, although mythical, exposes the arbitrariness with which cultures define handicap.

CLASSIFICATION OF HISTORICALLY OCCURRING IDEOLOGIES

The diversity of ideologies apparently held by various societies in responding to handicapped persons has been enormous, but they can be classified with surprising simplicity on two dimensions: value and potency. (This analysis was inspired by those of Rainwater, 1970, and Dokecki, Strain, Bernal, Brown, and Robinson, 1975). That is, all ideologies appear to make implicit assumptions about the *value* of handicapped individuals and about their *potency* as members of society.

It should be noted that these two dimensions have considerable precedence in the categorization of affective responses. Osgood, May, and Miron (1975) studied no less than 22 different cultures, which varied from Japanese to East Indian to Finnish to Iranian to American, and found that all 22 relied most heavily on the value dimension (e.g., good versus bad, pleasant versus unpleasant) to describe the qualities of an array of 100 persons, places, and things. Seventeen of the twenty-two used potency (e.g., strong versus weak, big versus little) as their second dimension for making these descriptions; the other five used potency as their third dimension. Another dimension, *activity* (e.g., active versus passive, sanguine versus phlegmatic), although less salient than the first two, was also culturally universal.

The conclusion that deviant minorities have elicited responses in all four combinations of high and low value and high and low potency supports the assertion made above that the responses of societies to their handicapped minorities are not universal, but are characterized by broad variations. Indeed, minorities can be classified according to the response that they elicit from the cultural majority, and, conversely, societies can be classified according to their characteristic response to these minorities.

The classification of ideologies according to the dimensions of value and potency is shown in Table 3.1. Reading from left to right across the table, ideologies are arranged according to the value that society places on those whom it perceives to be handicapped. Reading from bottom to top, the ideologies indicate society's perception of the potency of handicapped individuals to threaten cultural norms or to promote cultural enhancement. No claim is made that the spacing between pairs of these ideologies should be equal. Valuation, for example, should surely be nearer to deification, and segregation and discrimination should be closer together or even interchanged. As is always the case when words are used to represent constructs, clarifications are essential. These are made in the next sections.

Ideologies That Imply That Handicaps Are Bad or Degenerate

When handicaps are perceived to be degenerative, society's posture toward handicapped individuals varies according to its implicit assessment of their potency to impair the cultural mainstream. If handicapped persons are seen to be impotent, then society tends to abandon them, either abruptly, as in the case of euthanasia, or more subtly, as by excessive medication or institutionalization. If handicapped persons are seen to be threatening, they are met with more direct confrontation—an example is the involuntary sterilization of mentally retarded persons and supposedly hereditary criminals. Such genocide was legal in every one of the United States in the early 1900s. The rationale for this elimination of extreme deviants is that it is required for the protection of society. It has deep

Table 3.1. Classification of ideological responses of society to its handicapped citizens

Potency	Value		
	Degenerate	Neutral	Virtuous
Potent	Destruction	Integration	Deification
Neutral	Discrimination	Egalitarianism	Valuation
	Segregation	Prosthetization	Normalization
Impotent	Abandonment	Medicalization	Compensation

roots in the instincts of animals and appears in most human cultures. Animals ordinarily abandon or destroy any offspring that are grossly deformed. Primitive cultures apparently respond similarly. The Puritans, whose ideology has been so pervasive in setting the moral tone of the United States, followed the conclusion of both Martin Luther and John Calvin in asserting that deviant human conditions originated from Satan, and the only moral response was to purge deviant individuals from the community (Erikson, 1966).

This "moralizing perspective" has been reinforced in American if not in all of Western culture by the compatible perspective of "biological determinism," or social Darwinism (Rainwater, 1970). This perspective downplays the role of environment as a determinant of one's status and roles, and assumes that low status is biologically (genetically) determined. The obvious corollaries of this position are that the biologically weak deserve their low status, and that their destruction enhances the larger society.

While these extreme ideologies are often evident in social behavior, a more temperate posture is more common: devalued populations are often segregated for "the protection of themselves and others." Each of the 50 states has "due process" legislation that provides for the segregated institutionalization of certain groups of citizens (e.g., mentally retarded persons, mentally ill individuals, and convicted criminals). Unfortunately, segregation is a dynamic, not a static, condition: segregated structures, systems, and classes of people are inevitably subjected to ever-increasing devaluation, neglect, and abandonment. Furthermore, when members of the transgressed minority attempt to interpret the transgression to the majority, they are in danger of destruction. The author is aware, for example, of a young man who was shot in the leg and subjected to 30 days of solitary confinement because of his "escape" from an institution for the mentally retarded.

Ideologies That See Handicaps as Manifestations of Virtue

At the other extreme, handicapped citizens can be valued highly. For example, many cultures and subcultures value or even deify the simple loyalty and utter incapacity for duplicity that characterizes mentally retarded individuals (Wolfensberger, 1976). In his insightful reflections on the poor, Rainwater's (1970) apotheosizing perspective attributes to the disinherited "a special quality of existential humanity that eschews the artificiality of regular society . . . [Thus,] the disinherited are held up to the rest of society not as an example of its destructiveness and barbarity, but rather of its self-destructiveness, its artificiality, and its unreal and alienated ways" (pp. 21-22). This perspective appears to be at least as valid for handicapped individuals as it is for the larger class (the poor) to which most of them belong. Most people who have developed intimate relationships with moderately retarded individuals are struck with their sincerity, genuine good will, and personfication of virtuous human qualities.

Nevertheless, this is probably the least credible corner of the ideology rectangle. Extolling the virtues of handicapped individuals is almost inevitably qualified by the position that these virtues are but a single saving grace in a tragic and pitiful life. Thus, although recognition of their virtue undoubtedly brings society to increase its valuation of handicapped people, deification or apotheosizing is seldom genuine.

On the other hand, when handicapped persons are valued but perceived as impotent, they are provided with some form of compensatory support or charity. The reverse discrimination fostered by The Education for All Handicapped Children Act (Public Law 94-142) and Section 504 of the Rehabilitation Act of 1973 (Public Law 93-112) are two obvious examples, but virtually every piece of legislation passed in recent years mandates reverse discrimination in some form for those who are handicapped by genetic, environmental, or sociocultural forces. Compensation, reverse discrimination, and charity are a trilogy of responses whose central theme is pity. Humanism and good will are perverted to the debasement of the very individuals whom they would help. Handicapped individuals are ordinarily labeled, frequently segregated from their able-bodied peers, and compensated for their "pitiful" station in life. Although not all compensatory interventions fail, they are usually ideologically flawed by the incompatability of segregated programs and the integration ideals of normalization.

Normalization, the ideology that has received a great deal of recent support as the ideal for the provision of services to handicapped individuals, lies somewhere between valuation and compensation. It regards all members of the human condition as good and valuable, but it regards handicapped members as weak; however, for most handicapped individuals, the weakness is seen to be temporary and remediable given the proper compensatory or prosthetic services.

Normalization has been thoroughly interpreted by Wolfensberger (1969, 1972, 1976, 1980; Wolfensberger & Glenn, 1975a, 1975b) for remarkably broad application by human service professionals. According to Wolfensberger (1972), it is the "utilization of means that are as culturally normative as possible in order to establish and/or maintain personal behaviors and characteristics which are as culturally normative as possible" (p. 28). With equal emphasis on means and ends, the ideology is more easily implemented and evaluated than one that emphasizes only ends. Possibly, the popularity of normalization is due to its easy translation into the equality of opportunity principle that has been fundamental in the development of American domestic policy. If equality of opportunity is the foundation of normalization, its corollaries are: *cultural normativeness* of roles, expectations, forms of address, labels, environments, social services, and rhythms of daily, weekly, annual, and lifetime activities; *developmental* (as opposed to medical) *expectations,* with disabled persons seen to be developing individuals, not incurable invalids; *integration* of activities and services, since segregation denies culturally normative opportunities; *continuity* of services so that individuals can move along a continuum from supervision to independence; *separation* of handicapped groups and their services from one another, especially separation of the domiciliary function from others, since congregation of too many individuals or services, and/or juxtaposition of many different services, impairs integration and thereby forestalls culturally normative opportunities; and *smallness* of served congregations for the same reason (Wolfensberger, 1972). Given its historical undergirding and its internal consistency, it is not surprising that the normalization principle has pervaded the development of community services for developmentally disabled individuals.

Ideologies That Are Neutral on the Value Dimension

The middle column of Table 3.1 features ideologies that appear to ignore the value dimension in the posture that they take toward handicapped individuals. At the top of this column is the ultimate ideology, the absence of a differential response toward handicapping conditions, aside from the recognition of normative individual differences in their potential for social contribution. Medicalization, which regards a human handicap as a disease, is placed at the bottom of this column. This placement requires explanation in that medicalization has both good and bad components on the value dimension—it is not neutral. On the positive side, attention to personal health is a gesture that many cultures extend to their loved ones to demonstrate their care and regard. Furthermore, it is normative to provide medical care to an incapacitated individual. On the negative side, since most handicaps are "mild" and are associated with minor, usually normative, medical problems, it is probably a devaluation to classify handicapped people with the sick and infirm. Thus, advocates of normalization regard medicalization to be a pernicious perversion of sound medical care—a thinly disguised ploy to deprive devalued individuals of their basic freedoms. For these reasons, medicalization is ascribed neutral (i.e., balanced between high and low) value. With regard to potency, medicalization is seen to be the ultimate attribution of weakness, sickness being only one step from death.

Prosthetization is the provision of prosthetic devices, such as eyeglasses and crutches, to handicapped individuals in order to facilitate their seeking integration into the larger society. It is similar in intent to compensation: both have the goal of the application of extraordinary resources in order to remediate deficiencies. The critical difference between the two, as they are defined here, is that prosthetic appliances promote integration, whereas compensatory programs promote segregation. For example, a cerebral palsied individual could be given braces (prosthetics) that provide immediate mobility, or a specialized, segregated (compensatory) training program to train him/her to walk without braces. Prosthetization provides the supports necessary for an individual to participate in the mainstream of society; compensation removes individuals from the mainstream of society in order to remediate their weaknesses through training and other social and medical services. Prosthetization is the provision of extraordinary resources to promote integration; compensation is the provision of extraordinary resources in joint occurrence with literal or figurative segregation. Crutches, foster homes, subsidized employment, hospitalization insurance, push-button phones, ramps, hieroglyphic signs, and individualized classroom instruction systems are prosthetic; special transportation programs for the elderly, special education classes, group homes, sheltered workshops, and unemployment insurance are compensatory programs that segregate and ironically devalue their recipients.

The difference between these two approaches to the amelioration of a handicapping condition is profound. Compensation, by segregation, compounds the handicap by communicating to society and to handicapped individuals that unless they improve, they are unfit to participate in the society at large. Prosthetization, on the other hand, communicates that handicapped individuals are expected to participate in the larger society and, furthermore, promotes the development of intimate interactions among all citizens so that handicaps are seen to be common variations in the human condition rather than pitiful or repulsive pathologies.

Egalitarianism, the final ideology to be considered, seeks to avoid the excesses of both normalization and segregation on the value dimension. Its cornerstone is the equality of opportunity, and it stresses the absence of differential valuation of handicapped and nonhandicapped individuals. Like Rainwater's (1970) normalizing perspective, it "resolves the initial perplexity and anxiety [regarding disinherited minorities] by the simplest mechanism possible—denial" (p. 22). The cultural majority comes to view as normal that which was at first seen to be deviant or unnatural. "The disinherited are really just like you and me except perhaps that they are mistreated and poor, but these latter conditions do not result in other than superficial differences ... Except for behavior and attitudes that are simple, direct, and immediate responses to deprivation or prejudice, their views of life and their behavior are indistinguishable from those of others in the society" (pp. 22-23).

From this perspective handicapped persons are neither debased by discrimination nor enhanced by negative discrimination. The egalitarian ideal is a social order in which no opportunity is denied or offered solely on the basis of any handicapping condition. Handicapped individuals have all the rights and privileges (including prosthetic supports) that are accorded to the population at large, no more and no less. As with Rainwater's normalizing perspective, handicaps are seen to be normal and accepted variations in the human condition. In short, it is the ideology that presses society to integrate every individual into the community at large, adapting individual strengths to the maximum benefit of society.

The objective of egalitarianism is to promote equal opportunity for all citizens to participate in society. The conservative egalitarian has interpreted this to mean that nothing should be done to promote the integration of handicapped individuals into society. This position is not reasonable in that history is replete with examples of society's disposition to reject deviant individuals. The liberal egalitarian supports at least two mechanisms to promote integration in the face of this disposition to reject oddity. The first, prosthetization, was described above in detail. The second is affirmative action, here defined as the distribution of opportunities to individuals in proportion to their prevalence in society. For example, affirmative action is a guarantee that a woman who applies for a "foreman" position will be favored over an *equally qualified* man to the extent that her sex, ethnic origin, or handicap is underrepresented among the other forepersons in her company. Thus, as defined here, affirmative action is directed to the elimination of discrimination, not the adoption of reverse discrimination. Although affirmative action is very difficult to implement, draws attention to minority distinctiveness, and is vulnerable to abuse both by handicapped persons and by those who discriminate against them, it is nevertheless egalitarian in principle. However imperfectly it is applied, it would apppear to promote rather than inhibit integration.

EGALITARIANISM AS AN ALTERNATIVE TO NORMALIZATION

The advocates of normalization have aroused widespread interest in society's ideological posture toward its handicapped citizens. By stressing the importance of associating handicaps with enhancing imagery, these advocates support the valuation, and thereby the potency, of handicapped individuals. Resistance to medicalization further increases this potency. On the other hand, by supporting compensatory services, normalization advocates necessarily engage a counterforce, one that admits to the impotence of their proteges. It is necessary to distinguish here between normalization in theory and normalization in practice. In theory, normalization stresses, above all, integration of handicapped individuals into the physical and social interactions of the larger society, and especially their right to choose the degree to which they want to participate. However, in practice most advocates of normalization are service providers who see their segregated service agencies as centers in which their clients have normalized opportunities. Thus, on the issue of compensation versus prosthetization, there is little difference between egalitarianism and normalization in theory, but considerable difference in practice.

The primary difference between egalitarianism and normalization in theory is the stress that the latter places on associating devalued deviant individuals and groups with enhancing imagery. For example, in his material on normalization, Wolfensberger includes a slide that urges the developers of group homes to place them near such an "enhancing" image as a country club or an Episcopalian Church. According to Wolfensberger's "conservative corollary," dress, hair style, cleanliness, and so forth of handicapped individuals should be made to conform to the positive end of the normative continuum in order to compensate for the negative imagery that cultural norms associate with the handicap. There seems to be a measure of self-contradiction in this application of imagery. Why should the disinherited emulate the disinheritor? Why shouldn't the disinherited instead rebel against the association of minorities with any images, good or bad? Why shouldn't the quality of "human-ness" supersede all other qualities as the basis for human valuation?

Because of its current popularity among professionals interested in the integration of handicapped individuals into the community, normalization dominates the chapters that follow. However, the analysis in Chapter 15 suggests a framework for the ways in which handicapped citizens would benefit if society would take a more egalitarian posture toward them.

SUMMARY

This chapter discusses the ideologies that society has adopted in its responses to handicapped citizens. These ideologies are seen to vary on two dimensions, value and potency. Value refers to the worth of individuals as judged by the larger society, and potency refers to individuals' perceived abilities to effect social change. If handicapped citizens are seen to be strong and good, they are valued or even deified; if they are seen to be strong and evil, they are destroyed; if weak and good, they are provided with charity, or compensation; if weak and evil, they are ignored or abandoned. Normalization, the currently dominant ideology among human service professionals, apparently represents handicapped persons as good and weak. It was suggested that a more egalitarian ideology, as an alternative to both segregation and normalization, would more likely facilitate the integrated participation of handicapped citizens in society.

Part II
THE DEINSTITUTIONALIZED PERSON IN THE COMMUNITY

Chapter 4
Characteristics of Community Residential Facilities

Laird W. Heal, Angela R. Novak,
Carol K. Sigelman, and Harvey N. Switzky

Since 1850, when there were four public residential facilities (PRFs) in the United States, there has been an exponential growth in the number of PRFs; their numbers have increased from about 105 in 1960 to about 266 in 1976 (Conroy, 1977; Scheerenberger, 1978). The number of residents in these public facilities rose steadily until 1967, when it reached a high of about 200,000, but it has steadily declined since that time until today there are approximately 150,000. Butterfield (1976) indicates that this decline in population has been caused by the dramatic increase in releases from PRFs, since the number of admissions has remained stable or even increased slightly. Additionally, the decrease in the number of individuals in institutions for the mentally retarded cannot be explained by numerous transfers to public mental hospitals, because their populations of mentally retarded residents have declined at least as dramatically as those of PRFs (Butterfield, 1976). Parallel to the decrease in PRF populations has been the increase in the number of community residential facilities (CRFs). Of the 4290 CRFs studied by Bruininks, Hauber, and Kudla in 1977 (reported in 1979), 3256 had been in operation for less than 10 years.

A number of recent studies have addressed themselves to the movement of developmentally disabled persons from PRFs to CRFs. Nine of these, which are cited extensively throughout this volume, are listed and described in Table 4.1. Each column of this table shows basic methodological information about these studies, which vary broadly in purpose and quality. This chapter describes CRF facilities, their residents, and their staffs as they have been portrayed in these studies.

Much of the information contained herein has been adapted or quoted directly from Heal, L. W., Sigelman, C. K., & Switzky, H. N., Research on community residential alternatives for the mentally retarded. In N. R. Ellis (Ed.) *International Review of Research in Mental Retardation,* Vol. 9. New York: Academic Press, 1978.

Table 4.1. Essential information from nine recent studies of deinstitutionalization

Study	Data period	Target population				Instrument/ procedure	Topic of study	Respondents				Notes
		Location	Focus	Age	Notes[a]			N	n	% Rtn	R	
Baker, Seltzer, & Seltzer (1974, 1977)	Summer 1973	USA	CRF CS	Adult	Extensive search; foster homes included; ten models identified	Mail questionnaire	CRF	est'd 888	381	43	Ckr	R unspecified
						Site visit; Omnibus instruments	CRM CSS PSP	5	15	100	Ckr	R unspecified; 15 CRFs in northeast
Bell (1976)	Fall 1973 to Summer 1974	Texas	CRF IS	All	All released residents from all 10 Texas Ins	Mail questionnaire	CSS PSP	503	190	34	Res Ckr	R = Ckr when IQ <55; low and high IQ groups compared
Butterfield (1976)	1950–1971	USA	PRF	All	All PRFs in the USA	Source of data was not specified	PRF	?	?	NA	?	None specified
Gollay, Wyngaarden, Freedman, & Kurtz (1978)	1972–1974	USA	CRF IS	6–40	Released residents from 10 selected Ins	Inv with Res & Ckr; Ins data; questionnaire for Inv; AAMD ABS	CRF CRM	919	382	42	Res Ckr	"Nonreturnees"
							CSS PSP	323	58	18	Res Ckr	"Returnees" to Ins
Bruininks, Hauber, & Kudla (1979)	1977	USA	CRF	All	All CRFs in the USA	Mail questionnaire	CRF	5038	4427	88	CRF	R = residence manager

Study	Year	Country	Facility	Sample selection	Target population	N	n	% return	R	Comments
O'Connor (1976)	1973–1974	USA	GH CS	All	Comprehensive CRF sample, but limited to GH	GH 3582 CSS CRF	3412 611	95 95[b] 95	CRF GH Res	611 of 3325 nominees were GHs; 105, stratified by age, proprietorship, and size were chosen for Inv
					Mail survey of "nominees"					
					Inv with 105 GHs; AAMD ABS	GH CRM CSS	105 420			
Scheerenberger (1976)	1975–1976 Fiscal yr.	USA	PRF IS	All	100% sample of PRFs	PRF	239	100	PRF	R = superintendent or proxy
					Mail questionnaire on Res and Res transfers and Ins costs		239			
Scheerenberger (1978)	1976–1977 Fiscal yr.	USA	PRF IS	All	100% sample of PRFs	PRF	206 266	100	PRF	R = superintendent or proxy
					Mail questionnaire on Res and Res transfer and Ins costs					
Wyngaarden & Gollay (1976)	1972–1974	USA	Ins IS	All	All public and private Ins for the retarded	Ins IS	250 154	62	Ins	Presumably Ins superintendents
					Mail questionnaire					

Abbreviations: ABS = the American Association on Mental Deficiency's Adaptive Behavior Scale (Nihira, Foster, Shellhaas, & Leland, 1974). Ckr = caretaker of a resident. CRF = community residential facility, sometimes including the natural home. CRM = comparison of residential models. CS = community sample of residents; i.e., cases were located by searching for CRFs. CSS = community support services. GH = group home = a CRF (excluding the natural home, foster homes, and health care facilities) that serves 80 or fewer residents. Although O'Conner did not specify an upper limit, it is probably only a minor distortion to use the Baker et al. upper limit of 80 for definitional purposes. Ins = institution, public or private, ordinarily having more than 80 residents. Inv = interviewer or interview. IS = institution sample of residents; i.e., cases were located by finding the CRFs of individuals who had been released from PRFs. PRF = public residential facility. PSP = prediction of successful placement. R = respondent. Res = resident of a CRF, PRF or Ins.

[a] The target population was nationwide unless otherwise specified.
[b] When a random sample was selected for the study the percent return is less than n/N.

CLASSIFICATION OF COMMUNITY RESIDENTIAL FACILITIES (CRFs)

Table 4.2 shows a reasonably comprehensive taxonomy of residential alternatives presently available for developmentally disabled persons. This taxonomy is a revision of Scheerenberger's (1976b) list of categories used by superintendents of public residential facilities (PRFs) to classify the placement sites of their discharged clients. Because of variations in laws from state to state, each category includes a variety of residential options. A brief description of each category is provided below.

1. *Independent Living* refers to a site where an individual lives with a roommate, a spouse, or alone; usually an apartment or duplex, but occasionally a house.
2. *Natural or Adoptive Home* refers to the home of one's parents, usually natural parents, since Gollay, Freedman, Wyngaarden, and Kurtz (1978) found a negligible proportion of adoptive homes. Studies do not always discriminate between homes of parents and those of relatives, so this category occasionally includes both. The largest number of discharges, nearly a quarter of the total, are made to these natural homes.
3. *Other Relatives' Home* refers to the home of a resident's sibling, grandparent, aunt, uncle, or offspring.
4. *Friend's Home* refers to the home of someone who has befriended the resident or the resident's family.
5. *Foster Home* refers to a home whose "parents" accept the discharged individual in return for a stipend. The stipend is usually insufficient to provide a monetary incentive for the placement. These placements are often called family care placements, and are often made to homes that are approved by the institution rather than by the state's department responsible for family services.
6. *Group Homes* are homes that house as few as two or as many as 100 developmentally disabled children or adults. Typically, the number residing in one home is six to eight. Residences in several other categories are often called group homes.
7. A *Community ICF* (intermediate care facility) is licensed as a nursing home, making it eligible for federal Medicaid support (Title XIX of the Social Security Act and its Amendments). Two classes are distinguished according to size: 15 and under, and 16 and over. The larger homes must have a nurse (LPN) on duty at all times, whereas the smaller homes need only have one on call. ICFs, especially the smaller ones, often refer to themselves as group homes, and are usually classified as such in research on residential alternatives.
8. A *Convalescent Home* is a nursing home whose residents are expected to stay for a reasonably short period of time for rehabilitation before they return to the community.

Table 4.2. Taxonomy of residential alternatives for developmentally disabled individuals

	Scheerenberger (1976b, 1978)[a]: Discharged resident (%)		Baker, Seltzer, & Seltzer (1977)[b]: Community residential facility (N = 381) (%)	Hill, Sather, Kudla & Bruininks (1978)[c]: State & DC MR/DD coordinators (N = 51) (%)	Gollay, Wyngaarden, Freedman, & Kurtz (1978)[b]: Residents discharged to CRFs having 25 or fewer persons (N = 440) (%)	Hanley & Heal (Chapter 11)[d]: States' regulations (N = 84) (%)
1. Independent living	1.4	1.4	5.0	a. Staffed apartments 56.9 b. "Visiting professional" 9.8	a. Semi-independent 10 b. Independent 10	8.3
2. Natural or adoptive home	22.2	24.6	—	—	14 (See natural home)	—
3. Other relative	2.3	2.2	—	—	0	—
4. Friend's home	—	0.0	—	—	0 (See semi-independent)	—
5. Foster home	14.7	8.2	14.4	66.7	18	7.1
6. Group home	15.9	16.9	62.7	CRF 100.0	48	35.7
7. Community ICF	8.2	7.9	(See group home)	(See CRF) 0	(See group home) 0	16.7
8. Convalescent home	1.1	3.9	(See convalescent home)	(See nursing home) 10.0	—	0 (See nursing home)
9. Nursing home	15.6	7.0	(See convalescent home)	(See CRF) 45.1	—	13.1
10. County home	0.2	0.3	(See convalescent home)	0	—	0 (See nursing home)
11. Public residential facility	11.6	16.0	—	a. Institutional or regional center 100.0 b. Residential schools (children) 21.6	—	(See nursing home)
12. Private residential facility	0.7	—	a. Mini-institutions 1.3 b. Sheltered villages 2.4	a. (See CRF) 0 b. Sheltered villages 2.0	—	0
13. Work placement	4.1	3.2	4.2	(See CRF) 13.7	0 (See semi-independent)	—
14. Boarding home	1.3	2.1	0 (cf. group home)	—	0 (See group home)	19.0
15. Mental hospital	1.2	6.1	—	(See Institutional or Regional Centers) 0	—	—
16. Prison and other	0.2	0.2	—	—	—	—
TOTAL	100.0	100.0	100.0		100	

NOTE: — = not included in the study population; 0 = included in the indicated category.

[a] For the Scheerenberger study the first percent column indicates the percent discharged into each CRF category in fiscal year 1975–1976; the second column indicates the corresponding percent for fiscal year 1976–1977.

[b] For the Baker et al. and Gollay et al. studies, the percentages are based on the proportion of the sampled residences that fell into the indicated categories.

[c] For the Hill et al. study the percentages are based on the proportion of the states that have facilities in the indicated categories.

[d] For the Hanley and Heal study, the percentages are based on the proportion of states that have regulations relating to the indicated categories.

9. *Nursing Homes* include a variety of residential alternatives, all providing continuing medical care for anyone who needs it. The convalescent home and intermediate care facility are specially licensed nursing homes. Nursing homes are nearly always privately owned and are expected to make a profit for their owners.
10. The *County Home* is another type of nursing home, usually for the elderly who are unable to afford private nursing home care. It was a much more common institutional alternative for the elderly before Medicaid made nursing homes more readily affordable.
11. *Public Residential Facilities* (PRFs) are state institutions. Until recently these were very large, typically having about 1500 residents and occasionally having over 5000, but today they average only about 500 residents each, and many have fewer than 50.
12. *Private Residential Facilities* are a variety of privately owned and foundation-owned residential alternatives. Some of these are expensive, highly visible, multiple-treatment centers; some are largely custodial facilities; and some are communes that feature an idyllic life for handicapped and nonhandicapped co-residents.
13. *Work Placement* refers to placement where room and board are provided as a condition of employment. Presumably this category includes the "workshop dormitories" studied by Baker, Seltzer, and Seltzer (1977).
14. *Boarding Homes* are homes where the resident is provided room and board for a fee, but no other services are contracted. These homes house individuals of varying abilities. They are usually not classified as group or family care homes.
15. A *Mental Hospital* is an institution for mentally ill individuals. Although many placements were made to these facilities in the past, Scheerenberger's data (1976b, 1978) indicate that they are about 5 percent.
16. Other alternatives, including *Prisons,* account for less than 0.2 percent of the discharges from institutions for developmentally disabled persons.

Investigators of community residential facilities (CRFs) have made very few refinements of this list. For instance, in the category of private residential facilities, Baker, Seltzer, and Seltzer (1977) distinguished two subcategories: the mini-institution and the sheltered village. Neither of these is apparently visible to the PRF superintendent, since they were listed as placement sites for less than 0.1 percent of the discharged PRF residents during fiscal year 1975–1976. Although these alternatives are rarely utilized, they are of great ideological interest, and should probably be utilized in any inquiry into types of residential alternatives for developmentally disabled persons. The mini-institution is important because of the position embodied in the principle of normalization that the size of an institution is a crucial determinant of the quality of life of its residents. The sheltered village is important not only because it is somewhat incompatible with normalization ideology, but also because its various models have deeply rooted and historically persistent ideologies of their own. For instance, the rural, idyllic life style it represents has frequently been proposed in the past as one that is appropriate for mentally retarded individuals. Furthermore, the protected environment of the sheltered village is seen by many as the only alternative that provides both dignity and safety for these citizens. The sheltered village is, to a great extent, the modern manifestation of the noble plans that the builders of rural institutions held a century ago. The second refinement of Scheerenberger's categories is the division of "Independent Living" into "Staffed Apartments" and "Visiting Professional Apartments" (by Bruininks and his associates). This refinement seems crucial in permitting the investigator to indicate the degree of support provided to the resident in an apartment placement.

Perhaps the greatest weakness in the various taxonomies that have evolved is the failure to refine the group home category. Baker et al. (1977) divided the category into five subdivisions, four according to size and one according to the presence of disabilities other than mental retardation. Classification by size appears to be crucial, particularly in relation to normalization. However, a more ideal division by size would be one that was more in correspondence with licensing and other regulatory guideposts than that used by Baker et al. For instance, many if not most states treat a home differently if there are four or more unrelated persons under domiciliary care than if there are three or fewer. Furthermore, federal ICF regulations are different for homes of 15 or fewer than they are for homes of 16 or more (General Accounting Office, 1977). It seems, then, that group homes might best be divided into three categories for research purposes: 2–3, 4–15, and over 15 residents. An additional division of those with over with 15 residents might be made in terms of the management model: house parents versus manager. O'Connor (1976) indicated that larger group homes were more likely to have managers as opposed to house parents. Furthermore, the category "Intermediate Care Facility" should be distinguished from the others in that it is associated with mandated nursing services in addition to domiciliary services. Finally, the natural home should always be considered as a site for community placement, since about 25 percent of all persons released from residential facilities are placed into their natural homes (Scheerenberger, 1976b, 1978).

CHARACTERISTICS OF COMMUNITY FACILITY RESIDENTS

Turning to characteristics of the residents themselves, both O'Connor (1976) and Baker et al. (1977) reported that about 52 percent of CRF residents had come from PRFs, about 31 percent had come from their family homes, and the remainder had come from other residences. However, Bruininks, Hauber, and Kudla (1979), with a much larger and more recent sample, found that only 35 percent of the CRF residents had come from institutions. About 32.4 percent had come from their natural homes, 24.3 percent from other community placements, and 8.3 percent from unspecified sources.

Most CRF residents are between the ages of 16 and 30, although the entire age range is represented. About 55 percent of all CRF residents are male (Hauber, Kudla, Wieck, Masiee, & Kirwin, 1979), and approximately equal proportions of males and females are distributed to Baker's 10 models (Baker et al., 1977).

Soforenko and Macy (1977) found that the male population was, on the average, older than the female population—37 years compared to 28 years. They also found that the males had been institutionalized twice as long as the females—17.9 years to 8.5 years—and that the number of married males exceeded the number of married females by 14 percent, contrary to previous findings. Soforenko and Macy also found a higher rate of discharge for black persons than for the general institution population. Humm-Delgado (1978) found that racial minority clients were not receiving a proportionate share of community residence services.

The AAMD (American Association on Mental Deficiency) functioning-level classification of CRF residents in 1973 was about 2.5 percent profound, about 17 percent severe, about 28 percent moderate, about 30 percent mild, and about 23 percent nonretarded (O'Connor, 1976). These figures are consistent with those of Gollay et al. (1978) for residents who had been released from institutions from 1972 through 1974. Gollay et al. tabulated the number of adults (above age 18) and children (age 18 or below) in each of the four mental retardation categories. Their percentages for adults were 4 percent in the profound range, 19 percent severe, 34 percent moderate, and 43 percent in the mild categories; those for children were 8 percent in the profound range, 22 percent severe, 29 percent moderate, and 41 percent in the mild categories. Although CRFs have generally housed individuals with milder levels of mental retardation, there has been considerable variation from model to model. Persons placed in foster care placements and sheltered villages tend to have lower levels of functioning than those placed in mixed group homes, nursing homes, and workshop dormitories (Baker et al., 1977).

Figures from Bruininks, Hauber, and Kudla (1979) indicate a downward shift in ability levels since these earlier studies, with more lower-functioning residents living in community facilities; part of this downward shift may reflect Bruininks' superior case-finding. By mid-1977, 11 percent of CRF residents were classified in the profound range, 22 percent severe, 35 percent moderate, and 30 percent in the mild and borderline categories. Another fact that is certain to influence future community residential planning is that approximately 61.5 percent of current PRF residents are multiply handicapped (Scheerenberger, 1978), whereas only about 35 percent of O'Connor's group home residents were so classified. Soforenko and Macy (1978) point out that, although 61 percent of the total PRF population in their study was in the severe and profound range, only 10 percent of the deinstitutionalized group was in these ranges, reflecting what one would expect during a period of "rapid depopulation" of the institution.

BUILDING TYPES

Baker et al. (1977), as well as others whose studies were on a smaller scale, such as Wehbring and Ogren (1975), describe a broad variety of living facilities being used as CRFs. These include apartment buildings, former hotels, farm houses, town houses, ranches, and convents. The comparison of findings from different studies is made difficult by the fact that not all of the studies used the same definition of "community residential facility." O'Connor, for example, did not include foster family placements whereas Baker and Gollay did. Bruininks, Hauber, and Kudla (1979), in their 1977 national survey, excluded three categories from their definition of a community residential facility: natural homes; nursing homes, boarding homes, and foster homes that were not specifically licensed or contracted as developmental disabilities service providers; and apartment programs when no staff resided in the same facility with residents. Even so, they distinguished 37 different types of facilities fitting their definition of "community-based" living quarters that provide 24-hour, 7-day-a-week responsibility for room, board, and supervision of developmentally disabled persons. These distinctions between different definitions of "community residential facility," shown in Table 4.2, should be kept in mind throughout the present discussion. Despite the difficulty of comparison, these studies contain the most extensive current and nationwide research on CRFs available.

Bruininks, Hauber, and Kudla (1979) identified a total of 5038 CRFs (reported by Hauber, Kudla, Wieck, & Anderson, 1978) that had a total of 76,250 residents, for an average of 15 per residence. However, only about a fourth of these persons lived in CRFs having 10 or fewer residents, whereas an equal number lived in CRFs having more than 100 residents.

The buildings used as CRFs come in a wide variety of types. In Baker et al.'s (1977) study, only a small percentage (15 percent) were found to be new structures, built or purchased specifically for CRF use. O'Connor depicted the typical CRF as being a fairly large (7 to 20 rooms) and older (built over 20 years ago) home in a residential area or in a combined residential/small business area. In the Baker et al. study 54 percent of the group homes were old houses, and in the Gollay et al. study 60 percent of the individuals surveyed lived in single family dwellings.

Another aspect of the community residential facility environment is its interior and exterior appearance. Gollay et al. (1978) reported that over half of the CRFs studied were rated excellent on cleanliness, homeliness, and overall appearances; only independent living settings rated poorly on these factors. O'Connor reported 69 percent to be in good-to-excellent condition externally and to be homelike and in fair-to-good condition internally. Wolpert (1978) reported that most group homes in his study were better maintained, in such external aspects as appearance and landscaping, than surrounding neighborhood properties. It would appear that most community residences are considered generally neat, clean, and well maintained.

CHARACTERISTICS OF COMMUNITY FACILITY CARETAKERS

Many of the surveys have investigated the caretakers as well as the residents and building types of community residential facilities. Caretakers tended to be well educated: natural parents averaged 11 years of education, foster parents 12 years, and group home managers 15 years (Gollay et al., 1978). Seventy-three percent of the CRF caretakers in Scheerenberger and Felsenthal's (1977) study said that they took their jobs because of "personal satisfaction" or because of "a specific interest in mental retardation." Ninety-eight percent of the caretakers in the study by Gollay et al. indicated that they enjoyed working with mentally retarded individuals. As might be expected, only 42 percent of these caretakers indicated that they were pleased with the monetary benefits of the work. In Intagliata's (1978) study of foster family care providers, 34 percent reported that they had an altruistic motive in taking on this work. Forty percent had had no formal training but felt that raising their own children had been adequate preparatory background for this work. Half of his sample had not graduated from high school. He also found that a significant proportion (29 percent) of foster family care providers in New York State were over 60 years of age, and noted that this tendency was paralleled by Willer's (1978) findings. Willer, in his 1978 study of families who chose to take their natural children back into the home, found a slightly higher percentage of female heads of household over 60 than in younger age groups. Thus, foster family care providers appear to be more like natural parents than like the much younger trained staff in group homes and other larger facilities.

Berdiansky and Parker (1977) found that the openings of many group homes were delayed when the group home developers quickly exhausted their lists of applicants for the jobs of managers; their difficulties in finding qualified group home managers included setting standards too high for the positions, low salaries, the nature of the work, and vague job descriptions. However, the major problem that these developers listed for opening group homes was the difficulty of working with mental retardation centers to obtain "suitable group home residents."

The staff-resident ratio varies with the type of CRF. O'Connor found that the ratio of staff to residents was significantly higher in group homes for younger residents than in those for older ones, higher in those with fewer residents, and higher in nonprofit homes than in proprietary establishments. Group home staff-to-resident ratios averaged about 1:2 based on a 40-hour week, which compares favorably with the 1:1.6 for PRF resident care workers reported by Scheerenberger (1978).

ROLE OF NORMALIZATION
IN THE COMMUNITY RESIDENTIAL FACILITY

An account of the current status of the nation's residential services for the handicapped would be incomplete without noting the extent to which normalization ideology has pervaded decision making in the community residential facility movement.

Given its historical undergirding and its internal consistency, as discussed in Chapter 3, it is not surprising that the normalization principle has pervaded the development of community services for developmentally disabled individuals. State plans, such as that of the (Illinois) Governor's Planning Council on Developmental Disabilities (1977), include descriptions of a complete continuum of community residential alternatives. In practice, some 70 percent of the CRFs studied by Baker, Seltzer, and Seltzer (1974) and Gollay et al. (1978) were houses, whether new or old, that were set on residential streets. While one might question why the other 30 percent were not so placed, it is clear that normative settings were selected in the overwhelming majority of the cases. Gollay reported that 68 percent of the individuals in her study were within walking distance of a shopping district, and nearly that many were within walking distance of public transportation. Again, these figures fall short of the ideal of 100 percent, but individual constraints invariably prevent all facilities from following exactly the same model.

Baker et al. (1977) evaluated the extent to which each of their CRF models met normalization ideals. Not surprisingly, they found that apartments, smaller group homes, mixed homes, and homes for the elderly more nearly met these ideals than did the larger group homes, foster care placements, sheltered villages, and workshop dormitories. Humm-Delgado (1978) found that the best positive predictors of "normalization" for group-home residents were: younger staff, more highly educated staff, number of years of operation, and a lower percentage of the area's population being over 65 years of age.

Evidence of the recency of the impact of normalization on the CRF movement was offered by Baker et al. (1977), who found (contrary to Humm-Delgado) that group homes with a longer history of operation tended to be more restrictive, be less normalized, require fewer household duties from the residents, and have a lower quantity and quality of work activity for their residents. A related finding was reported by Wyngaarden, Freedman, and Gollay (1976), who found that individuals who had been released from institutions with long-standing deinstitutionalization policies had had less intensive prerelease programming, had fewer community services available, and depended on their releasing institutions for a greater proportion of their postrelease services.

De Silva and Faflak (1976) report on a 14-year-long release program of one institution, most of whose discharged residents had been in the borderline and mildly retarded ranges. Earlier placement options had consisted of government-funded boarding home programs and leaves of absences to natural or substitute families; only recently had the institution begun discharging residents directly into community residence programs with the residents paying their own rent or room and board. Releases into the boarding home and leave-of-absence programs had escalated in the most recent periods, and more moderately and severely retarded individuals were being included.

Of Soforenko and Macy's (1977) discharged population, 77 percent had been released before recent legal rights legislation had occurred and before deinstitutionalization had become a popular movement. They found very positive signs of a trend toward "self-mainstreaming": 52 percent of the clients who had been discharged over a 9-year period could not be located. Of the persons placed originally in group homes, only one-third still lived there; the number of persons placed initially into apartments had doubled by the time of the study. In Humm-Delgado's (1978) sample, fully 77 percent of the original group home residents had also moved out—into their own apartments, supervised apartments, and rooming or boarding homes.

Once administration ideology, then, has adopted normalization as a working principle, the integration of individuals into the community escalates. In recent years, the average size of community residences has been reduced, more lower-functioning residents have been integrated into the community, and apparently even the clients themselves have internalized the principle (Soforenko & Macy, 1977). As they are moved into normalized settings, clients subsequently choose more independent settings for themselves and disappear from facility lists.

CONCLUSIONS

This chapter reviews the research that describes various CRF models, their residents, and their staff, as they have evolved on the national scene. The impression left by this review is that a broadly diverse array of models has been developed. Yet, the movement has spread so quickly that research is only beginning to address the difficulties and complexities of classification of a wide range of alternatives, description of their differences, and understanding of the role normalization plays in successful community adjustment. The gathering of data beyond basic head counts and demographic figures, with more concern for service quality, will be necessary if community facilities are to continue as viable residential alternatives for developmentally disabled citizens.

Chapter 5
Factors That Affect the Success of Community Placement

Carol K. Sigelman, Angela R. Novak,
Laird W. Heal, and Harvey N. Switzky

As in any other form of human adaptation, the community adjustment of developmentally disabled persons is a process involving interaction between individuals and their environments (L. Phillips, 1968). The person brings certain skills and characteristics to the process, the environment exerts influence on individual behavior, and both person and environment inevitably change as a result.

Unfortunately, this concept of community adjustment is not incorporated into the bulk of existing research. First, adjustment is most often measured at a single point in time rather than longitudinally and so it is not really examined as a process. Moreover, although much attention has been devoted to individual characteristics as predictors of success and of individuals' accommodations to their environments, little is known about environmental accommodation to the behaviors of the individual or even about the effects of different environments (Freedman, 1976). Finally, as Freedman notes, the simple success-failure dichotomy, hinging on whether or not a previously "institutionalized" person remains in the community, has been used to operationalize what is certainly a more complex phenomenon.

Although more can and will be said about the limitations of previous research, the concepts of community adjustment introduced above guide the discussion below. First, characteristics of the individual being deinstitutionalized are considered, through allusion to previous reviews and examination of research that has been recently completed. Included here is evidence regarding the role of training received prior to deinstitutionalization, on the assumption that such training facilitates the acquisition of skills that then become part of the total

---

Much of the information contained herein has been adapted or quoted directly from Heal, L. W., Sigelman, C. K., & Switzky, H. N., Research on community residential alternatives for the mentally retarded. In N. R. Ellis (Ed.) *International Review of Research in Mental Retardation*, Vol. 9. New York: Academic Press, 1978.

complex of characteristics brought by the individual to the community adjustment process. Second, selected characteristics of the community environment are analyzed. Finally, interactions between individual and environmental factors are considered. This review is guided by the view that environmental variables and their interactions with personal factors have received too little emphasis heretofore (Freedman, 1976; Lambert, 1974; Sigelman & Bell, 1975; Sigelman, Bell, Schoenrock, Elias, & Danker-Brown, 1978.)

CHARACTERISTICS OF THE DEINSTITUTIONALIZED INDIVIDUAL

The published literature includes several major reviews on community adjustment of persons who have left institutions for the mentally retarded (Cobb, 1972; Eagle, 1967; Heal, Sigelman, & Switzky, 1978; McCarver & Craig, 1974; Shafter, 1957; Windle, 1962). The McCarver and Craig review was particularly comprehensive and analytical. Rather than duplicating their efforts, this chapter, following the lead of its earlier version (Heal et al., 1978), recalls their major findings and reviews some recent research that sheds further light on the difficulties of predicting community success on the basis of individual characteristics.

Briefly, the findings relative to characteristics and skills of clients were as follows:

1. There is no consistent relationship between adjustment to community living and age at the time of release. Windle (1962) concluded that age was generally positively correlated with success, but five of the 24 studies reviewed by McCarver and Craig (1974) found an inverse relationship, and nine reported no significant relationship in either direction.
2. There is a consistent absence of relationship between diagnostic category (organic versus cultural-familial) and adjustment.
3. Race, although examined in relatively few studies, is not predictive of community success.
4. Although intellectual level has been analyzed in numerous studies, most have reported contradictory findings. This area is discussed in more detail below.
5. Academic ability may be weakly related to community adjustment, but, as with intellectual level, the bulk of the research reports no appreciable relationship.
6. Personality appears to be related to community adjustment, although evidence is not extremely strong.
7. Personal appearance, although seldom examined, was positively related to success in three of four studies.
8. The presence of physical handicaps bears no consistent relationship to success of placement.
9. Vocational skills appear to be somewhat associated with community success.

10. Psychomotor skills, primarily performance IQ measures, appear to bear some relationship to adjustment, primarily to vocational adjustment, but the evidence is not compelling.
11. Social skills were significantly related to success in five of the six studies in which they were examined.

All told, McCarver and Craig were unwilling, given 175 published studies, to conclude that any one of these individual variables was an unambiguous predictor of community success. If knowledge is to expand, it is essential that reasons for the failure of previous research to confirm predicted relations be identified.

Community Adjustment and IQ

Surprisingly, intellectual functioning, which is correlated with academic ability and a variety of other skills, has not consistently predicted community success. However, presuming that IQ is related to adjustment, institutions often use it as a selection criterion, releasing first those individuals in the mild to borderline ranges of retardation (e.g., Goldstein, 1964; Soforenko & Macy, 1977; Windle, 1962). Although a positive relationship between IQ and community adjustment was reported in at least 12 studies reviewed by McCarver and Craig (1974) and was suggested by seven more, 13 studies reported no relationship, and one even reported a negative relationship (Hartzler, 1953). Aninger and Bolinsky's (1977) recent study also found no relationship between IQ and community adjustment. However, as is discussed below, it is unreasonable to look for a simple relationship, because IQ apparently is positively related to some measures of placement success and negatively related to others.

McCarver and Craig noted that most studies had focused on a restricted range of retarded persons, generally the mildly retarded, thus reducing the probability of uncovering significant relationships. This explanation is supported by a recent study (Bell, 1976) that included a wider range of IQs than did many earlier studies, and compared several aspects of the adjustment of discharged persons with IQs above or below 55. Higher-IQ subjects were more likely to be employed, less likely to live at home, and more likely to be active in programs and leisure activities. Their only major liability in comparison to the lower-IQ group was that they were more likely to be arrested. Windle (1962) also emphasized the prevalence of delinquency and personality problems among the higher-IQ level residents as the cause of this inconsistent relationship between IQ and placement success. Baker, Seltzer, and Seltzer (1977) confirmed the relationship between employment and IQ, as did Aninger and Bolinsky (1977). O'Connor (1976) reported a similar relationship between employment and level of functioning as determined by the Adaptive Behavior Scale (Nihira, Foster, Shellhaas, & Leland, 1974), finding that those residents in community residential facilities who were in paid jobs had higher levels of functioning than did those in other day activities or training programs.

Further clarification of the relationship between IQ and placement success has been provided by the Abt Associates project directed by Gollay (1976; Gollay, Freedman, Wyngaarden, & Kurtz, 1978; Wyngaarden, Freedman, & Gollay, 1976; Wyngaarden & Gollay, 1976). In a series of multiple regression analyses, Gollay (1976) found that level of retardation was a significant predictor of four out of five success of outcome variables. Compared to the less retarded individuals, *more* retarded persons were *more* likely to remain in the community and had *fewer* unmet needs. On the other hand, they had more problems and were allowed less independence in their residential settings. As Gollay suggested, it may be that more severely retarded individuals have a lower standard of achievement to meet in order to remain in the community. A Texas Tech University study directed by Bell (Sigelman et al., 1978) also found that more severely retarded clients were significantly more likely to remain in the community than higher IQ clients. They postulated, in accordance with Gollay's suggestion, that environmental factors are at work to lessen the demands for independent functioning that are placed on more severely handicapped individuals. They also concluded that clients of virtually any intellectual functioning level can "make it" in the community, as long as adequate supports are provided. However, by implication, these studies do not suggest that more severely retarded persons would be successful in more independent living environments.

The research of Bell (1976), Gollay (1976), and Sigelman et al. (1978) suggests that a reexamination of the role of intellectual competence in community adjustment is in order. The major difference between their and previous studies is that there was more variation in IQ scores and a more diverse set of outcome variables in their samples. They suggest that the impact of retardation level depends on the outcome variable at issue. Gollay and Sigelman recommend, as other reviewers have, that IQ not be the major criterion for release into the community, because severely retarded persons were found to succeed in the community with adequate support. At the same time, these findings suggest that intellectual level should be considered in matching client to type of residential alternative, so that demands for independent functioning match client competence.

Community Adjustment and Other Personal Variables

As is the case with intellectual level, age has not consistently predicted community success in previous studies (McCarver & Craig, 1974). However, in Gollay's (1976) multiple regression analysis, age emerged as a relatively powerful correlate of outcome. Although younger persons in Gollay's sample were more retarded than older ones, age, independent of retardation level, predicted placement outcome. Younger clients were more likely to remain in the community and had fewer problems and fewer unmet needs; older clients were more active in the community and experienced more freedom of decision-making in their residential settings. Children differed from adults with regard to aspects of their institutional backgrounds and characteristics of the communities to which they were returned; they were also more likely than adults to be placed in their natural homes. Hence, Gollay proposed that the community may be more accepting and supportive of children than adults. Considering age and IQ together, the evidence of Gollay (1976) and Sigelman et al. (1978) indicates that the success of younger, less competent persons is mediated by more moderate demands for independent functioning.

Nihira and Nihira (1975a, 1975b) have examined both age and intellectual functioning as correlates of problem behaviors in community residential settings. Of 1252 incidents reported as "serious" by 109 caretakers in family care and board-and-care facilities, 16 percent were judged to represent actual or potential legal or medical jeopardy. The "jeopardy" primarily placed the resident in question, rather than other persons, in danger. Legal problem incidents were experienced mainly by individuals in the mild and borderline levels of retardation, as was the case in Bell's (1976) research. Moderately retarded residents were underrepresented in the reports of problem incidents, and children and adolescents were more likely to have engaged in jeopardizing behaviors than were adults. Nihira and Nihira (1975b) found that positive behaviors, which they construed to be signs of adjustment, were not a function of intellectual level or of age.

Another method for determining whether personal characteristics are associated with community adjustment has been the study of reasons for failure. Sigelman et al. (1978) found that, when caretakers were asked why their clients had returned to the state school, 52 percent of the reasons were accounted for by behavior, health, and work adjustment problems. These reasons appear to reflect client deficiencies, but could also reflect caretakers' low tolerance for deviance; they perceived the clients' negative behaviors to be caused by deficiencies within the clients rather than by aspects of the home environments that the caretakers were responsible for. In a review of the research concerning foster family placements, Sternlicht (1978) surveyed individual resident characteristics affecting the success of foster care placement, and found that unacceptable behavior and poor health were the two most common causes of failure. Age related to successful placement in a curvilinear fashion: youths below approximately 15 years of age and adults above 50 were more successful than those at the intermediate ages. Lower IQ also seemed to be associated with successful placement, and independence in self-care was the most significant skill required for success.

The Adaptive Behavior Scale (Nihira et al., 1974) is designed to measure a broad range of personal and social competencies and liabilities, and should correlate with measures of community success, particularly if it is administered in the community setting rather than prior to release. However, Gollay (1976) found that high scores on Part I (measuring self-care and independent functioning) predicted only one of five outcome measures—degree of independence allowed in the residential setting. Scores on Part II (measuring undesirable personal and social behaviors) were associated only with problems in the community, an almost definitional relationship. However, those readmitted to their institutions received higher scores than those not readmitted on all 14 of the maladaptive areas. Although these overall findings are suggestive, there is clearly a need for further research on the relationships between *specific* competencies and adjustment in specific community environments.

Gollay's (1976; Gollay et al., 1978; Wyngaarden et al., 1976) study included an enormous list of individual characteristics related to successful community placement as well as to five indices of community adjustment. The most accurate characterization of her results is that the patterns of satisfactions and dissatisfactions, recreation activities, training activities, work activities, worries about placements, abilities, and physical characteristics were strikingly similar for those individuals who were successfully placed in the community and for those individuals who were returned to their institutions from unsuccessful attempts at placement. Nevertheless, several characteristics in addition to these did discriminate between these two groups. Although the activity profiles of the two groups were generally similar, those persons who were successfully placed participated in sports and watched sports more often, both before and after release, than those who were returned to their institutions. Maladaptive (Part II) Adaptive Behavior Scale scores, caretakers' ratings of adjustment, and ratings of problems of adjustment were predictably different for the two groups. Similarly, although they engaged in less interaction with the opposite sex, the successful community residents were rated by their caretakers to be significantly more competent in romantic relationships than were the unsuccessful residents. All of these ratings are somewhat suspect because they were made after the unsuccessful individuals had returned to their institutions; they could therefore have been biased by the selective memories of the informants. Nevertheless, similar ratings were generated by the community caretakers, the interviewers, and the residents themselves. Parenthetically, whether or not their residents had been returned to the institution, caretakers saw their own problems to be of about the same magnitude. That is, problems of individual residents predicted success of placement, but problems of caretakers did not.

Another interesting, although partially uninterpretable, finding was the effect of personal appearance. Interviewer ratings of stigmata, obesity, and other physical characteristics did not discriminate between successful and unsuccessful community placements; however, those appearance characteristics over which the individual had control (e.g., neatness, cleanliness, style of dress) discriminated significantly between the two groups. Again, the fact that the ratings were made after the residents returned to their releasing institutions restricts the interpretation: perhaps the same residents who were rated by Gollay's interviewers to be unkempt and unstylistically dressed had been quite the opposite when they were in their community placements.

Still another of Gollay's findings sheds new light on previous research. According to the presumptions of normalization, length of institutionalization should correlate negatively with community adjustment. However, McCarver and Craig (1974) reported that there is at best an inconsistent association between these two variables. Soforenko and Macy (1977) found that length of institutionalization neither deterred nor facilitated community adjustment. However, Gollay, who used a national sample with a broad age and IQ range, found that successfully placed individuals had lived at their releasing institutions significantly longer than had unsuccessfully placed individuals, although both groups had been released at the same age. Related to this finding was the fact that, prior to their current placement, individuals who returned to the releasing institutions had had significantly more readmissions to institutions than had those individuals who had not returned.

This pattern of findings puts into question the usual institutional criteria for selecting individuals for release. Those individuals who have had lengthy institutional placements (and whom Gollay found to be likely to succeed in the community) are those who have previously failed to meet the institution's criteria for community placement. Those individuals who have been released and readmitted several times have repeatedly met placement criteria and have repeatedly failed in their placements. Thus, the very people that institution staff have apparently judged ready for release are the people most likely to return to the institution. This interpretation suggests that the adequacy of the usual release criteria of IQ, competence, and age should be carefully scrutinized. Again, however, the compatibility of the individual and the community support system is probably crucial; one interpretation of the positive correlation between length of institutionalization and placement success is that placement officers may attend more to environmental supports in cases that they consider to be high risk, and may underestimate the support required by their more capable clients.

Prerelease Training

Another characteristic of community residents that has frequently been examined is the amount and quality of prerelease training and experience they have been given. Despite "common sense" expectations, there is surprisingly little evidence that prerelease training facilitates community adjustment. The only study identified by McCarver and Craig that related types of training received to community success was that of Madison (1964), who found no relationship. Nor has it been established convincingly that work experience in an institution is associated with successful community placement, although some evidence does point in this direction (McCarver & Craig, 1974; Windle, 1962). Recent studies have added evidence regarding the value of institutional training for community adjustment. Wyngaarden and Gollay (1976) found some type of prerelease program available in more than 90 percent of the 154 public and private institutions they surveyed, with the number of programs increasing from 1972 to 1974. Although broad educational programs were most commonly available, institutions had apparently developed many programs specifically aimed at deinstitutionalization; for example, 84 percent had independent-living skills training and 44 percent had "prerelease independent living units" (Wyngaarden & Gollay, 1976). About half of the 440 individuals in the Abt Associates target sample, who came from 10 of these institutions, had participated in one or more prerelease programs (Wyngaarden et al., 1976). Of Soforenko and Macy's sample (1977), 86 percent of the discharged population had received some form of programming in the institution.

Training and experience in the institution was a positive predictor of community outcome in Gollay's study (1976). Participation in day programs (work, school, and day activity programs) before release predicted fewer problems in the community. Moreover, a general institutional variable, intensity of institutional programming—which included per capita expenditure and average percentage of released residents who had participated in various programs—was positively associated with remaining in the community. Similarly, Bell's (1976) above-55 IQ subjects, who showed better community adjustment on nearly all outcome measures, had had more prerelease prevocational and independent living skills training (but less academic training) than the more poorly adjusted, below-55 IQ group.

A specific problem in the measurement of how prerelease training affects community adjustment is the perception of community care providers with regard to the adequacy and necessity of training. In Intagliata's (1978) study foster family care providers indicated that 96 percent of released residents did not use public transportation on their own; yet, 79 percent of those providers felt that the former residents were adequately prepared in travel skills. Possibly the care providers felt that independent travel was an unrealistically high expectation, or they did not want the residents to be able to travel independently, since then supervision would be more difficult. Family care providers identified problems of residents in the areas of eating, dressing, and toileting much more frequently 2 years after release than the institutional staff had at the time of release. This does not necessarily indicate that people placed in family care homes deteriorate in behavioral functioning, but rather may suggest that foster family care providers have a different frame of reference (their own normal children) than that of institution staff, who compare a resident to other retarded persons. Furthermore, these staff members are the providers of the supposedly adequate prerelease training. Also, possibly, the training may not generalize to the new settings.

This question of generalization relates to another issue of prerelease training: the degree to which an individual's skill levels change after s/he leaves the institution. Soforenko and Macy (1977) found that, across all skill areas they examined, 52 percent of their subjects maintained an adequate or normal level of functioning after release into the community. Twenty-two percent of the skill scores reflected a rise in functioning level after community placement, and only 10 per cent reflected a decline in ability. Forty-five per cent of the group were functioning adequately in money management, 70 percent were functioning adequately in grooming skills, 62 percent in interpersonal relationships, 73 percent in communication skills, 55 percent in time skills, and 41 percent in knowledge of community services. Twenty-three percent improved in vocational skills, and only 8 percent dropped in performance in this area. In transportation skills,

25 percent improved, and 12 percent declined. Twenty-four percent improved in "independent living" skills, and 9 percent dropped. Sixty-one percent improved in "general community adjustment," and 18 percent appeared less capable than at the time of release. Overall, then, this study suggests that skill levels are generally maintained or even raised after release from the institution. Contrary to Soforenko and Macy, Sigelman et al. (1978) found no marked improvements, and even some marked decreases in adjustment skills of individuals placed into community residential facilities. Fiorelli and Thurman (1979) found some empirical support for one of the tenets of the principle of normalization: that in more normalized living environments, the possibility of a client's progress toward habilitation is enhanced. However, they did not find as much behavior improvement as they expected in clients who had moved from an institution into a group home; the behavioral changes were complexly intertwined with differences in client/staff interactions. Cohen, Conroy, Frazer, Snelbecker, and Sprent (1977) found that, when a large group of individuals was moved from a state institution to a smaller community facility, the higher-functioning residents became more withdrawn, had setbacks in language development, and showed a pattern of generally lowered functioning. The lower-functioning residents increased both their adaptive and their acting-out behavior.

Schalock and Harper (1978) trained individuals in specific skills for independent living before placing them into visiting-professional apartments. They found that their more successfully placed residents were more highly skilled in five of their training areas: symbolic operations, personal maintenance, clothing care and use, socially appropriate behavior, and functional academics. However, other trained target skills were not found to be related to or predictive of independent living placement success; these included home maintenance, food preparation, time management, and community utilization. Crnic and Pym (1979) found that training alone was not enough to guarantee success in independent living; clients also needed adequate self-concept, the ability to cope with life stress, and appropriate social support systems.

Aninger, Growick, and Bolinsky (1978) have indicated that often new problems will arise in the community setting that prerelease training did not take into account or anticipate. New experiences and problems of their community residents that became areas of major concern to their supervisors included employment, sex, and marriage; minor concerns were nutrition (i.e., overeating) and loneliness. Seevers (1975) also discussed the need for training to help community residents cope with rejection, nonacceptance, prejudice, and indifference from other members of the community.

Summary

This selective review of individual factors in community adjustment suggests that new inquiries, although not substantially changing the information presented by McCarver and Craig (1974), aid in identifying reasons for the failure of many individual characteristics to predict outcome. In the case of intellectual functioning, analysis of findings requires consideration of the range of IQs in the sample and of the possibility that different levels of IQ have differing relationships to various outcome measures. One must also recognize that lower IQ and higher IQ persons are typically placed in environments that differ in the degree of support they provide. Similarly, in assessing relationships between age and adjustment, one must take into account and preferably control for the fact that younger clients are placed in different settings than are older clients and that demands for competence may consequently be less. The study of relationships between specific personal and social competencies and community adjustment remains at a primitive stage, and has perhaps been hampered (McCarver & Craig, 1974) by the frequent use of prerelease measures as predictors of adjustment in settings that are quite different in character from institutions. Recent evidence does point to the value of prerelease training and suggests the importance of monitoring adaptive behavior. Nevertheless, it should still be emphasized that research has fallen far short of being able to predict, on the basis of personal characteristics, who will and who will not succeed in the community.

CHARACTERISTICS OF THE COMMUNITY ENVIRONMENT

In view of the limited ability of individual characteristics and competencies to predict community adjustment, one might suppose that environmental factors play a large role in the adjustment process. The few studies that have focused on environmental variables (for example, Krishef's 1959 analysis of rural-urban differences in adjustment) confirm the potential of such research.

Five aspects of the community environment that are relevant to this discussion are: 1) community attitudes and behaviors toward residential facilities and their residents (discussed in Chapter 7 of this volume); 2) the availability and adequacy of a network of community support services (discussed in Chapter 6); 3) the articulation of community opposition in court zoning cases (discussed in Chapters 11 and 12); 4) the special role of "benefactors" (Edgerton, 1967) as an informal support mechanism (discussed below); and 5) characteristics of the residential service system itself (discussed below). Although these five topics do not exhaust the set of potentially relevant community variables, they comprise the most critical problem areas that have emerged to date in the deinstitutionalization movement.

Special Role of Benefactors

The unofficial counterpart of a service network (cf. Chapter 6) is an informal network of friends and helpers who can meet social needs and provide a 24-hour crisis intervention capability. In his intensive study of 48 former Pacific State Hospital residents, Edgerton (1967) concluded that the "ex-patient succeeds in his efforts to sustain a life in the community only as well as he succeeds in locating and holding a benefactor" (p. 204). By "benefactor," Edgerton meant a person who provides help with everyday coping problems and aids the released resident in "passing" (disguising his/her incompetence). Of the 48 clients Edgerton estimated that as few as three, and at most 10, could cope with community life adequately without a benefactor. Of the rest, 17 were characterized as "heavily but not completely dependent" on their benefactors, and 21 were "for all practical purposes, completely dependent." He detected a strong relationship between dependence on a benefactor and low social competence, but judged the client's IQ to be a poor predictor of both. Neither age of admission to the hospital nor length of time there predicted dependence.

Of the 50 persons who entered roles as benefactors, 30 were women, and 20 were known to have had prior experience with mentally retarded individuals. Thirteen were spouses or lovers, 12 were employers, 10 were close relatives, 10 were neighbors or landladies, and 5 were professionals who went beyond normal responsibilities. When asked why they had befriended retarded persons, the benefactors generally expressed some variation on the theme of altruism.

Twelve years after Edgerton's (1967) study, Edgerton and Bercovici (1976) revisited 27 of the original 48 subjects. They estimated that reliance on benefactors had substantially diminished, with 16 judged less dependent than previously, 11 dependent to the same extent, and none more dependent. They concluded that the devastating effects of stigma evident when the ex-patients first returned to the community had lessened, and that at the same time subjects had become more competent in coping with life. Whether or not original benefactors facilitated the learning process is unknown. Furthermore, the results themselves could be questioned in that they were based on the "unblinded" judgments of interviewers/observers from a single laboratory.

Although the roles of benefactor and of supervisor are often indistinguishable, other evidence points to the beneficial effects of unpaid advocate-helpers. A sociological study of retarded adults in Texas (Henshel, 1972) emphasized the value of benefactors, much as Edgerton did. Live-in employment placements and the availability of an advocate-supervisor were associated with fewer sociosexual problems among females in a study by Floor, Rosen, Baxter, Horowitz, and Weber (1971). Krishef, Reynolds, and Stunkard (1959) reported that 66 percent of successful community placement clients, as contrasted with 28 percent of unsuccessful clients, had good supervision in the community. However, Shafter (1957) found no relationship between amount of assistance from relatives and community adjustment. Although caretaker respondents from the Wyngaarden et al. (1976) study reported that nearly all individuals who had been placed in the community had one or more individuals to whom they "turned for support," successfully placed persons were far more likely (99 percent) to have identifiable friends in the community than were the individuals who were readmitted to their institutions (59 percent). Furthermore, successful cases were far more likely (64 versus 42 percent) to have daily supervision by a "case manager" (parent, house parent, institution case worker) during their first 6 months in the community.

In contrast, Soforenko and Macy (1977) found that only 3 percent of their discharged population sought assistance from institution staff after discharge.

However, 51 percent of the studied group were placed directly from the institution with either parents or relatives, although only 19 percent were still in this type of residence at the time of the study. Presumably, these parents and relatives initially acted as "case managers." Willer (1978) found that parents of individuals returned to their natural homes were better advocates for these community residents, searching more actively for community services and expressing more concern about the lack of availability of services than did family care or group home parents.

However, the parents in Willer's study expressed disappointment and confusion about not receiving any training in preparation for the resident's return home, or any training after the resident had been placed. Berdiansky and Parker (1977) noted that the developers of group homes also listed the difficulty of obtaining satisfactory manager training as a major problem. Bruininks, Kudla, Wieck, and Hauber (1979) reported that administrators of CRFs consider personnel management, including recruitment, retainment, and development of staff, as their most important problem.

In his more recent research on retarded adults in residential settings, Edgerton (1975) raised serious questions about the suitability of residential staff for benefactor roles. He found that residents of family care and board-and-care homes were apparently "caught up in elaborate and tenacious dependency relationships" with staff of the facilities where they resided (p. 132). This impression is consistent with that of Birenbaum and Seiffer (1976), who found that only 10 percent of 48 residents of a community facility claimed to have received help from community members; the majority depended instead on facility staff and agency personnel. Edgerton lamented staff control of resident funds, regimentation, and condescending treatment. More importantly, the needs of caretakers to remain financially solvent were often in direct conflict with a philosophy of client movement to greater independence. Edgerton's impressions are consistent with data suggesting that movement out of group homes is more likely in public than in privately operated facilities (Sitkei, 1976).

Humm-Delgado (1979) found staff of community facilities willing to admit to the inherent conflict in their roles. Although they wanted clients to lessen their dependence on others and increase their decision-making abilities, staff still saw their primary role as providing emotional support to clients and acting as parental figures.

Thus, the availability of benefactors or advocates appears to be both a blessing and a curse. Although benefactors may be a necessary environmental support mechanism, they may also reinforce dependency behavior and may sabotage progress toward self-sufficiency. This possibility applies not only to informal benefactors and staff acting as advocates, but also to persons working in one-to-one relationships through organized citizen-advocacy programs. Danker-Brown, Sigelman, and Bensberg (1979) found such advocates performing many services for their protégés even though neither they nor their protégés expressed a need for such services. As Kurtz (1975) noted, a "lack of empirical information about individual and community experiences with advocates makes it impossible to determine whether the citizen advocate role will eventually be a productive or counterproductive factor in community success'' (p. 391).

Characteristics of the Residential Service System

Although the residential service system is a component of the broader service delivery system, it is the component that more directly touches clients and that should be expected to have the most powerful impact on adjustment. Unfortunately, one cannot readily identify variables in residential settings that are associated with community success; instead, one can only identify problem areas that will require scrutiny if deinstitutionalization is to be a success.

Consider first the task of determining which types of residential alternatives most facilitate adjustment. McCarver and Craig (1974), focusing primarily on rates of return from vocational placements, home placements, foster homes, colony or halfway house placements, and group homes, could derive few firm conclusions. Very simply, because different kinds of clients are assigned to different kinds of placements, the role played by individual characteristics compared to the role played by environmental factors is never clear; hence, neither can be ruled out as a cause of type-to-type differences in community adjustment. Given this confusion, it is not surprising to find a self-contradictory literature. For instance, although Eagle's (1967) review concluded that foster home placements had no higher a failure rate than that in home or vocational leaves, several more recent studies have uncovered very high rates of return from foster or family care placements (Adams, 1975; Gollay et al., 1978; Intagliata, 1978; Keys, Boroskin, & Ross, 1973). Environmental factors also play a significant role in reinstitutionalization; these include caretaker illness (Meyer, 1951), the closing of the community facility (Keys et al., 1973), or inadequacies in care provided (Bjaanes & Butler, 1974; Browder, Ellis & Neal, 1974). It has been estimated that over one-third of community placement failures are associated with adverse environmental factors rather than with client problems (Eagle, 1967; Townsend & Flanagan, 1976; Windle, 1962).

For instance, Intagliata (1978) found that, although 67 percent of the community placements in his study were made to foster family care homes, the return rates from these homes within 6 months of release was 48 percent. The reasons, he suggested, were the major problems that caretakers listed: the amount of extensive supervision required (31 percent), the difficulty of getting any free time (20 percent), and the neglect of other family members (20 percent).*

It may be more instructive to study determinants of success for clients within each class of residential setting than to attempt comparisons of alternative models, since different types of facilities accommodate different types of clients. For example, Browder et al. (1974) studied only foster homes and found that acceptance of the child's handicap by foster parents was correlated with both availability of "necessary" services and improvement in the child's emotional

---

*Editors' note: More recent figures from New York State indicate, however, that actual return rates from foster family care are considerably less (Willer & Intagliata, 1980).

response. As another example, Intagliata, Willer, and Wicks (1979) found that, within the class of family care homes, particular homes could be identified that facilitated better community adjustment. Evaluating the quality of family care homes in New York State, they found that raters discriminated reliably among homes in terms of their judgments of resident growth, normal (i.e., conventional) behavior, use of community resources, resident independence, and availability of social support. These judgments of residence quality correlated with several characteristics of family care providers. By and large, high-quality providers were better educated, had more health-related training, were more disposed to seek out services and activities for their residents, were actively involved in their residents' treatment plans, had stable, well-organized homes, established "warm but not dependent relationships" with their residents, encouraged the residents to use community resources and to develop new skills, and became family care providers because of their past experiences with mentally retarded individuals.

Many variables also affect the quality of success of clients returned to their natural homes. Willer (1978) studied the characteristics of natural home placements as compared to alternative placements like foster family care or group homes. He found that the idea for community placement almost always originated with the institution. A sizeable majority of natural families felt that they were not in control of the situation and that their consent was not necessary; regardless of where their child was placed, they often felt the decision was wrong and they were opposed to it. When an individual was placed into his/her own home, that natural family was more likely to experience a crisis than was a family whose child was placed into a foster family care setting. Families that were less "structure-oriented" (Moos, 1974; Moos & Moos, 1976) and those that were of a "moral-religious" type were also more likely to experience a crisis. The main problems cited by those natural families who took their child back into the home were the difficulty in getting free time, the amount of supervision required, and neglect of other family members—the same problems Intagliata's (1978) foster family care staff identified. However, when families who had originally opposed the retarded individual's placement into the community were asked, "What would be your first choice of residence in ten years?" only a small percentage indicated that they would choose to have the individual returned to the institution. The individual's residence at the time of the study was the most likely choice of placement for the future.

Willer also discovered that the mothers of individuals returned to their own homes were suffering slightly in terms of their mental health, possibly as a result of the resident's placement in the home. That is, they were somewhat less well adjusted and displayed more symptoms of mental illness than the mothers of individuals who were placed into foster family care settings. Willer suggested that the burden of having an individual returned to his/her natural home is real and "that the mother pays a significant price for that burden" (p. 15).

Retherford (1975) found age, and Penniman (1974) found maturity, to be primary factors in predicting which foster parents would be successful in caring for discharged retarded residents. Both found that demographic variables such as sex, education, personal experience, marital status, religion, and number of children in the family had no predictive value, although they, like Willer, found that emotional stability was another important factor.

Problems of research design have also plagued attempts to study so basic an issue as the relationship of facility size to quality of care and resident functioning (Balla, 1976; Baroff, 1978). Both facility size (e.g., King, Raynes, & Tizard, 1971; McCormick, Balla, & Zigler, 1975) and size of the living unit independent of facility size (e.g., Harris, Veit, Allen, & Chinsky, 1974; Klaber, 1969) have been associated with level or quality of care and with institution-oriented compared to resident-oriented management practices—that is, the larger the facility or living unit, the lower the quality of care given and the more likely that the care given focuses on what is best for the institution rather than what is best for the resident. However, resident characteristics have not been controlled adequately in these studies. Moreover, even among community residential facilities, staffing patterns vary as a function of facility size (Baker et al., 1977; Brown & Guard, 1979; O'Connor, 1976) and may, along with other confounding variables, foster false conclusions about the effects of size per se; that is, more staff in a larger facility may enable the staff there to give higher quality care, but the relationship is difficult to determine.

Despite these weaknesses, size remains a most important variable from the perspective of normalization ideology. Consistent with expectations based on the normalization principle, Baker et al. (1977) found that group home size was negatively correlated with individuals' autonomy, responsibilities about a group home, staff-to-resident ratio, and quality of work placement. The fact that size was not correlated with the age, degree of retardation, or sex of residents strengthens the conclusion that facility size itself influenced degree of normalization. Moreover, a composite variable, which indexed both the quantity and quality of transfers from a group home, was also significantly correlated with its size. Average tenancies ranged from 2 years and 3 months for the small group home to 5 years for the mini-institution. Of the 10 alternatives in Baker et al.'s study, mixed group homes had by far the highest scores on the composite transfer variable, with an expected tenancy of about 7 months, and sheltered villages had the lowest, about 20 years. Workshop dormitories scored surprisingly high, with an expected tenancy of about 2.5 years. Homes for the elderly and foster homes had expected tenancies of about 2 and 3 years, respectively, whereas semi-independent living had an expectancy of 2.5 years. Thus, there is at least some evidence that smaller facilities are not only more normalized but may facilitate progress to still more normalized settings. However, further research will be needed to ensure that this is the case even when characteristics of residents are controlled.

INTERACTION BETWEEN PERSON AND SETTING

The foregoing sections have considered two environmental factors that affect placement success (see also Chapters 6 and 7). What has not yet been systematically examined is the possibility that one residential environment might be optimal for a client with one set of characteristics whereas another is optimal for a client with a different set of characteristics. This notion is consistent with some evidence already reported in this chapter. For example, IQ was correlated negatively with some of Gollay's (1976) and Bell's (1976) outcome measures and positively with others, which implied that community programs vary depending on the functioning level of the resident. Suggestive evidence from related fields also pinpoints the interaction of person and environment as a significant determinant of behavior. For instance, Raush, Dittmann, and Taylor (1959), studying the social interactions of hyperaggressive boys in a residential setting across six different behavioral settings (e.g., breakfast, structured games, arts and crafts), found that, although there were consistent individual differences across settings, and consistent effects of setting across individuals, the interaction of child and setting accounted for more of the variance in behavior than did the sum of the independent contributions of child and setting. Moos (1968) obtained similar results in a study of patients and staff in a psychiatric ward, then replicated the results in a second study, concluding that psychiatric ward subsettings may be more or less therapeutic depending on the patient groups exposed to them (Moos, 1969, 1975).

Directly relevant to community residential alternatives is Fanshel's (1961) work concerning the interaction between foster parent characteristics and success in working with different kinds of foster children. Foster parents who were rated by caseworkers to be more suitable for work with physically or mentally handicapped children had different characteristics from those considered suitable for work with aggressive children. Optimal foster parents for handicapped children were oriented toward dependency needs of children, preferred working with infants rather than older children, and had experience caring for large families of their own. These characteristics contrasted with those for foster parents who were optimal for work with aggressive children. Such homes had a strong father figure, but the foster parents were not rated high in ego functioning or democratic child-rearing style.

Willer (1978) found that individuals placed into their natural homes were much more likely to exhibit acting-out behaviors than individuals placed in alternative placements like foster family care; it is possible, however, that the natural families were simply more likely to report behavior problems. If the individual had been originally placed in an institution because of a behavior problem, s/he was much more likely to be returned to his/her own home; if s/he was placed into a family care or group home, the reasons for the original institutional placement were more likely to have been a physician's recommendation, parent illness, or one parent's death. Eyman and Call (1977) found definite interactions between the prevalence of behavior problems and whether an individual had been placed into an institution, a community facility, or his/her natural home. The more disturbed a retarded individual was, the more likely s/he was to be residing in a larger institution; the more severely retarded an individual, the more likely s/he was to commit self-injurious behavior, violence to others, and damage to property, unless s/he was nonambulatory. They conclude that, if a community placement is to be successful, the strongest prerelease training needs are for intensified individual attention and programming for behavior problems. It is also reasonable to assert that community facilities should be prepared to manage and ameliorate different types of behavioral disabilities.

Scheerenberger and Felsenthal's (1977) study is one of the few that address the question of the satisfaction and personal reactions of former residents placed into different settings; in this case, foster homes, group homes, and adult homes. Although there were no outstanding differences in the satisfactions and problems of the residents of the three types of facilities, there were striking differences in the amount and type of leisure-time activities engaged in, the degree of mobility in the community, and the ways in which spending money was utilized. It seems reasonable to conclude that in these areas clients were matched to environments that were appropriate to their needs, since even the more severely retarded clients in this study were apparently making a successful adjustment to community living, and few persons expressed any desire to return to the institution.

One might expect that the group home would impact differently on individuals coming from institutions and individuals coming from community settings (natural homes and other CRFs). However, Yaron (1974) found that residents originating from these two settings made comparable gains on nine measures of social, domestic, academic, and self-help competence. Whereas the community group started with superior scores, both groups gained significantly on nearly every measure after a year in a group home.

Yaron's results notwithstanding, further research in this area is certain to improve the matching of clients with residential settings. It is almost certain that the individual characteristics and skills reviewed above would be more predictive of adjustment if their interactions with environmental variables were controlled—for example, if studies focused on predictors of success in only one type of residential setting (e.g., Intagliata, Willer, & Wicks, 1979; Novak, Heal, Pilewski, & Laidlaw, 1980).

SUMMARY

Although the empirical information currently available for predicting the success of placement is of extremely poor quality, primarily as a result of the difficulty of collecting the data and manipulating critical variables, some individual characteristics tend to be associated with more successful placements than do others. Of all personal characteristics, problem behaviors appeared to be most predictive of placement failure. There appears to be very little empirical support for restricting placement on the basis of age or IQ, except that needs for community services and environmental supports appear to correlate with these variables. Generalizing from this statement, it appears that a most fruitful approach to optimizing placement success is to study the interaction of individual and environmental characteristics in order to specify the extent to which some settings optimize placement success for some individuals and different settings do so for others.

In conclusion, although research on deinstitutionalization faces great methodological and political challenges, issues in the area are amenable to empirical investigation. Furthermore, this investigation, more than most, has practical applications that are likely to influence public policy toward individuals who are developmentally disabled.

Chapter 6
Generic Services for Developmentally Disabled Citizens

Vernon T. Savage, Angela R. Novak, and Laird W. Heal

The underlying philosophy of this chapter is that the principles of "normalization" (Wolfensberger, 1972) and egalitarianism (Chapter 3) call for the full and complete utilization of generic services by developmentally disabled individuals and their families. There has been a proliferation of specialized community programs and services for this population, and paralleling this development has been the growing realization that specialized programs are not the sole answer to meeting their total needs (Heal, Sigelman, & Switzky, 1978; Scheerenberger, 1976a). Not only is the full utilization of generic services anticipated by "providing as normalized an environment as possible" (Wolfensberger, 1972), but three very practical considerations make continued dependence on specialized programs unrealistic: 1) economic considerations argue against establishing specialized programs; 2) adequately trained persons are usually not available to staff specialized programs; and 3) provision of the continuum of care required by the full range of handicapping conditions cannot be attained by a fragmented service network (Scheerenberger, 1970).

Providing all services "in-house" defeats the purpose of community-based residential programs. In order to approximate the breadth and depth of services provided by multipurpose institutions, community residential facilities (CRFs) must rely on a network of community services that is prepared to adapt itself to the full range of human handicapping conditions.

Perhaps the most compelling reason for a more complete utilization of generic services by developmentally disabled individuals is provided by Gollay, Freedman, Wyngaarden, and Kurtz (1978). Their data show a significant corre-

---

Much of the information contained herein has been adapted or quoted directly from Heal, L. W., Sigelman, C. K., & Switzky, H. N., Research on community residential alternatives for the mentally retarded. In N. R. Ellis (Ed.) *International Review of Research in Mental Retardation,* Vol. 9. New York: Academic Press, 1978.

lation between the number of developmentally disabled persons returning to an institution after having been placed in the community and the lack of adequate services in the community to support their placements. These data are discussed more fully below, but their most direct implication is the need to improve access to, and utilization of, generic services by developmentally disabled citizens.

CURRENT STATUS OF GENERIC SERVICES

A generic service is defined as any service that attends to the health, education, welfare, rehabilitation, or employment needs of a broad spectrum of persons in the community, including developmentally disabled individuals (Jaslow, 1967). Special programs designed solely or primarily for persons with developmental disabilities are excluded.

Very little research has addressed the question of the existence and use of generic services. Scheerenberger's (1970) study, the most comprehensive examination to date of accessibility to and utilization of generic services by a developmentally disabled population (i.e., mentally retarded persons), had four objectives:

1. To study accessibility of generic services.
2. To study variations in accessibility of generic services as a function of sociogeographic area and socioeconomic status.
3. To identify those problems encountered most frequently by professional persons providing generic services.
4. To determine which problems are encountered most frequently by parents as they seek to utilize generic services for their retarded children.

The sample surveyed included representatives from four generic service categories:

1. Medical, including physicians, dentists, and community health agencies.
2. Guidance and counseling services, such as mental health clinics and family agencies.
3. Religious services.
4. Sociorecreational services, such as parks, social centers, youth centers, and YMCA/YWCAs.

Parents of retarded children on a waiting list for the same services were also interviewed.

The sample was drawn from three sociogeographic service populations in Illinois, each having approximately 500,000 persons: one from middle-class, metropolitan Chicago neighborhoods; one from metropolitan Chicago poverty neighborhoods; and one from downstate communities. As shown in Table 6.1, a total of 736 professionals, agency representatives, and parents were contacted for interviews. The table indicates that the majority of agencies contacted did not serve mentally retarded or developmentally disabled individuals. Although the

Table 6.1. Total response distributed according to generic service category and nature of response

Category	Total sample contacted	Number responding		Serves the retarded		Does not serve the retarded		Don't know if served		Unable to participate for other reasons	
		(N)	(%)[a]	(N)	(%)[b]	(N)	(%)[b]	(N)	(%)[b]	(N)	(%)[b]
Generic Agencies											
Medical services											
Primary physician	110	108	98	22	20	67	62	8	7	11	11
Dentists	104	98	94	19	19	51	51	15	15	13	14
Community health	25	25	100	3	12	22	88	0	0	0	0
Guidance and counseling	32	32	100	14	44	17	53	1	3	0	0
Religious programs (church)	130	123	95	47	38	58	47	7	6	11	9
Sociorecreational agencies	103	88	85	19	22	55	63	10	11	4	4
Subtotal	504	474	94[c]	124	26[c]	270	57[c]	41	9[c]	39	8[c]
Parents	232	143	61	—	—	—	—	—	—	—	—
TOTAL	736	617	84	124	26	270	57	41	9	39	8

From Scheerenberger, 1970, p. 11, by permission of the author and the American Association on Mental Deficiency.
[a] Percent of total sample.
[b] Percent of responses.
[c] Average percentage.

highest recorded level of participation involved guidance and counseling agencies, this high level is somewhat misleading. Of the 14 agencies serving retarded individuals, six received some form of state aid for that purpose. Of totally voluntary agencies, the church was the most active generic agency providing services to retarded persons.

One generic agency that frequently expresses high interest in and concern for the retarded is the mental health clinic. As shown in Table 6.2, mental health clinics were one of seven generic service categories (pediatricians, mental health clinics, family agencies, parks, social centers, youth centers, and YMCA/YWCAs) where more than 1 percent of the total client population was mentally retarded (1 percent is taken here as the national prevalence estimate of mental retardation; Tarjan, Wright, Eyman, & Keeran, 1973). Generic guidance and counseling services reported that mentally retarded individuals comprised 6 percent of their caseload, presumably due in part to their receiving state aid to serve retarded persons. The relatively high percentage of retarded individuals served by social centers and YMCA/YWCAs is also misleading. Since most of these facilities were located in poverty areas, the high percentage of retarded persons served by many of the YMCA/YWCAs and social centers would appear to be a function of the facilities' locations in areas in which retarded individuals are disproportionately represented. Scheerenberger estimated that the retarded population served by those YMCA/YWCAs in nonpoverty areas was below 1 percent.

Scheerenberger concluded from his studies that generic services in the community are not available in sufficient quantity, are not coordinated with other generic and specialized programs, have low visibility, are not infused with expertise in mental retardation, are costly, and are not adequately complemented by specialized programs. In later publications (1975, 1976b, 1978) he reported that the primary reason for over half of the readmissions to public residential facilities was the presence of shortcomings in various community services, including the lack of follow-up services.

O'Connor's (1976) data on 611 group home and supervised apartment facilities presented a somewhat more optimistic picture with respect to availability of services. As shown in Figure 6.1, of the 10 services used directly by residents, only educational counseling was rated by more than 10 percent of the facilities to be needed but not available. Twenty-two percent of the facilities lacked but wanted a directory of community services, and 19 percent lacked but wanted a referral service to identify and obtain needed services.

An optimistic picture was also presented by Humm-Delgado in her survey or residents in Massachusetts group homes (1978). Seventy-eight percent of residents' 23 "support" services were from generic community agencies; these included services in the areas of physical health, emotional health, recreation, and training self-help skills.

However, wide gaps in the generic service network become evident when adequacy of available services are examined, and these gaps have been detected by several researchers. Almost 90 percent of O'Connor's respondents reported at

Table 6.2. Summary: Generic services for retarded individuals and their families

	Respondents serving MR (N)	MR served—percentage of total clients (%)	Referral to other agencies (%)	Accept referrals of MR (%)	Counseling parents about MR (%)	Counseling siblings about MR (%)
Primary physician						
General practitioner	11	0.28	100.0	64	81	18
Pediatrician	11	2.00	100.0	100	54	37
Dentists	19	0.43	55.0	89	10	0
Guidance & counseling services	12	6.00	90.0	50	50	50
Mental health clinics	6	9.00	80.0	100	100	100
Family agencies	6	1.10	100.0	—	—	—
Religious services	47	0.40	51.0	100	80	15
Catholic	16	0.30	73.0	100	80	18
Jewish	8	0.60	28.0	100	86	12
Protestant	23	0.40	44.0	100	78	15
Sociorecreational services	19	7.00	2.7	0	0	0
Parks	7	2.60	57.0	—	—	—
Social centers	5	7.00	—	—	—	—
Youth centers	3	1.30	100.0	—	—	—
YMCA/YWCA	4	12.00	—	—	—	—

From Scheerenberger, 1970, p. 12, by permission of the author and the American Association on Mental Deficiency.

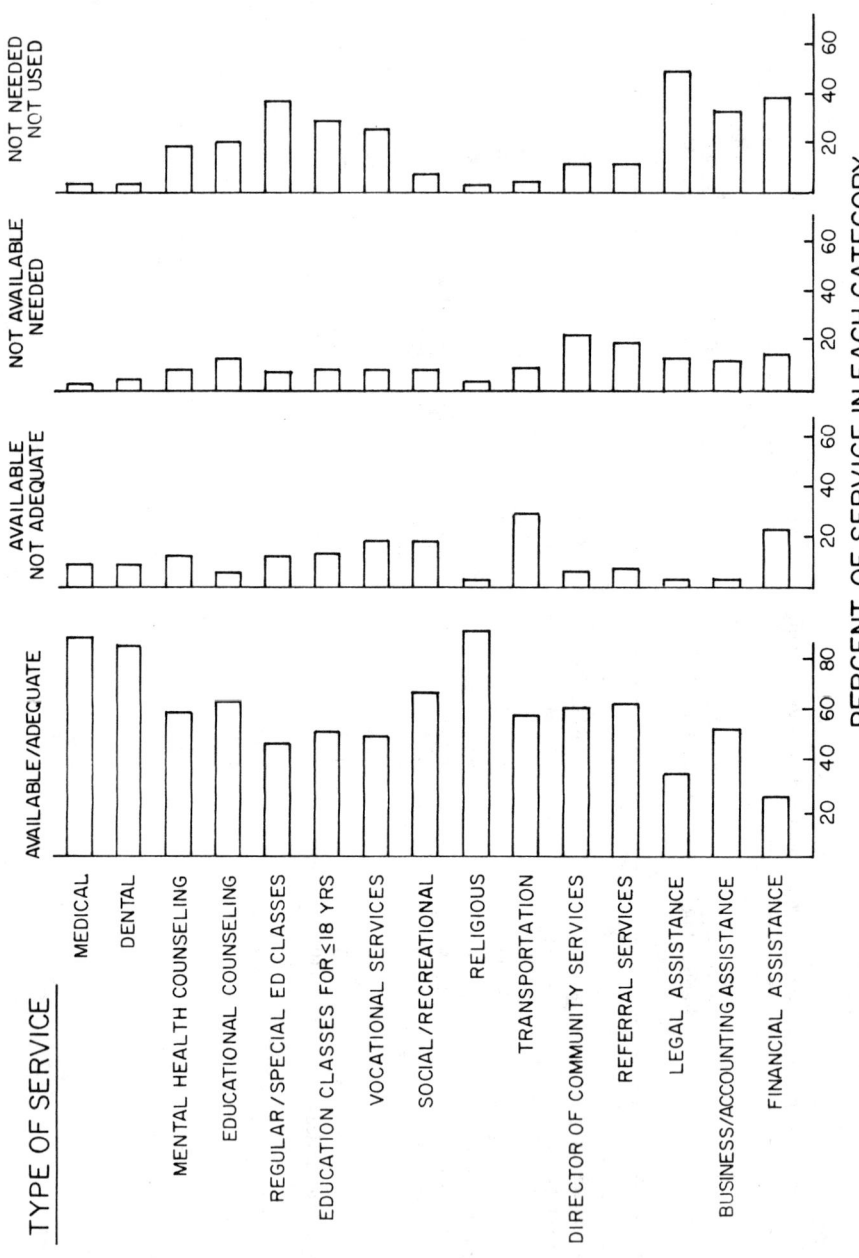

Figure 6.1. Utilization and adequacy of community services. Respondents were 105 group home managers. Adapted from O'Connor (1976).

least one community support service to be "unavailable or inadequate"; nearly half reported four or more such services in that category (see Figure 6.1). Services frequently judged inadequate included transportation (judged inadequate by 30 percent), vocational services (19 percent), sociorecreational programs (18 percent), and mental health counseling (14 percent). Medical and religious services were largely adequate. O'Connor estimated that from 24 to 40 percent of the residents would benefit if transportation, vocational services, educational services, sociorecreational programs, or mental health counseling were made adequate.

Surveys of parents and community agency personnel have uncovered other problems in the community service network. In New York State, Intagliata (1978) found that 73 percent of foster family care providers had no trouble obtaining medical services for retarded persons in their care. The principal problem areas identified were lack of transportation and speech services that were either unavailable or too expensive. In Willer's (1978) survey, families that accepted retarded children back into their natural homes reported gaps in vocational services, speech therapy, and recreational therapy, and complained that medical and psychological services were too expensive. Polivka, Marvin, Brown, and Polivka (1979) found that only 16 percent of services that were identified as needed in individual habilitation plans of group home residents were not provided. However, it is both disconcerting and disturbing that 47 percent of the services actually provided to clients were not identified as needed to reach habilitation goals; these unneeded services were concentrated in the areas of "personal adjustment" training, mobility training, and recreation and cultural services.

In his study of generic services, Scheerenberger (1970) found mentally retarded children to be underrepresented in the client populations for medical, guidance and counseling, religious, and sociorecreational services, particularly in poverty areas; he also identified lack of information about options and lack of access to services as factors that could increase the probability of institutionalization. Similarly, one British study found that 29 percent of 100 families would have kept their children at home if needed services had been available (Tizard & Grad, 1961); familiarity with and ready access to a service network might have substantially reduced the need for institutional placement.

Another major problem was indicated by Willer's (1978) natural parents, who expressed considerable anger at having been left to "fend for themselves" by the institution, after having accepted their retarded children back into their homes. They felt lost in a maze of community agencies and services, of whose existence and methods they felt they had little knowledge.

Soforenko and Macy (1977) pointed out the difficulties of determining how often generic services are used by discharged residents. Of all of their subjects who had been released from institutions, three-fourths had been placed into the community before mandatory legislation had been passed and before district service operations to maintain contact with them had been well established.

Consequently, knowledge of their whereabouts was lost. This group of released clients was so large that Soforenko and Macy presumed that they had been assimilated into the mainstream of society and that their utilization of generic services was indistinguishable from that of the general public.

In their survey of foster care providers, Justice, Bradley, and O'Connor (1971) found that, although approximately three-fourths of them used medical, educational, and planned activity programs for one or more residents, both day care services and sheltered work or vocational training programs were virtually nonexistent. Foster parents identified public misconceptions, inadequacies of school programs, and the lack of other supportive services as principal problem areas. By comparison, residents' behavior problems were perceived to be of relatively minor significance. In another study of foster families, lack of transportation, cost of services, and distance to services emerged as major problems (Browder, Ellis, & Neal, 1974). Although previously cited studies (O'Connor, 1976; Scheerenberger, 1970) suggest that medical services are more adequate than many other services, physicians appear to be unfamiliar with generic services for developmentally disabled individuals that might decrease the need for institutionalization, and they continue to recommend institutional placement (Kelly & Menolascino, 1975; Olshansky, Johnson, & Sternfeld, 1962).

As mentioned above, the mental health clinic is one generic agency that frequently expresses high interest in and concern for retarded persons. Yet, reports by Burton (1971) and Savino, Stearns, Merwin, and Kennedy (1973) challenge the depth of that interest and concern. Burton reported that during three fiscal years, 1963 to 1965, a total of 1040 retarded persons had been seen at clinics in the state of Kentucky. Most of the services provided were essentially limited to evaluation and diagnosis without further treatment. Seventy-six percent of all the retarded individuals seen received no treatment, 10 percent received individual therapy, 8 percent received chemotherapy, and 6 percent received some other form of therapy. In view of the relatively small number of retarded clients who actually received treatment, Burton concluded that those "who have criticized the strategy of assigning to mental health clinics the major responsibility for providing community programs are justified" (p. 38). He showed that these clinics fulfill their role of initial evaluation, and then most often resort to referring retarded candidates to "other agencies possessing the expertise for treatment or service outside the realm of mental health clinic responsibility" (p. 40).

Savino et al. (1973) have also described the lack of planning and lack of provision of services to mentally retarded persons within the current structure of community mental health programs. They describe the plans of the federal government to establish a vast array of community centers for mentally ill individuals, and the service networks that have been in existence in New York and California for over 15 years; yet they show that retarded persons remain underserved. Among the major problems they describe that impede the provision of services to retarded individuals through these community mental health programs are cultural biases against the retarded, lack of training among professional persons, prejudices of psychiatrists for treating only "good candidates for psychotherapy," fragmentation and duplication of services, and lack of a modern method of system design.

It would appear that, although professional persons from a variety of specialties and agencies profess obligations and responsibilities for developmentally disabled individuals, this sense of obligation has yet to be manifested in actual delivery of services to this population. The principle of normalization (Wolfensberger, 1972, 1980), with its explicit call for deinstitutionalization, can be implemented only if an adequate generic service network is available to support the developmentally disabled individual in the community. Existing research indicates that the four recommendations advanced by Jaslow (1967) concerning generic service agencies have yet to be fully instituted: 1) open every generic community agency to retarded individuals insofar as the agency's competence and ability permit; 2) train every health worker to work with mentally retarded (cf. developmentally disabled) persons; 3) place a mental retardation specialist, either full-time or part-time, in every generic agency of any size or significance; and 4) establish a coordinating mechanism within each community to ensure balanced services. Bradley (1978), Cohen (1975), Datel and Murphy (1975), Scheerenberger (1976a), and Wiegerink and Pelosi (1979) offer useful guidelines to generic service program administrators who desire to implement these recommendations.

GENERIC SERVICES AND COMMUNITY ADJUSTMENT

The preceding discussion focused on accessibility to and utilization of generic services by developmentally disabled citizens. However, the question remains of whether or not empirical evidence exists to support the assumption that developmentally disabled individuals benefit from the utilization of generic services. Too often, ideologies such as normalization are embraced, and programs and strategies that stem from these ideologies are implemented (e.g., more complete utilization of generic services by a specific population), but no consideration is given to their empirical justification. If the lives of developmentally disabled citizens are enhanced by using generic services. we are justified in advocating full use of these services by this population. However, if empirical studies show no significant differences in the lives of those developmentally disabled individuals who utilize generic services as compared with those who do not, then perhaps our energies should be invested in developing a more comprehensive network of specialized services.

The following discussion is in part based on two assumptions. First, it is preferable to have individuals in a community setting as opposed to an institutional environment, the former being more congruent with the principle of normalization and, more generally, with equality of opportunity to participate in the nation's democratic institutions. Second, community adjustment of developmentally disabled individuals can be indexed using admission and/or readmission data—in other words, those developmentally disabled individuals who maintain residence in the community have more successfully adapted to a "normal environment" than those who have, for whatever reason, returned to an institutional environment.

Keys et al. (1973) conducted a 14-month study of individuals placed in the community, the number who returned, and their reasons for return. All subjects were former residents of Fairview State Hospital, California. During the 14-month period, the average number of former residents on leave was 1270. Only 126 (9.9 percent) were readmitted, and only 1 percent of these were "repeaters" (i.e., those residents who repeatedly left and entered the institution). A major reason for return (27.8 percent of the cases) involved medical problems, which included "placements where medical needs could not be met in the community, acute medical episodes, and routine medical/dental needs" (p. 56).

Scheerenberger's (1975, 1976b, 1978) studies specifically addressed the question of the reasons for readmission. As shown in Table 6.3 (from the 1976b study), the primary reasons underlying unsuccessful placements, as reported by 135 public residential facilities, were community rejection of the retarded and the lack of community services. In the 1975 study, shortcomings in various community services appear to have been the primary reason for over half of the readmissions to public residential facilities.

Perhaps the most compelling evidence for the role of generic services in facilitating community adjustment comes from the research of Gollay (1976) and her associates. Caretakers' estimates of support services provided in the community were positively associated in multiple regression analyses with their ratings of higher resident activity level in the community, fewer problems in adjusting to community living, more independence in the living environment, and fewer unmet needs. Her data indicate that reinstitutionalization is significantly correlated with the lack of adequate services in the community to support the place-

Table 6.3. Primary reasons for readmission during fiscal year 1975–1976 as reported by 150 PRFs

Reason	N	%
Community rejection	20	13
Lack of community services	78	52
Activity centers and sheltered workshops	(18)	(23)
Behavior management programs	(20)	(26)
Counseling	(8)	(10)
Family support	(6)	(8)
Formal educational programs	(22)	(28)
Health services	(18)	(23)
Failure to adjust	74	49
Family unable to cope	24	16

From Scheerenberger, 1967b, p. 18.

ment. Figure 6.2 shows that a larger proportion of the respondents who did not return to the institution (NR) rated community services to be adequate for 10 of the 11 services that were considered. Another relevant predictor (Gollay, 1976), the releasing institutions' estimates of services and training provided in the community, was a composite measure based on services received or needed and available, staffing of the residence, and the extent to which parents or staff used supportive services. This measure was associated with greater likelihood of remaining in the community, fewer problems adjusting to placement, and more independence in the residential setting. Overall, measures of community support and training options (in and out of the residential setting) were among the best predictors of community adjustment in this study. Moreover, Wyngaarden, Freedman, and Gollay (1976) found that placements were more likely to be successful when there was in the community a residential facility that was either more closely or less closely supervised than the one in which the resident was placed. The implication is that a continuum of residential alternatives forestalls the decision to return residents to their releasing institutions. In addition, Polivka et al. (1979) found that movement to more or less restrictive settings was intimately connected to the availability of state funds for support services; there was substantially more reinstitutionalization when funds for support services decreased. They also found that there was little movement to less restrictive settings, but that the norm for client movement was from one setting to another of similar restrictiveness, typically "shopping around" from one group home to another.

Another significant finding in Wyngaarden et al.'s (1976) research was that those clients who received follow-up casework and more training and services from the institution staff rather than from community resources were less likely to remain in the community (see Figure 6.3), had less independence in their residential settings, and had more unmet needs. The individuals who eventually returned to the institution (R) had had a higher proportion of their services provided by the institution for 10 of a possible 11 services. Conversely, the individuals who remained in the community had the greater proportion of their services provided by community agencies for 10 of the possible 11 services. Gollay's data also indicate a positive relationship between the frequency of clients' contact with case managers and their likelihood of staying in the community. The individual who remained in the community was more likely than the individual who returned to the institution to be supervised daily by a "case manager." Such findings support the need for follow-along services, especially by a community agency. Finally, Gollay et al. (1978) reported that 99 percent of those who remained in the community, but only 59 percent of those who returned to their releasing institutions, had "friends in the community." They concluded that those who returned "appeared to be more lonely and less socially involved in the community than those who remained" (p. 145).

Although the data of Gollay and her colleagues are impressive, they are weakened by the retrospective method used to record them. Retrospective data

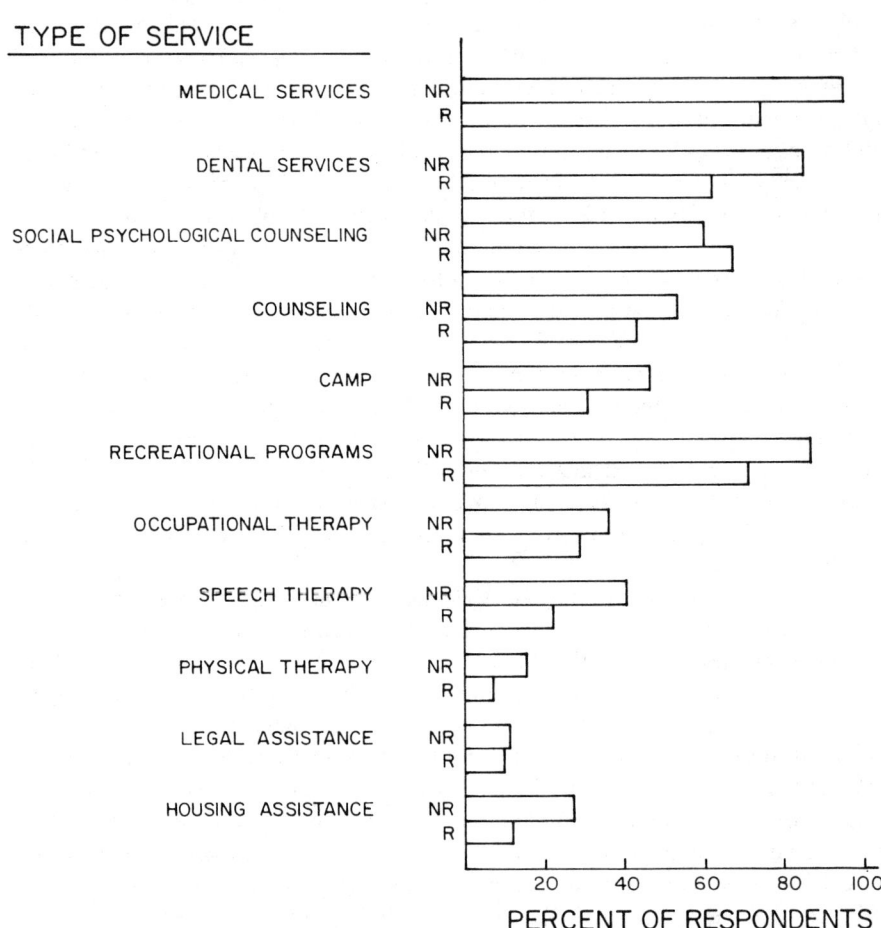

Figure 6.2. Availability of community services. Respondents were the community residential caretakers for 382 persons who were successfully placed and 58 who were returned to their releasing institutions. From Wyngaarden et al. (1976).

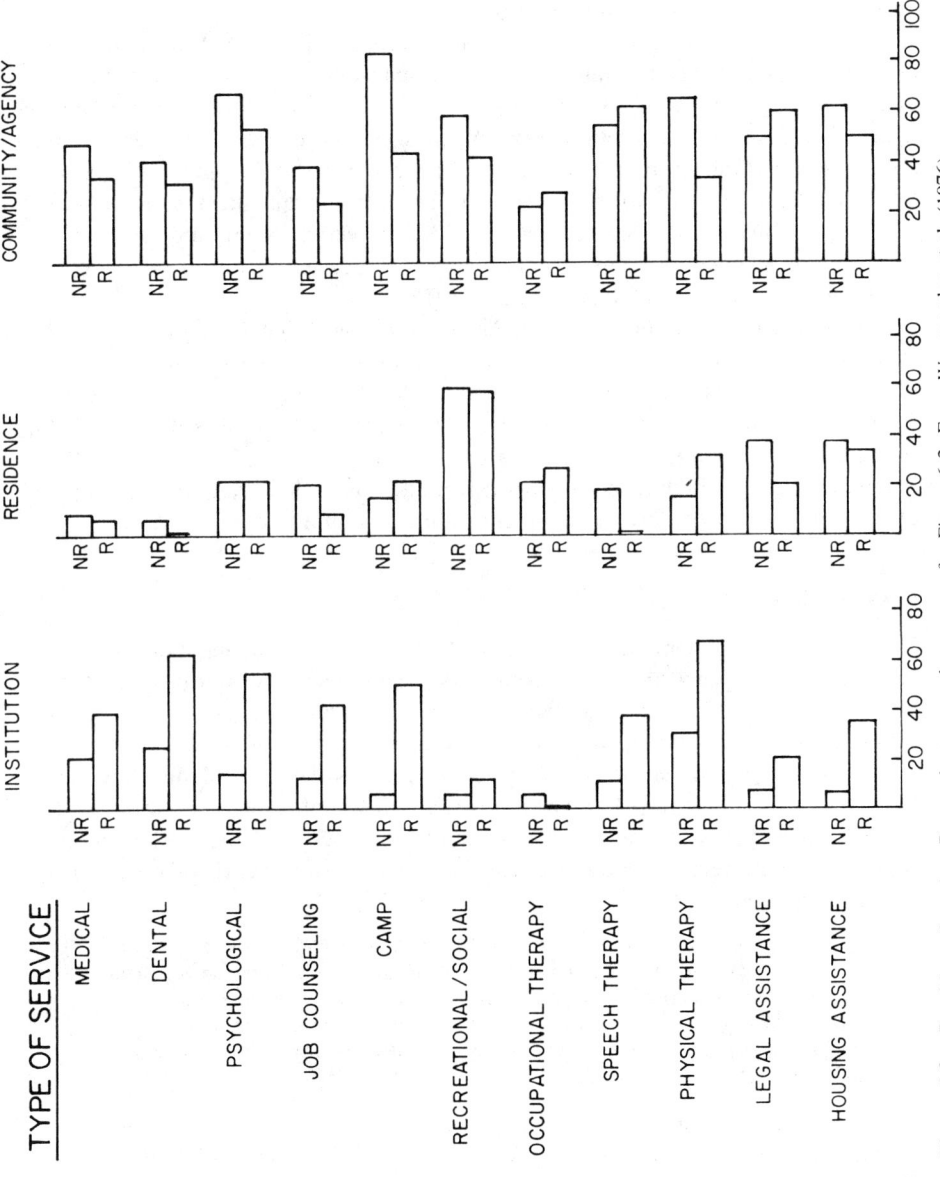

Figure 6.3. Providers of service. Respondents were the same as for Figure 6.2. From Wyngaarden et al. (1976).

are suspect in any case, but are especially subject to distortion in this study; their respondents, who were community-based residential caretakers, would appear to have had a vested interest in attributing successful placements to themselves and unsuccessful placements to other factors.

In other research, Sigelman, Bell, Schoenrock, Elias, and Danker-Brown (1978) also found that the rate of reinstitutionalization was higher for clients placed within 30 miles of a state school, and farther removed from community mental health/mental retardation services, thus leading to more dependence on the institution. Data from O'Connor (1976) show that handicapped individuals who have been placed into the community need and obtain substantial support service (see Figure 6.1). Her data also provide the overwhelming impression that services are adequate to meet the needs of the individual; this impression is consistent with the data of Gollay et al. (1978).

Gollay and her associates avoided the conclusion that institutions should stay out of the lives of former residents, and proposed that the institution and community services should coordinate to provide a total service network. In their interpretation of these data, Heal et al. (1978) concluded that it is possible that the institution intervenes only when a client is in jeopardy of returning to the institution. Thus, a high level of support from the institution might be the consequence, not the antecedent, of incipient failure of community placements.

CONCLUSIONS

The vast array of generic services, although constituting a treatment and service resource of huge proportion, has yet to fully meet the needs of our developmentally disabled population. Although a number of models identifying required services have been developed over the past several years, none has been cited more frequently than that proposed by the President's Panel on Mental Retardation in 1962. This model advocates a full array of direct services, both specialized and generic, for developmentally disabled citizens. Although the research with respect to generic services is meager, two very broad conclusions can be supported:

> ... generic services have yet to fulfill their role as providers of service to the developmentally disabled.... Unless expansion and integration of an accessible and adequate, generic and universal community service network keeps pace with the development of community residential models, there is serious question whether deinstitutionalization will prove more beneficial than institutionalization. (Heal et al., 1978, p. 236)

The four recommendations advanced by Jaslow (1967) appear to have merit. Guiding models for community service agencies interested in intensifying their services to developmentally disabled individuals have been proposed (e.g., Bradley, 1978; Fanning, 1973; Hersh & Brown, 1977; Kenowitz & Edgar, 1977; Sells & West, 1976). Datel and Murphy (1975) describe the Virginia model of "service-integrating mechanisms" for processing of clients, which is based on the collaboration of all state human service agencies and their community counterparts for the purpose of implementing orderly deinstitutionalization. Both Cohen (1975) and Scheerenberger (1976a) offer useful recommendations to administrators to rectify shortcomings in various community services. A network of generic services must be developed that not only is accessible to persons with developmental disabilities but is also capable of providing adequate service.

Generic services appear to be essential to successful placement in a community residential facility, but definitive statements are impossible without systematic examination of the possible consequences of both adequate and inadequate generic service networks. The full utilization of generic services by developmentally disabled citizens and the realization of Wolfensberger's (1972) principle of normalization cannot be accomplished until the existing shortcomings in community service networks are fully identified and eliminated.

Chapter 7
Physical and Social Integration of Developmentally Disabled Individuals into the Community

Francis A. Moreau, Angela R. Novak, and Carol K. Sigelman

Integration of developmentally disabled persons into the community is a complex process, yet it is a highly important one if deinstitutionalization is to meet its goals. In much of the literature discussing this process, the emphasis has been on studying the characteristics of the individuals who are placed into the community (Heal, Sigelman, & Switzky, 1978; McCarver & Craig, 1974). A few major studies have focused instead on the community environments into which these individuals have been placed (e.g., Baker, Seltzer, & Seltzer, 1977; Gollay, 1976; Gollay, Freedman, Wyngaarden, & Kurtz, 1978; O'Connor, 1976; Wyngaarden, Freedman, & Kurtz, 1976). Table 4.1 (Chapter 4) gives summary information about several major studies that have had this environmental focus, including the types of facilities sampled, and the IQ ranges of the residents studied. This chapter examines this research specifically in light of physical integration and social integration of developmentally disabled persons. Particularly relevant to social integration is the question of community attitudes toward persons with handicaps and toward residential alternatives; this area is also discussed.

NATURE AND EXTENT OF PHYSICAL INTEGRATION INTO THE COMMUNITY

In her national survey, O'Connor (1976) reported on the geographical location of community residential facilities (CRFs, but excluding natural homes, foster homes, and nursing homes) and found that 46 out of 50 states had at least one such facility. Six states, however, had over half of all of the CRFs in the United

---

Much of the information contained herein has been adapted or quoted directly from Heal, L. W., Sigelman, C. K., & Switzky, H. N., Research on community residential alternatives for the mentally retarded. In N. R. Ellis (Ed.) *International Review of Research in Mental Retardation*, Vol. 9. New York: Academic Press, 1978.

States: Michigan, New York, Nebraska, California, Washington, and Minnesota (in order by total number of CRFs). When arranged according to ratio of the number of facilities to the population, the order changed to: Nebraska, Washington, Colorado, Kansas, Minnesota, and Oregon. In all, O'Connor found 611 CRFs that met her classification criteria. She reported that the majority of the CRFs in her survey were located in cities with populations over 2500, where community services and programs might be expected to be sufficiently diverse to serve developmentally disabled clients. Baker et al. (1977) pointed out that 36 percent of the CRFs in their national survey were in cities with populations of less than 10,000; although 80 percent of the people of the United States were living in cities with over a million people, only 1.6 percent of the CRFs were in cities of this size. The data from these surveys indicate that most of the CRFs are located in urban environments of moderate size.

Optimally, a CRF site should have the following characteristics: a pleasant and safe neighborhood, availability of public transportation, proximity to places of employment, existence of programs meeting special needs, and low costs. However,

> Large, old houses within a suitable price range frequently are in older less desirable neighborhoods. On the other hand, older neighborhoods (near the central business district) have a mixture of different types of people, and persons who are somewhat different are more easily tolerated. (Wehbring & Ogren, 1975, p. 21)

The conflict is often between choosing a location that permits both physical and social integration into the community, but that still protects individuals with handicaps and provides the necessary services for their survival. The group homes in Berdiansky and Parker's (1977) study, for example, were usually located in central or transitional zones of cities or large towns in fairly stable, usually white, neighborhoods, inhabited by lower-middle and upper-middle-class families. A total of 22 percent of the homes were in deteriorating neighborhoods characterized by transience, high unemployment, or dependence on welfare agencies.

Presumably, the location of a CRF within the community affects the services rendered to its residents and also the amount of integration that can be expected. Gollay et al. (1978) found that two-thirds of the CRFs in their study were located on residential streets and were less than a half-mile from a shopping center. Very few CRFs were found in rural areas (10 percent) and over half of these were natural/adoptive or foster homes; these rural homes fell short of the ideal in that 60 percent of them were more than a half-mile from a shopping center. As pointed out by Bank-Mikkelson (1969) in Denmark and Grunewald (1969) in Sweden, placing CRFs near or in cities provides back-up services for the residents; nevertheless, natural and foster home placements, although rural, can provide the support necessary for successful community integration.

Closely related to the location of the CRF is the availability of transportation. One of the aims of integration into the community is to provide more opportunities for greater independence on the part of developmentally disabled persons, and transportation is essential to doing so. Forty percent of O'Connor's respondents and 35 percent of Gollay's reported that transportation was inadequate or unavailable for community residents. Lack of transportation was also cited by Browder, Ellis, and Neal (1974) as being a community service deficiency. Similarly, Wehbring and Ogren (1975) found lack of transportation to be a major problem for foster and group home placements: "Residents were also trained to use public transportation, but often service is infrequent or inadequate." (p. 35). Physical integration of developmentally disabled individuals into the community is undermined by the lack of transportation; its availability is essential in order for persons who live in the community to use other generic services independently. Very few developmentally disabled individuals can drive and, even when public transportation is available, limited scheduling, high cost, and individual handicaps create obstacles to independent living.

Edgerton (1967), in his classic study of deinstitutionalized adults living independently in the community, stated that many of his subjects lived in the inner city because transportation was available there or was made unnecessary by the nearness of most services. These neighborhoods, however, tended to be in lower socioeconomic areas and possibly placed the security of the individuals in jeopardy.

The problem of where to locate developmentally disabled persons becomes more complicated as additional variables are considered. For instance, the use of transportation might be hampered by negative attidues toward disabled individuals on the part of those already using it; the location and type of facility used as a CRF can be severely restricted by local ordinances and laws; and the decision of where to locate in the community might be further restricted by economic considerations.

In summary, the geographical location of the CRF in the United States, the size of the city, the type of neighborhood, and the availability of public transportation are physical characteristics of community facilities that have been considered in studies describing the physical integration of developmentally disabled individuals into the community. This physical integration may determine in part the nature and extent of their social integration into the community, which has also been studied.

NATURE AND EXTENT OF SOCIAL INTEGRATION INTO THE COMMUNITY

Even optimal location of an adequate community facility does not necessarily imply that individuals will be more integrated into the community than they were when living in an institution. Murphy, Renee, and Luchins (1972), studying foster homes in Canada, found that there was often no interaction between residents and other individuals or facilities in the community. In Browder et al.'s (1974) study in the United States, children in foster home placement were also found to be far removed from the social life of the community.

Social Activities

In their attempt to find out how extensively residents of CRFs were integrated into the community, Scheerenberger and Felsenthal (1977) questioned 75 residents of foster, group, and adult homes. Their results showed that these individuals had formulated new friendships both within and outside their homes and visited places outside their homes, although rarely unaccompanied; when asked specifically about their activities, 89 percent reported going to the grocery store, 94 percent to the park/zoo and 89 percent to church. Thus, Scheerenberger and Felsenthal substantiated at least some degree of social integration.

However, it is possible that, although CRF residents were going to town, they were not actually interacting with any members of the community. In Gollay et al.'s sample (1978) of 440 deinstitutionalized persons, for instance, individuals had very little interaction with the community. When questioned about their spare-time activities, these residents cited watching television and/or listening to the phonograph most often (98 percent), and they cited group activity (going to meetings of clubs or organizations) least often (18 percent). Vacations, parties, going to friends' houses, and religious services were enjoyed by 72 to 84 percent of the residents; nearly half didn't participate in any sports or go to sporting events. These results indicate a wide variety of social activities; however, very few of the activities actually included interactions between residents and nonhandicapped members of the community outside the residential setting.

The residents in Baker et al.'s (1977) study of 381 CRFs listed their most common activities as: watching TV and listening to the radio, doing chores, swimming, fishing, playing games, talking to other residents, walking around the neighborhood, and just "hanging out." Both the Baker et al. and O'Connor studies reported that about 90 percent of CRF residents have some household duties, although for about 15 percent these were limited to cleaning their own rooms. It can be easily recognized that not many of the above activities involve interaction with community residents. Almost all types of activities were represented, but, as Baker et al. remark, "Like most other community dwellers they spend their leisure time most often with peers they know from work, from their community residence, and from their previous residences" (p. 224).

O'Connor also did extensive research into the community social activities of CRF residents. In her study of 611 CRFs, she found going to restaurants and snack bars the most popular activity (85 percent), with indoor and outdoor recreation (80 percent), going shopping (77 percent), and attending church (67 percent) next in order of preference. Involvement in organized community groups or clubs was not common (27 percent). She pointed out that somewhat limited use of public transportation (47 percent) could have restricted many of the opportunities for community interaction. O'Connor also noted that three-quarters of the residents took part in recreational activities in the community, but over half of these were in activities offered solely for persons with developmental disabilities, not for the community at large. She also noted that about 15 percent of the residents in her study had no leisure community activities.

Social Contacts and Friendships

In addition to looking at the social and recreational activities of CRF residents, researchers have studied their social contacts with others, including friends, relatives, work associates, and benefactors within the community. About three-quarters of O'Connor's residents had some social contact with their own families, almost half on a regular basis. Fifty-seven percent reported having friends outside the facility and 80 percent of those residents actually visited their friends. Nearly all facilities (97 percent) allowed residents to entertain friends from the community, although approximately half had restrictions as to when and where within the facility entertaining was allowed (O'Connor, 1976). Baker et al. reported the same close supervision and restrictions on residents' social contacts with members of the opposite sex. About half of the facilities in their study had a curfew of 10:00 p.m. or earlier; almost all had some curfew or set bedtime. Most did not permit the consumption of alcohol, and a few (6 percent) did not permit the entertainment of nonresidents of the opposite sex in the CRF. A large majority (83 percent) of the residents needed permission in order to leave the CRF overnight or to go on a vacation. In contrast, Scheerenberger and Felsenthal's (1977) respondents from group homes, foster homes, and adult homes indicated that they had considerable choice regarding freedom to come and go, to select their clothing, to spend their money as they pleased, to decorate their rooms, and to show affection to others. Gollay (1976) found that the extent to which restrictions were placed on residents was more closely associated with residents' problems in the community ($r = 0.42$) than with individuals' level of retardation, suggesting that group home restrictions are possibly imposed to deal with individual problems that arise rather than because the residents have handicaps.

In Wyngaarden et al.'s study (1976), 90 percent of the individuals who continued to live in the community had "good friends from the community," but less than half of the individuals who returned to the institution had had such friends when they were living in the community. Her questionnaire, however, did not clarify whether or not these "good friends in the community" could be staff members or fellow residents. Thirty-four percent of the community residents had friends from the institution from which they had come. Some caretakers mentioned that residents had relatives as "friends" (26 percent), but only a few named nonhandicapped individuals in the community as "friends" of the residents. Scheerenberger and Felsenthal (1977) found 82 percent of their residents had "a special friend" and, of these, 70 percent were in the respondent's group home. These results tend to indicate that friendships are formed most often within the CRFs and not as often with neighbors or people outside them. Thus, although developmentally disabled individuals have involvement in community activities, it appears that they rarely interact with persons outside of their residences or outside of a network of disabled persons.

Dating and/or romantic involvement has also been studied as a dimension of social interaction. O'Connor reported that slightly over one-fifth (22 percent) of the residents in her study dated, with fewer than one-tenth dating on the facility grounds. Gollay et al. (1978) reported that 27 percent of community residents had had romantic relationships since leaving the institution; however, she also reported that having guests for dinner and going out on dates were the least common leisure activities. Again, she did not report how many of the relationships were with individuals outside the CRFs.

Employment

Another aspect of social integration into the community is employment, which is a major way in which adults participate in the life of the community and build social ties. Only 10 percent of CRF residents in O'Connor's study were competitively employed, whereas 48 percent were in workshops or training programs. Gollay et al. reported 13 percent as competitively employed, 42 percent working in sheltered workshops, about 25 percent placed in daytime activity programs, and 10 percent having little or no employment. Of Intagliata's (1978) discharged residents, 82 percent attended either a sheltered workshop or school during the day; however, most evenings and weekends were spent at home, in direct relation to the very low level of resident mobility in the community.

Obviously, more competitive employment is needed to foster integration with community members at least during and optimally outside of productive work hours. It is hoped that interaction on a daily basis with nonhandicapped coworkers would remove many of the attitudinal barriers between members of the community and CRF residents. Integrative employment is not possible as long as the majority of persons with developmental disabilities work only in segregated sheltered settings.

Education

Along with employment, education is one of the major means of social interaction available in our culture. For developmentally disabled individuals, educational integration presents a paradox: while they require a curriculum that is more specialized than that of the average student, their exclusion from the "normal" educational process automatically segregates them from opportunities to learn to get along with their less handicapped peers. As one resident responded when asked if there was anything he wished he could have been taught before moving into a CRF, "Oh, they (the institution) could have taught me to get along with people and to get acquainted a little better" (Wyngaarden et al., 1976, p. 40).

CRFs often have available to them a wide variety of educational programs; a resident's age and functioning level, and the types of programs available, dictate whether the individual attends the community school system or seeks special training elsewhere. Of Gollay et al.'s respondents, who ranged in age from 6 to 40, 40 percent were involved in school placements, with most in public schools. Very few, however, were in regular classes; half attended classes in specialized schools, and about a quarter were in special classes in regular schools. Scheerenberger and Felsenthal (1977) found 75 percent of their subjects enrolled in a formal educational program, and one-third of O'Connor's subjects attended school as their primary endeavor, with nearly half of these being in special education classes. In her study, 47 percent of the residents were in some form of a school program. (As shown in Table 4.1, Scheerenberger and O'Connor studied all age ranges.)

These data, although useful, do not indicate the amount or quality of interaction between developmentally disabled students and regular students. Many handicapped students appear to attend only special classes and therefore may have only minimal social contact with nonhandicapped students.

Recent research indicates that education indeed has a strong potential for aiding social interactions and social integration. Bruininks, Rynders, and Gross (1974) showed that, when sex of peer raters was controlled, no appreciable differences were obtained in the levels of peers' social acceptance of integrated mildly retarded pupils as compared to nonretarded pupils. Budoff and Gottlieb (1976) demonstrated the positive effects on mildly retarded children after integration into regular classes. After 1 year, the reintegrated children were more internally controlled, felt that others perceived them as more competent, and expressed more positive fellings about themselves as students than children who had been retained in special classes. As a means of integrating disabled individuals into the community, education is capable of playing a very positive, well-defined role, especially given the "education in the least restrictive environment" mandate of the Education of All Handicapped Children Act of 1975 (Public Law 94-142).

COMMUNITY ATTITUDES TOWARD RESIDENTIAL ALTERNATIVES

A critically important factor affecting the integration of developmentally disabled individuals into the community is community attitudes. For physical and social integration to occur, members of the community must be willing to accept, or at least tolerate, handicapped persons in their midst. Heal et al. (1978) have reviewed the role of community attitudes in the establishment and maintenance of community residential facilities; evidence of this role is found in both the attitude literature and in accounts of facilities' experiences. The next two sections discuss these two lines of evidence.

Attitude Research

Sigelman (1976) has described the difficulty of ascertaining the true attitudes and behavior of community residents toward persons with developmental disabilities, particularly those with mental retardation. She perceives that the problems arise from conflicting data about attitudes and from research indicating that overt behavior can and often does contradict expressed attitudes.

Stigmatization of mentally retarded persons has been documented in numerous studies (e.g., Gottlieb, 1975; Gottwald, 1970; Harth, 1973). Although these studies indicate the presence of stigmatizing views in the community, there is contradictory and extremely inconsistent evidence about the extent to which these negative attitudes translate into opposition to the integration of developmentally disabled citizens into the community. Gottwald (1970) reported that 48 percent of a national sample identified most mentally retarded persons as "good neighbors," and that only 8.6 percent felt that having mentally retarded adults in the neighborhood would tend to reduce property values. Lewis (1973), on the other hand, found that only 23 percent of those he surveyed recommended community living for an educable-trainable level person, 36 percent unconditionally called for their institutionalization, and 41 percent suggested that the decision should be conditional. Respondents in the Lewis survey were even more intolerant toward severely retarded persons living in the community, with 74 percent unequivocally rejecting such a proposal.

Attitudes toward group living arrangements for persons with mental retardation have also been mixed. The President's Committee on Mental Retardation (1975), in a commissioned Gallup Poll, found that fully 85 percent of the respondents "would not object" to a home on their block for six mildly or moderately retarded persons prepared for community living. In contrast, Sigelman (1976) found that only 44.7 percent of a stratified sample in a conservative southwestern city wanted the law to allow homes for retarded adults in residential districts. The discrepancy between the two studies could be attributed to differences in phrasing of questions; for example, it is possible that the public distinguishes between passively accepting group homes and actively asserting that they should be allowed. Kastner, Reppucci, and Pezzoli (1979) conducted interviews about attitudes toward retarded persons and toward community integration under "control" and "threat" conditions, where the "threat" condition consisted of interviewing persons who lived on a city block where a house was for sale. Before the interview began, respondents were asked to express their opinions in the interview "if that house was being considered for the location of a new group home." Respondents in the "threat" condition expressed significantly more negative attitudes on questions centered on immediate personal neighborhood interests, or that implied bringing retarded people more closely into their "personal space," than they did on broad questions about mental retardation or general issues like equal rights. These studies, like those measuring broader attitudes toward disabled persons, suggest that community receptivity regarding residential alternatives is more enthusiastic from a distance than from next door.

There is also no clear evidence indicating which types of people are likely to be good neighbors to persons living in community residential facilities. In an attempt to identify individual correlates of positive attitudes, Sigelman (1976) found that young persons, liberals, frequent church attenders, and Blacks (as compared with Anglos and Mexican-Americans) were most favorable toward group homes, and that there was a tendency for renters and those living with their families to be somewhat more favorable than home owners. If used by program planners, these data might suggest locating homes in black or ethnically mixed neighborhoods, with many young adults who rent rather than own homes and who perceive themselves to be liberals—the very kind of transitional urban neighborhood where many group homes are now located (O'Connor, 1976).

However, not all previous findings are consistent with Sigelman's. Although Gottwald (1970) found the same relationship between age and attitude in his study, females were more positive toward mentally retarded persons than were males, and persons with higher income and education more positive than those with lower income and education. Although Blacks were more favorable to group homes in the Sigelman study, they were more likely to express rejecting attitudes or call for institutionalization of retarded persons in Lewis's (1973) research. Harasymiw, Horne, and Lewis (1976) found that young and old, professional and lay persons, were equally tolerant toward disabled groups. What distinguished the level of acceptance was the degree to which a handicapped individual could conform to the majority standards, such as work productivity and living standards; the individuals who most conformed to the majority standards were the most accepted.

Few firm conclusions can be drawn from this attitude research; relationships detected in one study are often contradicted in others. To date, the search for a profile of the "good neighbor" for CRFs has been less than an overwhelming success. The attitude literature offers little guidance for those seeking to locate a facility where integration will be maximized.

Even if correlates of attitudes toward persons with developmental disabilities and toward community integration were consistent across studies, however, one must be concerned with the relationship between attitudes and behavior. For instance, Rothbart (1973) found that Eugene, Oregon, residents who lived within a mile of a halfway house for ex-convicts were less favorably disposed toward it than were those who lived 3 or 5 miles away, even though they were just as liberal in their attitudes concerning prison sentences. In addition, favorability toward a proposed housing project decreased as the proposed site moved nearer to the respondent's home and began to affect the respondents directly; although 80 percent approved the need for low-income housing projects, fully 53 percent opposed a specific proposed project within a half mile of their homes. The more concrete and personal an attitudinal item is, the more likely it is to predict behavior (Harrelson, 1970); still, the relationship between attitude and behavior is tenuous enough so that in one case a planned community facility was opposed even after neighbors had said in response to a direct question that they would accept it (Sigelman, 1976). In summary, the attitude literature appears to be an inadequate source of information about levels of community acceptance, characteristics of accepting neighbors, and the probability of active opposition.

Community Facilities' Experiences

Further indication of the magnitude of the problem of obtaining community support comes from studies based on the experiences of existing facilities. Justice, Bradley, and O'Connor (1971) and Tinsley, O'Connor, and Halpern (1973) found that community nonacceptance and misconceptions headed the list of problems identified by caretakers in family and group homes. Based on a survey of state institutions, Morrissey (1966) singled out lack of community acceptance as a major cause of failure in foster home programs. The individuals in the Gollay et al. (1978) study who returned to their institutions after "failing" in community placements rated their neighborhoods to be significantly less friendly than those who remained successfully placed in the community. Holmes (1979) found neighbors of apartment cluster programs were more accepting than neighbors of group homes, whose development had been impeded by negative community reactions. One-third of the 611 community residential facilities studied by O'Connor (1976) reported that there had been opposition at the time of their establishment. In 83 percent of the cases, this protest came from neighbors, although 11 percent reported opposition by businessmen, local officials, or community leaders. Opposition was apparently not a function of the type, size, or extent of normalization of the facility, nor of the age of the residents. Very similar results were reported by Baker et al. (1977), who found that 35 percent of their 381 responding community facilities reported opposition, usually from neighbors. Ironically, they found a modest correlation ($r = 0.18$, $df = 329$, $P < 0.001$) between the number of sources of opposition and the number of approaches used for community preparation, indicating that the more extensive the preparation of the community for a facility, the more likely the community will be to oppose its establishment.

Unfortunately, these studies do not indicate how many facilities never opened in the first place or were closed because of community opposition. All focused on operating facilities that apparently survived any opposition they experienced. A recent estimate that at least 50 percent of all community-based programs for ex-mental patients are blocked because of neighborhood opposition suggests, however, that opposition is a significant obstacle to deinstitutionalization (Rutman & Piasecki, 1976). Keating (1979) has written of the intense opposition in New York City against the establishment of group homes for former residents of Willowbrook; this opposition includes attempted arson, physical assault, vandalism, and bomb threats. Six of the 51 group homes in Berdiansky and Parker's (1977) study did not open because of community opposition. The principal fears expressed by the neighbors toward all these group homes were fears of physical harm, loss of property value, and sexual deviance; there was also a high level of intolerance toward racial-sexual integration. Each of these issues was raised in one-fourth of the cases where opposition was reported, and was resolved in less than half of the cases in which it occurred. However, Wolpert (1978) reports that many of these concerns are unfounded. In his controlled study, group homes did not affect property values or property turnover. Also, their functioning in a neighborhood was inconspicuous; group home residents were generally not noticeable on the street; and group homes were generally maintained better than surrounding properties.

It is not clear whether one can expect that any amount of social integration between developmentally disabled persons and their neighbors will occur once residents are placed in the community; or whether contact with developmentally disabled persons improves attitudes and, more importantly, affects behavior toward them. As discussed earlier, preliminary evidence suggests that the amount of community contact with group home residents is limited. Although 57 percent of O'Connor's (1976) sample and 94 percent of Gollay et al.'s (1978) subjects had friends outside their residences, it was not determined how many were neighbors or nonhandicapped members of the community. In one large community facility studied by Birenbaum and Seiffer (1976), only one of 48 residents had a girlfriend who was not from either the residence or a workshop setting, and it was concluded that "the surrounding community has not been the source of many new friendships" (p. 93). Although neighbors of the facility were not hostile, staff members were apparently sensitive to this possibility, discouraging residents from standing around idly, and encouraging them to dress appropriately. Here, the very staff consciousness that was intended to reduce negative neighborhood attitudes may also have reduced resident-community social interactions.

In O'Connor's study, 89 percent of the facilities claimed that opposition had decreased since the time of opening, primarily because of the behavior of residents and secondarily because of efforts by the facility staff. A study of neighbors of family care homes for retarded individuals in Fresno, California, indicated that attitudes of 58 neighbors were generally positive and, according to Mamula and Newman (1973), "illustrated that once mentally retarded residents had lived in a neighborhood, they tended to be accepted" (p. 60). Again, resident behavior may have been influential, because care-providers' records indicated that 96 percent of the residents had had no recorded behavior difficulties in their neighborhoods. A California State Department of Health study (reported by Lauber & Bangs, 1974) also concluded that, as negative-minded community members and agency personnel become more familiar with program objectives and residents, their opposition decreases. Another study reported by Lauber and Bangs (1974), conducted in Green Bay, Wisconsin, found that rates of approval of group homes in prime residential neighborhoods were similar for those community members who knew of a family or group care facility and for those unfamiliar with them, suggesting that, at the very least, experience with facilities did not result in more negative attitudes.

Although Gottlieb and Corman (1975) found that adults who had had no previous contact with mentally retarded persons were more likely to favor segregation of the retarded in the community than those who had had contact, some evidence indicates that it is the quality rather than the quantity of contact that is most instrumental in changing negative attitudes (e.g., English, 1971; Gottlieb, 1975; Vurdelja-Maglajlic & Jordan, 1974). Unfortunately, negative stereotypes often affect the quality of interaction; behavior incidents that may be inconsequential for the nonretarded may be judged intolerantly if engaged in by a retarded person (Goroff, 1967), or may be deemed "problems of retarded persons" rather than everyday problems (Edgerton, 1975). Kastner et al. (1979)

found that individuals who wanted contact with or who had already been exposed to retarded persons expressed more positive attitudes toward retardation and community integration than those who had not had experience, whether this contact was actually visiting a group home, knowing a retarded individual personally, or simply reading factual information on mental retardation. Mamula and Newman (1973) found positive attitudes among neighbors who had lived next to retarded individuals for at least 2 years; they reasoned that the neighbors had learned from experience that retarded persons are not a neighborhood liability.

Apparently, then, neighbors become accustomed to community facilities, although they tend to oppose them before the fact. Sigelman (1976) concluded that the more that preparation, planning, and discussion about retarded persons goes on in a neighborhood, the more likely it is that organized opposition to group homes will occur. Thus, these findings support the practice of many agencies of simply moving in unannounced without informing neighbors and thereby forestalling organized protest (Baker et al., 1977). On the other hand, Berdiansky and Parker (1977) point out that this approach increases a group home's vulnerability in the event of a "news leak," and many developers have regretted their surreptitious approach, just as others have regretted their elaborate information campaigns. They suggest that, if a community facility is planned in the suburbs or in rural areas, at least an informal canvass should be done to determine whether the community has recently fought the opening of a similar facility, to gauge the intensity of attitudes, to discover the existence of potentially antagonistic organizations, and to check the viewpoint of powerful people in the neighborhood. Less care needs to be taken in heterogeneous neighborhoods in the inner city and in transitional zones.

In summary, negative attitudes toward persons with developmental disabilities and toward their living facilities exist, as evidenced by attitude surveys and as witnessed by the experiences of residential facilities. Although the apparent unpredictability of community opposition reduces opportunities for the strategic placement of facilities in receptive neighborhoods, program planners can at least be heartened by the preliminary evidence that opposition dissipates once the facility has been established.

CONCLUSIONS

The principle of normalization advocated by Wolfensberger (1972) emphasizes the independence of the developmentally disabled person, and requires both physical integration and social integration into a culturally normative setting. The research of Baker, Bruininks, Gollay, O'Connor, Scheerenberger, and their associates indicates that this integration is progressing at an ever-increasing rate. Their studies give an overview of the national scene; in specific areas of the country, even greater strides have been taken to make integration a reality.

An example is a program in Omaha, Nebraska, that uses "live-in friends" as supporters for retarded individuals. In this program the retarded person lives with a nonretarded person who acts as a "friend," but not as a supervisor or controlling agent. The program has been extremely successful, and an evaluation of it concludes: "The major problem is not the adult's retardation; it is the fact that he lacks the experience of living in a real community" (Perske & Marquiss, 1973). Wehbring and Ogren (1975) also noted in their study of seven exemplary CRF facilities that: "Learning about the community may be one of the significant lessons of the community residential experience. It is part of the larger lesson that people who happen to be retarded are a part of the human condition, and they have something to contribute if we but have eyes to see it" (p. 227).

However, many contradictions remain. For example, a coworker in a sheltered community asked, "Why train a retarded person to fit into an abnormal outside community, where he will feel stress and run a high probability of being exploited? Why force a retarded person to live like that because many normal people live like that?" (Baker et al., 1977, p. 119). One can also raise questions that revolve around a tension between the goal of integration on the one hand, and the training and service needs of developmentally disabled persons on the other. While trying to give individuals a more normalized life in a CRF, staff, out of necessity, establish rules and restrictions that interfere with living normally but that may serve to protect residents from threats in the community for which they are not yet prepared. Placing developmentally disabled individuals in special education classes segregates them, yet putting them in regular classes without adequate special educational interventions hardly meets their needs.

Physically placing individuals with developmental disabilities into the community may not provide them with opportunities for greater independence, for more contact with nonhandicapped persons, or with more opportunities for the community to accept them. The goals of normalization, including physical and social integration, must be carefully evaluated in terms of the best interests of each individual. In the process of pursuing these goals, developers of community residential facilities must grapple with the many inherently difficult ideological questions involved. They must consider the risks involved as well as the other needs of clients, which may not be well served by an exclusive emphasis on normalization, and they must ask probing questions about what is individually optimal. The kinds of studies discussed in this chapter—supplemented, it is hoped, by further studies of specific aspects of physical and social integration—can help to determine how the opportunity to participate in society can be achieved for every citizen regardless of handicap.

Part III
TRAINING FOR INTEGRATION

Chapter 8
A Behavioral Approach to Integrating Individuals into the Community

Richard P. Schutz, R. Timm Vogelsberg, and Frank R. Rusch

The principle of normalization (Nirje, 1969; Wolfensberger, 1972) has become the major philosophical impetus of the community integration movement. Unfortunately, normalization has often been misinterpreted to mean that a normative community placement will automatically be beneficial to developmentally disabled individuals. Simple exposure to the "patterns and conditions of everyday life which are as close as possible to the norms and patterns of mainstream society" (Nirje, 1969, p. 181) will not guarantee acquisition of the vast array of competencies associated with successful community living. For instance, in their study of 160 community residential facilities, Butler and Bjaanes (1978) concluded that facilities with few or no training programs to facilitate the normalization process can be just as restrictive and debilitating as a large state institution.

The deinstitutionalization process involves much more than the physical removal of an individual from one setting and his/her placement into another (Wolfensberger, 1972). In preparation for a smooth transition from institutional life to the more independent lifestyle of a community-based living arrangement, personal needs of the individual, such as social and vocational skills training needs, must be taken into account. Furthermore, this preparation should be guided by an assessment of the factors deemed important for successful integration by the community into which the handicapped individual is placed. Accordingly, this chapter reviews skill areas that have been reported in the applied research literature, followed by a brief discussion of some efforts to use these findings to program for community integration. The chapter concludes with a statement of the need to acquire, on a continuing basis, measures of social acceptance in order to assure that there is a correspondence between the needs perceived by the community and the goals, procedures, and results delivered by behavioral training.

A BEHAVIORAL APPROACH

An important factor in the complex community integration process appears to be the preparation of developmentally disabled persons to function as independently as possible in a variety of community settings. Clearly, there is a need for community living skills training, especially for the moderately or severely retarded and those mildly retarded individuals with long histories of institutionalization. Recent studies have also provided evidence of a favorable relationship between institutional training for community adjustment and successful community placement (Bell, 1976; Gollay, Freedman, Wyngaarden, & Kurtz, 1978). Conversely, unmet training needs have been reported to be a contributing factor in former community residents' readmission to institutions (Baker, Seltzer, & Seltzer, 1977).

One of the more significant advances in the education and training of developmentally disabled persons in the past decade has been the increased acceptance in the fields of special education and vocational rehabilitation of the use of behavioral principles to change behavior. These principles refer to procedures that increase or decrease (depending on the goal) the frequency of a selected behavior by systematically arranging environmental events that precede and follow it (Rusch & Mithaug, 1980). It has been repeatedly demonstrated that these training and management procedures can make desirable behavior much more likely and can dramatically expand the adaptive behavioral repertoire of virtually all mentally retarded individuals (Birnbrauer, 1976).

In addition to providing a set of training and management techniques, this approach entails the use of concise behavioral definitions and objectives, the conceptualization of the habilitation process, and the use of methods for evaluating these techniques (Browning & Stover, 1971). Rusch and Mithaug (1980) have characterized the behavioral approach as including: an objective analysis of an individual's behavior; direct, repeated observation and measurement of behaviors; the use of replicable training and management procedures; and the treatment of behavioral performance in three training phases (acquisition, maintenance, and transfer). This approach has been applied in such diverse settings as classrooms (Becker, Engelmann, & Thomas, 1975), penal institutions (Bassett & Blanchard, 1977) and city street crosswalks (Vogelsberg & Rusch, 1979); in the treatment of a wide variety of individual social, educational, and sexual behaviors (Barrett, 1977; Goldfried & Davison, 1976; Lovaas & Bucher, 1974); and in the management of human service programs (Davidson, Clark, & Hamerlynck, 1974). This section details several successful efforts to train community-relevant skills that have utilized a behavioral approach.

Community Mobility Skills

One area in which adaptive community skill training has been investigated is travel training. This skill area refers to mobility about the community by such means as walking and riding buses. Cortazzo and Sansone (1969) described a travel training program that trained pedestrian skills and travel skills for various means of public transportation, including trains, subways, and buses. The basic program included teaching identification facts, pedestrian techniques, travel routes, money usage, and conveyance identification. Parent counseling was also provided. The authors reported that, of the 378 mildly and moderately mentally retarded persons enrolled in the program over 3 years, 199 learned to travel independently.

Page, Iwata, and Neef (1976) trained five mentally handicapped males (average IQ 61) to acquire complex pedestrian skills using a simulated model of the community in a classroom setting. The training method consisted of preinstruction and demonstration. Measures of generalized pedestrian skills were collected under actual traffic conditions on a city street. Pedestrian behavior was divided into five skills: 1) recognizing intersections, 2) recognizing pedestrian lights, 3) identifying tri-colored traffic lights, 4) crossing intersections with stop signs, and 5) crossing intersections without stop signs. An average of 5.3 hours of training over 21 sessions produced positive results for each person during a 2–6-week follow-up.

In another pedestrian skills study, Vogelsberg and Rusch (1979) provided preinstruction, feedback, and practice to three severely handicapped adolescents to teach them to cross partially controlled intersections. Data were collected on four training clusters: approaching (walking to and stopping on the curb), looking (looking behind, in front, left, and right), stepping (stepping off the curb when traffic was not present), and walking (walking quickly across the street). Components of the instructional package were systematically faded to promote skill maintenance. Generalization measures of pedestrian behaviors collected on untreated, partially controlled intersections, suggested that all individuals used their newly acquired behaviors appropriately.

Sowers, Rusch, and Hudson (1979) trained a severely mentally retarded adult to use the public transportation system in Seattle to get to and from work daily. Bus riding was divided into 10 separate task sequences: 1) crossing controlled intersections, 2) crossing uncontrolled intersections, 3) using bus tickets, 4) walking to and from the bus stop and home, 5) identifying the correct bus, 6) boarding, 7) riding, 8) getting off the bus, 9) transferring, and 10) walking to and from work and the bus stop. Instruction was provided in the natural environment and consisted of modeling, verbal instructions, and feedback.

In another travel training study, four moderately retarded adults were trained to ride a city bus to and from different community destinations, including a fast food restaurant, where they ordered a meal (Marholin, Touchette, Berger, & Doyle, 1979). Training procedures included prompting, modeling, corrective feedback, and social reinforcement. Training was conducted in the natural environment, with general preinstructions concerning what was to occur during each training session. Training resulted in increases in correct responses by each of the adults.

Domestic Skills

A number of authors have developed instructional programs to facilitate acquisition of domestic skills. Brown, Bellamy, and Sontag (1971) described a number of field-tested public school programs for training cooking, housekeeping, and laundry skills to moderately handicapped adolescents. Sitton (1972) prepared a manual to assist handicapped adults in the management of housekeeping chores such as laundry, care of furniture, and washing walls, windows, and woodwork. Fredericks, Baldwin, Heyer, Alrick, Bunse, and Samples (in press) also developed curricula for severely handicapped adolescents and adults in such domestic skill areas as cooking and home management.

Domestic skills training has also been addressed in the research literature. Robinson-Wilson (1977) designed an illustrated, color-coded recipe system that promoted independent cooking. This system, which utilized illustrative pictures for each preparation step, temperature controls, and ingredient measurement tools, was used to train three severely mentally retarded adults to prepare three separate recipes.

In the area of housekeeping, E. L. Phillips (1968) demonstrated the use of a token economy to increase several cleaning behaviors in predelinquent boys. Among the targeted behaviors were cleaning and maintaining one's room and cleaning the bathroom in a group home. Data indicated that cleaning skills increased as peer managers contingently distributed points, which were then exchanged for a variety of self-selected privileges. This investigation also reported the use of a response cost component, in which points were subtracted from those points earned for occurrences of inappropriate behavior.

Employing a multiple-baseline design across behaviors, Bauman and Iwata (1977) trained two mildly handicapped adults to self-monitor housekeeping tasks when provided schedules. Systematic fading of training, i.e., systematically increased reliance on self-scheduling and self-recording, led to maintenance of treatment gains. The authors also reported the efficacy of self-scheduling and self-recording in the maintenance of other domestic skills (e.g., cooking).

Self-Care Skills

A number of training manuals and curriculum guides have been developed that address self-care skills. Hamre (1974) prepared an instructional model for training severely handicapped persons in grooming skills, including hair care, treatment of acne, fingernail and toenail care, shaving, and menstrual care. Sample programs consisted of a task analysis, performance criteria, instructional sequences, needed materials, data collection and teaching procedures, and field-test results. Langworthy, Anderson, Bryne, Hathaway, Holum, and Swenson (1974) developed a training manual addressing similar grooming areas and instructional procedures. A curriculum guide covering a variety of grooming skills (e.g., bathing, use of deodorant, and hair care) has also been prepared by Bender and Valettuti (1976).

Research concerning self-care skills training has been conducted primarily with institutionalized severely and profoundly mentally retarded individuals. Self-dressing has been successfully trained by ward staff (Martin, Kehoe, Bird, Jensen, & Darbyshire, 1971; Treffry, Martin, Samels, & Watson, 1970), although these skills have been shown to deteriorate when maintenance is not systematically programmed (Ball, Seric, & Payne, 1971). A dressing program developed by Azrin, Schaeffer, and Wesolowski (1976) provided a forward sequence of steps, with graduated and intermittent physical guidance, use of clothing that was graduated in size, and an emphasis on natural reinforcers. This program was employed with seven profoundly mentally retarded adults who learned to dress and undress themselves after an average of 12 training hours over 3 to 4 training days. Systematic training and reinforcement procedures have also been successfully employed in training severely retarded persons to acquire toileting skills (Azrin & Foxx, 1971; Sloop & Kennedy, 1973), oral hygiene skills (Abramson & Wunderlich, 1972; Wehman, 1974), and menstrual care skills (Hamilton, Allen, Stephens, & Davall, 1969).

Brickey (1978) reported a program that taught moderately and severely mentally retarded adults to self-administer medication in residential and vocational settings. Fourteen persons were taking medications for epilepsy; 6 were doing so for losing weight, hyperactivity, or Parkinson's disease. The program consisted of nine phases, beginning with the establishment of a stable dosage and ending with the purchase of medication at a pharmacy. The training techniques included preinstruction, verbal prompts, color coding (in several cases), and verbal acknowledgment. The results indicated that all participants were successful in achieving all but the last step of the program—transaction at a pharmacy. Results from a subsequent pilot study indicated 50 percent of the participants of the earlier study successfully completed the pharmacy step within a 6-month training period.

Money Management Skills

Research concerning money management skills training with mentally retarded persons has primarily addressed coin recognition and making change as opposed to managing a checking account. Bellamy and Buttars (1975) taught moderately retarded adolescents to apply academic counting skills to money counting. All students learned rote counting skills and then applied these skills to selecting correct amounts of change. Orr (1977) demonstrated that mildly mentally retarded adolescents in a classroom setting learned to manage money by receiving a weekly salary based on attendance and school work. These individuals were required to budget money for monthly obligations such as housing, transportation, and personal care.

Tony Cuvo and his colleagues have reported several monetary skills training efforts. For example, Lowe and Cuvo (1976) developed a procedure to teach four mildly to moderately retarded persons to sum the value of 51 separate coin combinations. The authors employed modeling, imitation, and manual guidance in instructing trainees to count coins first individually, and then in combination with other coins. Results suggested an improvement in coin-counting performance. A 1-month follow-up probe indicated that these newly acquired skills were maintained. Trace, Cuvo, and Criswell (1977) taught mentally retarded adolescents coin equivalency by employing a three-component response chain: naming, selecting and counting, and depositing target monetary values into a coin machine. Individuals receiving training improved significantly in coin equivalence performance and maintained these skills.

Telephone Skills

Acquiring telephone skills may be particularly valuable, because the telephone can serve as a means of obtaining help if needed, or as a means of interacting with friends and relatives. Leff (1974) noted the utility of telephone skills in his report of a program in which 60 moderately retarded individuals learned to dial a phone and maintained the skill. Smith and Meyers (1979) taught telephone skills to 60 institutionalized persons with moderate to severe mental retardation. These individuals were instructed to perform such tasks as placing emergency telephone calls and making appointments. The authors noted little difference between those persons who received verbal instructions plus modeling and those who received modeling alone. The authors also noted no difference between individual and group training, suggesting the benefits of group instruction in terms of time and program cost.

Leisure Skills and Social Activities

Teaching leisure time activities has been the focus of various research studies. Recently, task analysis, data-based instruction, and contingent reinforcement have been used successfully to teach mentally retarded persons such physical activities as swimming (Bundschuh, Williams, Hollingworth, Gooch, & Shirer, 1972), bowling (Seaman, 1973) and cross-country skiing (Sinclair, 1975). Other authors have directed their attention toward studying the relationship between participation in recreational activities, such as basketball and dancing, and social acceptance (Eichenbaum & Bednarek, 1964; McDaniel, 1971). Several authors have also suggested the importance of creative arts as a programmatic area to introduce to mentally retarded persons (Burmeister, 1976; Maynard, 1976).

Paul Wehman and his collegues have reported a number of recreational programs ranging from specific skill training (Wehman & Marchant, 1977) to the examination of differential environmental conditions on leisure time activity (Wehman, 1978). For instance, Wehman (1977) reported two studies, one focused on developing isolative play and the other on developing cooperative play with six institutionalized, profoundly retarded adolescents. Each study reported the use of an across-subject multiple-baseline design with results indicating that stereotypic behavior was reduced through increases in appropriate play. Wehman, Renzaglia, Berry, Schutz, and Karan (1978) reported two studies demonstrating the acquisition of physical fitness and table game leisure skills. Specific instructional directives and appropriate task analyses were provided in data-based programs involving the training of three exercises and four table games. The results of each program indicated that severely mentally retarded individuals can acquire a diverse repertoire of leisure skills in a relatively short period of time.

There has also been an increased interest in teaching more effective interpersonal communicative behaviors (Hynes & Young, 1976; Perry & Cerreto, 1977). In one such study severely retarded persons were successfully taught to initiate social activity requests over the telephone (Nietupski & Williams, 1974).

Sex education has also received some attention. Recently, Hamre-Nietupski and Williams (1977) reported the results of a 3-year sex education program involving severely mentally retarded adolescents in three public schools. A model-test-teach design and a test-teach design were used to instruct adolescents in five instructional areas: 1) bodily distinctions, such as body parts and sexual distinctions, 2) self-care skills, such as premenstrual training, 3) family members and relationships, 4) social interactions, and 5) social manners. The sex education and social skills acquired as a result of this data-based behavioral program facilitated appropriate adult heterosexual social activities.

Vocational Skills

The vocational habilitation literature has primarily reported research concerning skill acquisition and production-oriented training in sheltered settings. The majority of research regarding skills training has focused on demonstrating the ability of mentally retarded persons to acquire a variety of difficult and potentially remunerative vocational skills. For example, recent studies by Bellamy, Peterson, and Close (1975), Crosson (1969), Friedenburg and Martin (1977), Gold (1972, 1976), Hunter and Bellamy (1976), Irvin (1976), and Martin and Flexer (1975) have demonstrated that mentally retarded individuals can learn complex vocational tasks requiring multiple discriminations of form, color, color-form compounds, and size, as well as judgment and the use of tools. Also illustrative of the numerous vocational training projects is the Specialized Training Program (Bellamy, 1976), which has empirically demonstrated the efficacy of stimulus control, shaping, and chaining techniques in vocational training.

Karan, Wehman, Renzaglia, and Schutz (1976) provided similar empirical support for the improvement of workshop performance of severely mentally retarded persons through specialized instruction. A number of studies have demonstrated the effectiveness of a wide variety of positive consequences to increase productivity, such as money (Schroeder, 1972), music (Cotter, 1971), choice of work assignment (Zimmerman, Overpeck, Eisenberg, & Garlick, 1969), and knowledge of performance (Jens & Shores, 1969). Other production-oriented studies have examined task analysis (Gold, 1972) and the development of more efficient job methods and work station design (Martin & Flexer, 1975). Recent studies have also demonstrated that mentally retarded persons can learn to decrease interfering behaviors that distract coworkers (Mithaug, 1978a; Schutz, Wehman, Renzaglia, & Karan, 1978).

A recent trend in vocational habilitation research is the investigation of procedures for training mentally retarded adults for nonsheltered, competitive employment. As has been the case with sheltered workshop studies, this research has focused on the acquisition and maintenance of specific vocational skills, primarily on those tasks associated with various service industry occupations. For example, mentally retarded persons have been successfully taught to perform janitorial tasks (Cuvo, Leaf, & Burakove, 1978) and kitchen laborer tasks (Rusch, Schutz, Lamson, & Menchetti, 1979; Sowers, Thompson, & Connis, 1979). Continuous work on designated tasks throughout the entire work day (Rusch, Connis, & Sowers, 1979) and speed of task completion have also been trained within nonsheltered vocational settings (Rusch, 1979a).

Completing job tasks and producing at an acceptable rate have been regarded as essential for successful occupational adjustment (Rusch, 1979b). However, several studies have addressed the identification and training of social and vocational behaviors that comprise a broader classification of occupational survival skills. For example, mentally retarded adults have been taught to manage their workday routines independently through the use of time management cards (Sowers, Rusch, Connis, & Cummings, 1980). Employer procedures, including sending workers home for inappropriate work behavior (e.g., verbal abuse toward a supervisor), have also been found to be effective with mentally retarded workers (Schutz, Rusch, & Lamson, 1979).

General Comments

Community skills training and the development of skill-sequenced curricula are relatively new areas of inquiry. Despite this brief history, the studies presented above demonstrate that even those individuals labeled as severely handicapped can learn functional community living skills. However, although this research has been shown to alter behavior of potential relevance to community adjustment, collectively it does not provide for a complete empirical basis for community habilitation efforts at this time. Additional behavior change programs that directly enhance community functioning are needed. In several of the studies reviewed here, the research setting was largely an institutional or simulated one, set up expressly to obtain the results reported. Greater attention must be directed toward the evaluation of skill attainment in community environs where individuals actually live and work.

Continued research efforts are also needed to refine the principles on which training techniques are based, to expand the set of available techniques, and to define useful procedures for broader aspects of community integration. Although a behavioral approach offers a useful conceptual framework for the development of viable community skills training, the majority of the studies reviewed above do not take into account the requirements of the community. In order to integrate developmentally disabled persons it is absolutely essential to devise community skills training efforts based on the actual or potential community environ. For example, it would be appropriate to train persons to ride a bus only if the community that they will enter has a mass transit system. Functional community skills training programs require a knowledge of the requirements of the community. Vogelsberg, Anderson, Berger, Haselden, Mitwell, Schmidt, Skowron, Ulett, and Wilcox (1980) provide an example of this community-referenced approach to training relevant community skills. Vogelsberg et al. (1980) developed an independent living skills inventory of skills necessary to select, set up, and survive in an apartment. The major areas addressed are:

I. Selecting an independent living situation
   A. Individual information list
   B. Legal concerns
   C. Financial consideration
   D. Where to look for an apartment
   E. Environmental considerations
   F. Physical setting
   G. Landlord considerations
   H. Steps to finalizing
II. Setting up an independent living situation
   A. Initial preparation
   B. Materials inventory
   C. Acquisitions
III. Surviving in an independent living situation
   A. Organizing a schedule
   B. Skills specific, room by room
   C. Transportation
   D. Safety
   E. Money Management
   F. Communication
   G. Leisure time
   H. Miscellaneous concerns

Schalock (1979a) and Bock and Weatherman (1976) have developed criterion-referenced assessment instruments to evaluate an individual in reference to specific behavioral skills that promote community participation. Target behaviors represent the results of task analyzing environmental demands relative to functional behaviors required for independent functioning. These instruments provide a functional diagnosis, summarizing an individual's strengths and weaknesses within several behavioral domains (e.g., clothing care and use, food preparation). Either of these tools can be employed in initial placement evaluations or on a regular basis for continuing individual and program reviews (Schalock & Harper, 1977; Schalock, 1979b).

Although efforts to develop functional community skills assessments are relatively new, they are based on the requirements of the community—the understanding of which is a necessary requisite for individual community integration and survival. These three community-referenced assessments, which suggest zero-instructional inference (Brown, Nietupski, & Hamre-Nietupski, 1976), represent approaches that yield instructionally relevant information regarding individual performance, given the myriad of community skills necessary for successful integration. Comprehensive efforts to develop larger programs utilizing a behavioral approach are few in number; the next section of this chapter describes some of these efforts.

COMMUNITY LIVING PREPARATION PROGRAMS

Behaviorally based community training programs have been interjected all along the deinstitutionalization continuum. These programs can be found within large institutions (Lent, 1968; Martin, 1974) as well as in group homes (Close, 1977). These programs typically consist of highly structured skill training components, with progressively more normalized routines engineered to ease the transition to greater autonomy and increased responsibility.

Bates (1977) reported on an institution-community transition program in which community adjustment training was provided to 50 severely and profoundly mentally retarded residents in such skill areas as basic toileting, dressing, and eating. All behaviors selected for training were task analyzed and taught in a step-by-step manner with continuous data collection. In addition to this training, the program included parent training in the use of behavioral principles and community resource information. The results of this program indicated that 21 residents were successfully placed in community-based residential facilities; one was returned to the natural home.

Community-based residences have also been the setting for specific skills training. Although programs vary widely, the most common setting has been the group home. For example, Close (1977) randomly selected four men and four women from an institution to live in a group home. These individuals were severely and profoundly mentally retarded adults who exhibited gross deficits in self-care and appropriate social interaction. Each of these individuals worked in a sheltered workshop while residing in the group home, which necessitated a cooperative interagency effort to coordinate training throughout the day. Results of this community integration effort indicated overall increases in relevant skill areas by comparison to matched pairs of adults who continued to reside in the institution.

A number of home-based parent education programs have also been developed within recent years. Hanson (1976) reported a parent-implemented training program for infants with Down's syndrome. Target behaviors consisted of normal developmental skills, including motor behavior, cognition, personal and social behaviors, and communication. The program included weekly home visits by child development specialists who initially assessed the infants and formulated training objectives based on normal developmental scales. Parents received training in behavioral approaches, including observation and data collection procedures. Results of this early intervention effort indicated that, by applying behavioral principles, parents facilitated the acquisition of developmental milestones that were near the normal range.

Another home-based program, the Portage Project (Shearer & Shearer, 1972), has implemented a behavioral training approach for handicapped preschool children. This program also involved parents in the education of their children. An experimental comparison of randomly selected program children and children enrolled in classrooms for culturally and economically disadvantaged children indicated that significant gains were made by the experimental group in mental age, IQ scores, language and academic development, and socialization (Peniston, 1972).

The programs sampled here suggest that specific community living skills and adaptive behavior training can be successfully implemented in a variety of settings. However, it is obvious that many issues remain to be resolved regarding family (e.g., Hobbs, 1975) and residential services, and the integration of individuals into normal settings (for example, see Chapters 5 and 10 of this volume).

SOCIAL ACCEPTABILITY

The behavioral approaches presented in this chapter are typified by their objective analysis of behavior, their reliance on data that are collected directly and often, and their use of behavior modification strategies that, when applied, develop new modes of behaving or change the actual occurrence of behavior. Today a behavioral approach is also typified by the inclusion of a measure of social acceptability. Social acceptability, in the context of community integration, refers to the consumers of the deinstitutionalization movement judging its goals, its procedures, and its overall impact. Consumers include the clients being integrated, the clients' families and friends, employers, neighbors, and the general public.

Although Baer, Wolf, and Risley (1968) outlined the components of a behavioral approach that included consideration for the assessment of social acceptability, this component has not received the wide usage originally intended (Wolf, 1978). The delay in actual use and development of a component of social acceptability may be related to the fact that what is considered socially important includes a subjective value judgment that only society is qualified to make, and that efforts to measure this judgment reliably have lagged behind the measurement of overt behaviors (see Chapter 7 for a more thorough discussion of attitudinal research).

This chapter has overviewed a number of extant community skill areas to which research has been directed. Collectively, these studies represent an effort to investigate the training of behaviors that are socially relevant. Several of these studies represent efforts to utilize the immediate community of potential consumers, e.g., employers, to validate their goals, procedures, and results (see Schutz, Rusch, & Lamson, 1979). The need for future research to examine behavior that is relevant, and therefore socially important and not merely convenient for study, will undoubtedly advance the development of quality integration efforts. Efforts directed toward the use of behavioral principles applied to relevant behavior and shown to be effective will promote the acceptance of deinstitutionalized individuals.

Determining which behaviors are important to acquire and whether actual changes in these behaviors are perceived are problems facing behavioral researchers. A number of forces will work against obtaining accurate, valid, and usable feedback from potential consumers. Three forces in particular deserve mention here. First, it is possible that behavior identified by potential consumers as relevant will later be determined to be different from the behavior originally identified as salient. For example, mobility about the community may be considered important; however, mobility per se may later be viewed as unimportant by comparison to a broader definition of mobility that includes not only riding to work on a bus, but also walking to and from the bus stop alone. Second, although certain select behaviors may be identified and changed, the overall acceptance of an individual may be predicated on secondary behaviors (e.g., cleanliness; see Chapter 5) that were not identified but that influence overall success measures. Finally, consumer groups, e.g., neighborhood associations, could provide inaccurate feedback to prevent or sabotage integration. Each of these forces provides unique and challenging problems for behavioral researchers. These problems, however, should serve only to generate interesting and qualitative answers to aid the development of relevant community skills and the overall process of integrating developmentally disabled persons.

CONCLUSIONS

Behavioral training, with its management of events that precede and follow target behaviors, has been successfully applied to a number of skills that appear to be crucial for participation in community life. However, preparation does not guarantee integration. A complete behavioral program necessarily includes efforts to measure not only training effects but also social acceptance of training practices and their results. The success of deinstitutionalization may be undermined by either failure to utilize the most effective behavioral training procedures or failure to develop community support for the goals, procedures, and results of these programs to train persons to live in community residential settings. Baer et al. (1968) suggested that behavioral programs, when effective, often lead to social approval and adoption. Public attitudes toward developmentally disabled persons have always been a major factor in their care, education, and training. The history of changing attitudes that our society has had concerning developmentally disabled persons also reveals parallel changes in residential services for these individuals. Although changes are oftentimes slow, training efforts like those described above have brought increased community awareness that developmentally disabled persons have far greater potential than was previously realized. Furthermore, these training efforts have promoted the view that deinstitutionalization is a practical, approachable, and humane goal.

Chapter 9
Issues in Communication Research Related to Integration of Developmentally Disabled Individuals

George R. Karlan

Integration of developmentally disabled citizens into the community through changes in either residential or vocational services will place dramatic new demands on the linguistic and communicative skills of the integrated individual. At a minimum the individual will need communicative skills to gain access to the most basic goods, services, and information. Mobility, with any degree of independence, will be restricted unless the individual can ask for and provide minimal identifying information. Unless isolated within the community, the individual will encounter increased opportunities to utilize language in its social functions, which include its use as the mediator of interaction and its use in conversation. Finally, language is especially important to direct or instruct. This final function will undoubtedly facilitate the preparation of individuals for integration into the community. As a means of specifying exactly how the individual should respond or behave, language has tremendous universality and portability within the target settings.

In contrast to these requirements and functions, much of the language intervention research with more severely retarded or developmentally disabled persons has focused on training receptive and expressive language skills, per se. For reviews of research in this area, see Harris (1975), Snyder, Lovitt, and Smith (1975), and Guess, Keough, and Sailor (1978). This research has examined techniques for developing these skills largely without consideration of their use in communication. Concern for the pragmatic, uses of language is a relatively recent development in the study of child language acquisition (Bates, 1976a) and has received almost no attention in research relating to those with severe language deficits (Rees, 1978). However, the functional aspects of communication acquire considerable importance in planning for the integration of moderately and severely developmentally disabled individuals into community settings.

It will be necessary, then, to bridge the gap that exists between the development of linguistic behaviors and the development of communication skills.

The terms "verbal skills," "language skills," and "communicative behavior" in the discussions to follow should by no means be taken to be synonymous with "oral language skills." Many of the developmentally disabled adults who would be likely candidates for community residential placement do display the skills necessary to communicate orally, although there is a wide range of such abilities. However, some individuals within this population are commonly referred to as nonverbal because they do not possess the capability or cannot be taught to use primitive oral skills. For this group, the strategies and requirements outlined in this chapter still pertain; however, adaptation is necessary to provide an alternative channel, other than oral, by which these persons can express themselves. Such alternatives have been referred to as auxiliary communication techniques and include two broad categories, manual signing (Stremel-Campbell, Cantrell, & Halle, 1977) and graphic forms of communication, e.g., communication boards and books (Harris-Vanderheiden & Vanderheiden, 1977). Because such techniques are used to provide alternatives for expression, the discussion of the use of language in skill training requires only the caution that auxiliary techniques might be difficult to integrate with self-instruction approaches. With social uses of language, it is important to be sensitive to the additional demands placed on the audience (those with whom the speaker is communicating through auxiliary channels) in receiving and interpreting the communication. For further information the reader is referred to the sources cited above.

This chapter examines what is known and what will need to be discovered in order to meet the language and communicative needs of those developmentally disabled persons making the transition from institutional to community-based service alternatives. These are individuals who might traditionally be classified as moderately or severely retarded, who may have physical as well as behavioral handicaps, and who have had an extensive history of institutional experiences. Finally, to stress a fundamental point, increased attention to the education, vocational training, and community integration of this population is relatively recent; therefore, subsequent discussion reflects established practice where possible, but in greater part reflects speculation based on the application of still-evolving thought. Whatever the source, the intent is consistent: to lay the foundation for the training of effective communication skills necessary to successful community integration.

RECEPTIVE LANGUAGE AS A TRAINING TOOL

Preparation for entry into the community will certainly require that the developmentally disabled person be trained in new, and possibly more complex, skills. One method for conducting such training entails the presentation of language, in the form of phrases or sentences, to tell the person what to do. Training persons to respond to language with appropriate nonverbal motor performances has been referred to as training in instruction-following (sometimes direction-following) (Frisch & Schumaker, 1974; Mithaug, 1978b; Striefel, Bryan, & Aikins, 1974; Striefel & Wetherby, 1973; Striefel, Wetherby, & Karlan, 1976, 1978; Whitman, Zakaras, & Chardos, 1971). Because such tasks do not require the trainee to *produce* any language behavior, but merely to *receive* and comprehend language, they are designated as receptive language tasks.

Instruction-Following

Language is a set of symbols (words) having specific referents (objects, actions, etc.); when these symbols are combined (sentences) the relationships occurring among words (syntax) indicate further relations (complex meanings). For example, the words *man, broom,* and *push* have specific, easily visualized referents; when combined into *man pushes broom,* a new relationship emerges and with it a new image. Huttenlocher (1974) has represented the task of the child learning to comprehend language as involving a process in which words must be recognized as separate units in the sentence. These units each correspond to specific referents. The particular order of these units (the sentence) represents a unique referential relationship. In order for the sentence to be understood, words and word order must be recognized, the referential association must be recalled, and the appropriate behavioral indication of comprehension produced. For example, *put the spoon in the cup* requires that an auditory discrimination be made among words, that each noun (spoon, cup) encountered result in the recall and selection of the correct object, and that the action (put) and relational (in) words result in placement of the named objects into the proper relationship.

Problems in Training Instruction-following requires that such responding be guided only by the linguistic information. However, Huttenlocher (1974) has identified several sources of extralinguistic information that might affect responding: redundancy, preference, and restricted or common relational characteristics of the task. **Redundancy** refers to the situation in which the instruction is given during the occurrence of a sequence of behavior; the person, responding to the nonverbal flow of events, coincidentally performs what would appear to be instruction-following. With handicapped individuals, this might occur when a chain of behaviors is being trained; a behavior in the chain, rather than the instruction, might serve to cue the next performance. For example, in the complex chain of behaviors required to prepare a simple breakfast, an individual might correctly pour out a glass of milk from a carton and still not understand the instruction *pour the milk into the glass.* This is due to the inevitability of this behavior following the instruction *put a glass on the table,* when the milk carton is the sole object already on the table. **Preference** becomes a factor when a single instruction is presented; a response that is performed with a high probability regardless of the instruction (e.g., drink the milk) will always appear to be correct when the instruction for that behavior is presented. The last type of nonlinguistic cue is perhaps the most common; the very way in which a task is arranged may serve to suggest either habitual or *restricted* solutions. If presented with the instruction *put the spoon in the cup and stir* and given a spoon, a plate, and a cup, even a severely retarded individual might perform the correct response, although he or she might have attended only to *spoon* from the entire instruction. This is possible since the motion of stirring with a spoon in a cup is a habitual, or common, response. On completion of sweeping a floor, presentation of the instruction *put the broom in the closet* may reveal little more than attention to *broom–closet*. There is a restricted relationship in the context; it would be difficult to place the broom under or on top of the closet. Any evaluation or training of comprehension skills will require that such sources of extralinguistic determinants be minimized. In fact, consideration of these factors clarifies many of the discrepancies and explains much of the difficulty encountered in interpreting the available research on instruction-following with severely retarded persons.

Research on Instruction-following One of the earliest of the instruction-following studies was conducted by Whitman et al. (1971) with institutionalized severely retarded children. A combination of reinforcement, physical guidance, and fading procedures was utilized to increase appropriate motor responses to 10 instructions. Instructions included simple directives (stand up, come here, clap hands), identification of body parts (point to your nose), and simple relational directions (put the pencil in front of the box; put your hands under the table). In addition to increases found as a result of direct training, Whitman et al. (1971) also reported increases in responses to untrained instructions. This research seemed to indicate that to produce instruction-following behavior one need only present the instruction, physically guide the individual through the response, then systematically withdraw physical assistance. Furthermore, the development of some instruction-following responses leads to the emergence of correct responses to new and unrelated instructions. However, two objections can be raised relative to the procedures and results obtained in this study. First, although no reinforcement was available during baseline, some correct responses were observed. In addition, instructions were selected that the institutional staff thought the children were capable of following. It could be argued, then, that the children already possessed instruction-following skills and were simply noncompliant during baseline, and that reinforcement, used as part of the intervention package, merely increased motivation and hence compliance. Second, the children were presented with only those objects that were needed to perform the responses. It is therefore possible that some responses were made on the basis of the common or restricted functions of the materials.

Striefel and Wetherby (1973) and Striefel et al. (1974) replicated the design of Whitman et al. (1971) but introduced two changes to the procedures. Reinforcement for correct responses was used during the baseline phases to control for motivation. Also, the number of objects among which the individual had to choose in order to respond was increased. This required increased attention to the instruction being presented. Striefel et al. (1974) and, to a lesser extent, Striefel and Wetherby (1973) observed some responding during the initial baselines.

More importantly, no generalization was observed in either study as a function of training; in the generalization set, those instructions to which no response had been made during the initial baseline continued to receive either no response or an incorrect response during the final assessment. In each of these studies an additional, and critical, analysis was conducted in order to determine which particular words in the instructions were controlling responding. Probes were conducted that were composed of variations on the verbal instructions; these variations consisted of only verbs, only nouns, verbs plus the preposition (put in), preposition plus the noun (in box), preposition only (on) and recombinations of different instructions. In this last variation, two instructions (e.g., wipe table, move chair) would be recombined to form two new instructions (wipe chair, move table). Analyses of all responses, correct and incorrect, revealed that in many cases an entire response was under the control of a specific word. In the above example, if *wipe chair* were presented as a probe item after training *wipe table* and the chair and table were both present, the table (the training object) would be wiped.

Striefel et al. (1976) suggested that, if instructions are generated by recombining the individual words from different grammatical classes of words (e.g., verbs and nouns) and if several objects are available for selection, appropriate learning of word-referent associations would be fostered from the outset. In order to evaluate when an instruction could be considered learned, they established a criterion that required that a correct response to the instruction being trained be performed repeatedly as a part of a sequence of responses to instructions that had already been trained. The instructions in the series had a special characteristic; they contained words that were common across instructions. For example, if the instruction *wipe table* were being trained, learning would be considered complete when correct responses occurred to the instructions *wipe table, wipe chair,* and *move table,* when *wipe chair* and *move table* had already been trained. These instructions would be presented several times each in a random sequence. In the above example, the three instructions represent a minimum set; each of the training words, *wipe* and *table,* occurs in an instruction with two other elements, *wipe* with *table* and *chair,* and *table* with *wipe* and *move.* The results of this study, unlike those of Striefel and Wetherby (1973), indicate that, if instructions are used that have common words, the individual words will come to control specific responses without those responses having been individually trained. That is, training on *wipe,* then training on *table,* need not precede training on *wipe table.*

Generalization The most important implication of the instruction-following research for practical application is what it reveals about generalization of instruction-following skills. Certainly, it is impossible to train an individual to respond correctly to each and every instruction he or she may encounter during and after integration into community employment and residence. It is critical, then, that generalization be established; the individual will need to make correct responses to new instructions.

Striefel et al. (1976, 1978) addressed the problem of generalization through an analysis of what constitutes a "new" instruction. Because the associations between words and referents are completely arbitary, the meaning of a single word in isolation cannot be inferred by a person's simply hearing the word. Either new meaning must be explained through more language or the referent for the word must be made apparent in a variety of contexts. With instructions, however, a new instruction can be created by combining words whose referents may or may not already be known; such an instruction is "new" because it represents a unique combination never before encountered by the individual. The greater the number of previously known words in a "new" instruction, the greater the probability that a particular appropriate response, not itself seen before, will be performed. Previous knowledge of components can be acquired through the experience of instruction-following. Striefel et al. (1976) structured a set of instructions and arranged the training sequence so as to maximize the possibility that generalized behavior would develop. Simple imperative instructions consisting of only verb-noun phrases were selected for training two severely retarded adolescents. The actual instructions were generated from a set of 12 verbs and 12 nouns. Training was cumulative; only one instruction was introduced at a time, but previously trained responses were practiced every session. An ideal learner would require training on only the first 12 verb-noun combinations (V_1N_1, $V_1N_2 \cdots V_1N_{12}$) and each subsequent verb combined with one noun (V_2N_1, V_3N_1, $V_4N_1 \cdots V_{12}N_1$) in order to have the basic knowledge to respond to all other "novel" instructions. Although the ideal was not achieved, substantial generalization was observed in two severely retarded adolescents. Mithaug (1978b) presented similar findings for generalization involving prepositional (object-preposition-object) phrases; prior experience with the constituents of the instructions and experience with some phrases resulted in generalized responding to untrained phrases.

Finally, several studies reported by Striefel et al. (1978) were concerned with how best to train instruction-following skills. The evidence suggested that some initial training on individual components (verbs, nouns) facilitates the development of subsequent instruction-following. However, the most benefit can be gained by maximizing the relevant contrasts as quickly as possible. For example, appropriate stimulus control would be most quickly developed if responses to an instruction set such as *wash the pots, wash the bowls, dry the pots,* and *put away the bowls* were trained concurrently. Presenting several objects as alternative choices promotes generalization to such instructions as *dry the bowls, wash the cups,* and *put away the pots.*

The previous discussion was directed toward the development of important instruction-following capabilities in individuals who may have extremely deficient receptive language skills. Two additional areas warrant further discussion. First, the instructions previously discussed consisted of simple imperative directives; their structures specified simple predication (wash dishes) or, at most, positional relations (put the broom in the closet). Several additional classes of instructions can be identified that might be encountered in normalized language settings. These more complex classes of instructions include compound and multiple instructions and instructions requiring an individual to make varying degrees of inference as a prerequisite to making a response. A second area of concern relates to the actual words used in and relations specified by the instructions. The training research previously reviewed utilized content that was selected arbitrarily or by convenience. The settings and tasks in which instruction-following training is used to develop the skills needed for community integration will dictate the selection of content. A systematic approach to the process of determining content based on observed or perceived need is discussed below (see "Selecting Content for Remediation").

Complex Instructions The use of complex instructions may arise in part from a desire to economize on words or to give maximum direction to large "chunks" of behavior. The result of such intentions can be the use of compound instructions or the delivery of a sequence of instructions, all of which are presented before the response to any one can be made (multiple instructions).

Compound instructions are most likely to occur where obvious redundancy can be reduced. If two or more actions are to be carried out with the same objects, economy of expression can be obtained by instructing someone using a compound verb, e.g., *sweep and mop the kitchen floor.* Other forms of common compound instructions might include:

1. Compound predicate objects—*Bring the broom and dustpan to me.*
2. Compound locations—*Sweep the floor in the kitchen and in the dining room.*
3. Compound prepositional objects—*Put the dishes on the counter and the table.*

Research into training responses to these varieties of instruction is virtually nonexistent. Logical analysis of the demands presented by these instructions suggests that skills may be required that are essentially extralinguistic. The most obvious of these is short-term memory; the greater the amount of time required to complete one unit of the response, the greater the memory demands to recall what to do next. Interacting with ability to recall the original instruction might be the necessity of changing settings in order to complete the response. It could be hypothesized that shifting to a new location introduces additional demands not present when the context is constant. For example, *sweep the floor in the kitchen and the dining room* would presumably be more difficult than *sweep and mop the kitchen floor.* On the other hand, the functional relationship between objects or the visual presence of the necessary objects could serve as prompts to facilitate completion, e.g., *bring the broom and dustpan, put the napkins and garbage in the trash.* Although by no means exhaustive, these variables would seem to be reasonable points of departure for an analysis of failure to respond to compound instructions.

Compound instructions and, to a greater extent, multiple instructions represent an opportunity to exercise control over behavior while minimizing supervisory effort. This is especially true when the completion of an instruction produces enduring changes in the environment that can be evaluated at one time as evidence of completion of the entire sequence of instructions. Lent, Holvoet, Ferneti, Keilitz, and Tucker (1973) have compared the abilities of groups of moderately retarded and normal adolescents to respond to multiple directions. Instructions were presented in sets of one, two, three, four, and five instructions. Both groups were equally able to follow single instructions and showed equal deficits in responding to five-instruction sequences. With sets having two, three, or four instructions, moderately retarded adolescents were significantly poorer both in performing the responses and in performing responses in the order established by the instructional sequence presented to them. These findings are relevant in that some settings or tasks will require only the ability to comprehend, remember, and correctly respond to a series of instructions regardless of the precise sequence, whereas other tasks and settings will require attention to substance and precise order. In addition, although less intense supervision may not be expected during the initial phases of community placement, successful sustained integration may require that individuals be given skills, such as multiple instruction-following, that allow placement into more loosely controlled settings.

Inferential Instructions Instructions that require certain inferential acts on the part of the respondent depend on the nonlinguistic context to provide the cues that are inferred but not contained in the instruction itself. An instruction intended to elicit aid that has the form "Bring me that thing" requires the listener to infer what is needed either by observation of what is missing or by following some glance or gesture. Other examples of inference-requiring instructions (with missing information indicated in parentheses) are *Go help Joe* (do what?), *Put the silverware away* (away where?), *Fill the glasses* (with what?), and *Get a laundry basket* (from where?). A special case of this type of instruction is the indirect instruction. Recent studies of the pragmatics of language use (Bates, 1976a, 1976b; Rees, 1978) have indicated that the speaker's intentions in uttering a sentence are usually apparent. However, the indirect speech act represents a case where literal interpretation does not coincide with communicative intent. The speaker who says "Go and check for the broom" may have little interest in receiving a report on the whereabouts of the broom, wanting instead the broom itself. Feedback that is intended to elicit appropriate corrections can also take such a form. The person learning to sweep the floor might be told "You missed some crumbs under the table"; such feedback, while precise in its observation, may be nonfunctional in achieving the intended goal—having the person return and sweep the crumbs. The value in recognizing instructions that require the listener to identify indirect intentions is in determining why a person might fail to respond or might respond incorrectly to an instruction. Although the potential of persons who are going to be integrated into the community may encompass the potential to learn to respond to indirect instructions, our current technology may fall short in the capacity to train such a skill. At best, one could identify the most common and specific examples and assure, through direct training, that responses could be made to the examples identified. It would be most appropriate to minimize the incidence of inference-requiring instructions in these settings by modifying the setting itself.

Training Technology for Multiple Instructions Developing the skills necessary to respond to compound and multiple instructions may be within our current technological capabilities. Two techniques that can be applied to this problem are the use of systematic shaping to increase short-term memory and the introduction of prompts to facilitate the completion of complex tasks.

The techniques previously presented as being relevant to the problem can be operationally defined in terms of the passage of time occurring while one or more responses are completed, and the occurrence of intervening responses. A possible training sequence would first involve evaluating, or training, performance along the time variable. The time interval between the occurrence of the instruction and the opportunity to initiate the response can be systematically increased without an intervening task. After stable levels of responding are exhibited or established, intervening tasks can be introduced. There are two levels of intervening tasks; tasks requiring skills that are well established in the individual's repertoire may provide less interference than tasks requiring skills that are still being acquired or are newly acquired. Training would be structured to enable the presentation of one task while the individual is completing a different task; for example, just after a person has started scraping leftover food from dinner plates, a trainer says "When you are finished, take out the garbage." Initially, intervening tasks would require already well established skills; later, intervening tasks requiring newer skills would be added. This type of training could prepare the individual to begin receiving sequences of instructions. Each task performed following the presentation of the compound or multiple instruction becomes an intervening task for the next response in the sequence. A systematic training strategy requires that, with multiple instructions, training be initiated with two-instruction sequences and the length of the sequences be increased according to established criteria.

The use of additional cues as so-called pacing prompts (Bellamy, Horner, & Inman, 1979) has been advocated for vocational training. Such prompts are used to pace the individual through complex tasks. For example, during community mobility training, a person learning to pull the buzzer to signal the bus driver of the approach of his/her desired stop might be presented with pacing prompts. These prompts might combine gentle nudges with verbal cues like: "Look, there is the drugstore two blocks before your stop; look for the pull-cord." "Look, now we are at the stoplight before your stop; put your hand on the pull-cord." "Look, there is the pizza place just before your stop; pull the cord." Eventually such prompts are faded by eliminating those nearest the terminal response and continuing away from it. With complex instructions, verbal reminders as to the portions of the response yet to be performed can be introduced frequently. The number of such prompts is then decreased contingent on correct responding. Through these means, the pacing prompts are systematically removed, and final control over complex responding rests with the instructions themselves.

Selecting Content for Remediation

The researcher's selection of language behaviors, i.e., words, instructions, requests, descriptions, and so forth, has often been arbitrary. That is, common words have been selected that represent materials at hand and phrases or sentences are generated from these. Often a language-teaching task is devised and the messages are conveniently fitted to it. Recently, however, discussions of the social importance of behavior change have addressed the issue of socially validating, i.e., establishing the appropriateness of, target behaviors and performance criteria (Kazdin, 1977; Wolf, 1978). The essence of the arguments raised in these discussions is that selection of goals and criteria requires either the detailed observation of the relevant context or the solicitation of input from potential "consumers," that is, those who will be interacting with the individual. Surveys of the requirements of vocational performance in sheltered and nonsheltered settings have been undertaken (Johnson & Mithaug, 1978; Karlan, Rusch, & Menchetti, 1980; Mithaug & Hagmeier, 1978; Rusch, 1979a). Of these studies, only one (Karlan et al., 1980) has focused on surveying the language skills that potential employers perceive their employees as needing in order to meet minimum job requirements. This survey focused on only one job setting, food service employment (e.g., kitchen laborer). It would seem that, as a preparatory activity, compilation of the minimum language and communication needs of the developmentally disabled adult being transitioned into community living arrangements should be undertaken. This effort will provide the richest source of content for language remediation.

EXPRESSIVE LANGUAGE AND SKILL TRAINING

Thus far, the analysis of language as a training medium has focused exclusively on the directive functions of language presented to the individual and how these functions can be established. Another paradigm exists by which control over the behavior of the individual can be established. Self-control, as it is commonly used, refers to the ability of a person to regulate his or her own behavior. As a component of skill training, it should be possible to use language produced by the individual to modify or regulate his or her own behavior.

General interest has existed for some time in self-directed uses of language (Luria, 1961; Vygotsky, 1962). Only more recently has interest turned toward self-instruction as a means of remediating behavioral problems; that is, a subject is trained to instruct himself to replace an inappropriate response with one that is socially acceptable (Meichenbaum, 1973). Israel (1978) has reviewed the characteristics of research in this area and has discussed the conceptual implications of those characteristics. That discussion and one by Karlan and Rusch (1980) have attempted to clarify the procedural and conceptual approaches to this intervention methodology.

Self-instruction

Initial investigations of the correspondence between the production of verbal self-instruction and the performance of nonverbal behavior were based on either of two strategies. In the simpler strategy, changes in verbal behavior were produced, then observations were made of the nonverbal behavior in order to determine whether the desired change had occurred. In the second strategy, more direct attempts were made, usually by explicit directions to the person to self-instruct, to get the individual to change on-going behavior, e.g., to increase the rate of lever-pressing by saying "faster, faster" to himself/herself. These studies presumed that there would be a relationship between verbal and nonverbal behavior. Finally, research emerged that directly examined this functional relationship; procedures were employed to develop the appropriate correspondence between verbal and nonverbal behavior, i.e., the functional relationship (Israel & O'Leary, 1973; Risley & Hart, 1968; Rogers-Warren & Baer, 1976). From this research, the process by which verbal self-regulation is developed can be summarized. The verbal behavior must be established or its existence verified. Then, reward contingencies are modified to produce reinforcement only when a positive correspondence is observed (the person does what they have said they will do). Finally, the ultimate goal, persistent correspondence, is evaluated by again reinforcing only the occurrence of verbal behavior. Self-regulation is said to occur when an appropriate level of verbal-nonverbal correspondence is maintained while only direct consequation of the occurrence of verbal behavior takes place. Israel (1978) notes further that two procedural sequences are possible. A person may state what will be done, and then do it (say-do). Conversely, a person may report what has already been done (do-say). After discussing the research relating to each sequence, Israel concludes that the verbal-nonverbal sequence (say-do) may be the more efficient strategy for training in that it seems to lead to more rapid development of correspondence.

Karlan and Rusch (1980) have presented some implications of this research in relation to the two major goals of behavioral intervention: increasing, or promoting, appropriate behavior and decreasing, or inhibiting, inappropriate behavior. Past research on direct correspondence training has focused on increasing behavior; positive correspondence is attained when increases in verbal behavior (saying that X will occur) result in correlated increases in nonverbal behavior (X occurs). On the other hand, research on direct correspondence training to inhibit inappropriate behavior appears to be absent. Such training would involve developing a situation in which the person states that X *will not* occur and the nonverbal behavior does not occur.

Implications for Community Integration

Self-instruction is a form of additional cue that could be used to facilitate the development of complex skills. As was suggested for complex instruction-following, the learning of skills that do not require intensive supervision or that will be performed in less structured settings will undoubtedly benefit the individual who is making the transition into the community. Furthermore, if the correspondence between verbal and nonverbal behavior can be evaluated through examination of permanent products or more durable conditions of the environment, then more direct observation of the process by which the product or condition is produced need not be undertaken. An individual could be presented with preinstruction (Schutz, Keller, Rusch, & Lamson, 1979) consisting of the opportunity to verbally rehearse the nonverbal behavior needed to perform the task. In effect, the person practices telling what *will* be done. Correspondence would be determined by judging the appropriate outcome measures. For example, a person learning simple housecleaning (bedroom) might verbally rehearse the following sequence: "Dirty clothes in hamper. Strip beds. Dust furniture. Vacuum floor." In this sequence the order of task performance is irrelevant. For other tasks, the process by which products or conditions are produced may be important. For example, unloading from a commercial dish-washing machine requires a sequence of activities involving loading, moving, and replacing storage racks; the proper sequence of steps is critical in order to unload the machine at a rate that ensures continued employment for the worker. Furthermore, it may be inconvenient or even inappropriate to intervene with such behaviors in natural settings. Under these circumstances, verbal rehearsal of the process serves as preinstruction but the process itself must be observed in order to determine correspondence. It would also be possible to "practice" the process in simulation and then have the individual deliver self-instructions just before undertaking each target component. Correspondence could be determined for the immediately subsequent nonverbal behavior during simulation and for the behavior as it occurs in the natural setting. Any of these approaches would yield a much less intrusive intervention than would procedures in which behavior is developed or controlled through the use of trainer instructions, physical prompts, or models.

It would probably be mistaken to assume that the use of self-instruction requires sophisticated expressive language skills. It is possible that even persons with language skills limited to one- or two-word expressive utterances could be trained to self-instruct; it would be critical to ensure that the verbal expressions selected for the instructions are very concrete. One-word instructions are generally more ambiguous than are the instructions of two words, and two-word instructions are more ambiguous than instructions of three words or more. Therefore, when one- or two-word self-instructions must be used, they must relate specifically to the precise nonverbal behaviors desired. Although it is necessary that a consistent instruction be associated with the nonverbal behavior, it is sufficient that a discriminable, although not clearly articulated, verbal expression be produced. The use of less precise articulation is consistent with the view that self-instruction represents "private language." Articulation needs to be understood only in so far as a trainer needs to understand what is said to judge correspondence. Correspondence itself is the criterion by which the value of the articulation to the behavior is judged.

LANGUAGE IN ITS SOCIAL FUNCTIONS: COMMUNICATION

> Language is a shared system with rules for correct use in given contexts. The knowledge of these rules and the ability to apply them are ... referred to as "communicative competence." (Rees, 1978, p. 194)

The characteristic of language that is the source of its importance as a behavior system is that it influences or controls the behavior of humans. Skinner (1957) recognized this essential fact by describing verbal behavior as that behavior that produces a consequence through the behavior of another person. A simple scenario will illustrate this point: if a child is thirsty, a request for water will not be addressed to the kitchen sink, but rather to a person who can reach the cup and the faucet. The verbal behavior (asking) successfully produces the consequence (a glass of water) only through the mediating behavior of another person (getting, filling, and giving the glass of water).

Investigations of child development have shown that the ability to regulate the attention of another person begins to develop very early, well before linguistic behavior begins to develop (Bruner, 1975). Bates, Benigni, Bretherton, Camaioni, and Volterra (1977) determined that the skills most predictive of the onset of communicative language were the use of objects to control adult attention and the use of adults to gain access to objects. The key component common to these behaviors is the ability of the child to seek out the audience and direct attention. The child either uses the object to get the attention of the audience, and in so doing may bring the object into the presence of the audience, or s/he seeks out the audience and brings it into the presence of the object. Later, when more formal communication develops, the child need only seek out the audience. Language makes it unnecessary to bring the audience to the object or the object to the audience; rather, the problem or concern is directly communicated by the use of language.

From such evidence, it becomes obvious that inabilities to use language among more severely disabled persons may rest in the failure to recognize the need for an audience and in the absence of skills necessary to control audience attention. Institutions, because of their established service and care routines, offer far fewer opportunities for the use of language than do community residential and vocational settings. In order to make transitions to and succeed in community settings, individuals will need to be trained to recognize the need to communicate with another person and to seek out and gain audience attention.

Such training can be accomplished in conjunction with the development of initial expressive behaviors. Once preferred or important objects, persons, or activities have been identified, the individual can be trained to make a verbal response in the presence of the desired object, person, or event. To develop functional communication, changes are subsequently made to the context along two dimensions. The desired referent must eventually be withdrawn so that the verbal response will be used as a request in the absence of the referent. Additionally, the physical proximity of the audience must also be withdrawn, or at least varied, in order that the communicator be required to find an audience before emitting the necessary verbal behavior.

Engaging an audience in order to ask for something is only one aspect of the social application of language. Rees (1978) has identified several other communicative uses of language. These include getting a person to do something (such as delivering goods and services or altering attention or action); describing ongoing events; getting a listener to believe or feel something; expressing the speaker's own intentions, beliefs, or feelings; indicating readiness for further communication; and entertaining. The communicative functions outlined by Rees may be broadly classified into two groups: those functions that bring about change in the environment or in persons, and those functions that produce more verbal behavior. A particularly useful function in this second area is the use of language to elicit information about language itself.

Guess, Sailor, and Baer (1977) have described a remedial language intervention strategy that emphasizes both language that produces change and language that produces information about language. They identify four dimensions of functional intervention: reference, control, self-extended control, and integration. **Reference** represents the most basic level of learning: the associations between specific words and the objects, actions, or relations to which they refer. **Control** communicates intended change in the environment or in the behavior of person(s). Guess et al. (1977) teach this through the development of request forms ("I want _____"; "I want you to _____"). **Self-extended control** is intended to produce specific information; requests are based on the speaker's determination of what he does not himself know. It is developed by teaching persons to use ''wh-'' questions (what [name, color, doing, size, etc.], whose, where, when). **Integration** is accomplished by exposing language learners to situations that require both the use of known language and the search for unknown information, and then by requiring the learner to make use of this newly acquired information. Requiring the use of newly acquired words assures that information acquisition is functional. These four dimensions comprising this remedial strategy have been integrated into a comprehensive language intervention curriculum, which was developed within institutional settings (Guess, Sailor, & Baer, 1976, 1978).

Pragmatics of Language Use

More comprehensive examination of the functions of communication and how they develop has been undertaken in the study of the pragmatics of language use (Bates, 1976a, 1976b; Rees, 1978). Pragmatic theory attempts to account systematically for how language works.

In the use of language, what is said may be less important than what is not said or is implied. The assumptions or presumptions that are made by the speaker but not specifically stated can be critical to comprehension. For example, if an individual were given a sequence of instructions, one of which was to *Clean up the broken glass,* it might be assumed by the speaker that, regardless of its order in the sequence, that instruction will be followed first. The speaker presumes that the listener shares his view that broken glass is dangerous and therefore requires immediate attention. Preparations for the integration of persons into the community will require identification of messages that are assumed to take priority over any other instruction. Semantics play a part in establishing what the speaker assumes is shared information. In the earlier example *broken* describes a condition of the glass, but it also connotes a dangerous situation. Identification of words that, in certain settings, commonly change the importance of an instruction will allow persons who do not initially understand the implications of such words to be taught their significance. However, not all presuppositions that may be encountered in a setting will be constant, and therefore they cannot all be discovered in advance. In these circumstances the individual will need to identify what is ambiguous and to request further information. This represents the use of what Guess et al. (1977) called self-extended control and integration skills. The development of normalized interaction between those in the community and those entering the community requires attention to more subtle aspects of social-verbal interaction.

Language and Conversation

Probably the ultimate use of language as a social skill is reflected in conversation. Conversation occurs entirely at the level of verbal behavior. Context, in the sense of the physical presence of referents, may be entirely absent. In fact, context is usually created as a function of conversation. The context will be established either specifically in the initial stages of conversation or by the experience held in common by the conversants and implied by initial discourse. Once the conversants implicitly agree on a context, then other social skills related to interaction become involved. These skills help to guide the interplay of behavior necessary to sustain, and then terminate, the conversation.

Before continuing with a discussion of the development of conversational skills, an observation on content is presented. A personal history of rigidly structured, non-normalized living and working environments would undoubtedly serve to greatly restrict the conversational content available to disabled persons. The greater the "mismatch" between the former environments in which the individual worked or resided and the environments available to him or her on transition to the community, the greater the probability that conversation will be inhibited. Such a mismatch would probably be of greater hindrance than speech and language deficiency itself. Restricted environments are probably also related to one of the more persistent problems of moderately handicapped persons who are capable of basic-level conversation: topic repetition (Rusch, Weithers, Menchetti, & Schutz, in press) Topic repetition consists of perseverative references to the same topic including, in its extreme, persistent use of one sentence or sentence fragment ("I got a watch for my birthday"). The fact that exposure to a variety of events or major life changes for the institutionalized person are infrequent may contribute substantially to such "broken record" behavior.

Like all social interaction, conversation requires that individuals learn appropriate initiating skills, e.g., greetings ("How have you been?") and opening gambits ("Say, did you hear what happened to Harry?"). However, unlike other social interaction, such as game playing, which is governed by the organization of the nonverbal activity, conversation must be supported by the "flow" of the information. Grice (1975) has identified a "cooperative principle" of normal conversation: all participants accept the purpose and direction of the discussion. The essence of this principle is that each turn in a conversation should be a brief episode in which some bit of information, relevant at that moment, is exchanged.

Connectedness of the conversation is maintained by each participant's being responsive to the behavior of the other in each exchange. Thus, turn-taking skills are critical; turn-taking involves awareness of the behavior of another and of the consequences of that behavior. Such awareness establishes and maintains direction. It is also necessary that the participants be able to redirect conversation either to new topics or, more frequently, to restatements because of confusion, or "communicative distress." Such requests for restatement ("What? Huh?") then require exchanges in which the confusion is clarified (repetition, paraphrase, qualification) and confirmation is sought ("Okay?"). Bedrosian and Prutting (1978) show that moderately retarded adults, in speaking to a normal adult, may be capable of demonstrating these types of behavior, but do so only in a submissive, rather than dominant, role in the conversation.

The development of conversational skills in persons being integrated into the community will be likely to improve the quality of the resulting interactions. It is clear, however, that such skills must be considered within the more general realm of social interaction skills, nonverbal as well as verbal. Conversation represents the intersection of the ability to represent and convey information about the world through language and the ability to initiate and sustain interaction with another individual. Although this intersection requires the coordination of a very diverse and complex set of behaviors, careful analyses of the requirements of the environment and a systematic application of training technology should result in the achievement of this coordination by developmentally disabled persons.

SUMMARY

The intent of this chapter has been to expand the consideration of language beyond a discussion of the training of purely "linguistic" skills. Language requires, and deserves, a consideration of more than how to train word-object or word-action associations, how to teach production of wh- question forms, and so forth. Beyond word meaning and syntax, effective communication training requires an understanding of the uses to which language can be put.

As discussed in relation to instruction-following and verbal correspondence training, language can be a powerful training tool. When language is used for training, consideration must also be given to the issue of generalization; how do trained behaviors serve as a basis for the generation of new and untrained behavior? The use of language as self-instruction was considered in relation to its use as a means of increasing self-reliance and decreasing dependence on more restrictive training techniques.

When considered in the context of communication, language entails both very basic and very sophisticated social interaction abilities. In its most elemental form, communication requires that the individual develop both the ability to get the attention of another person and the ability to affect the action of that other person. Higher level skills are required when communication is used to acquire information about communication itself. Independence for an individual increases as he or she can identify and solicit information about what is unknown but needed during the course of events. Unknown information may be words or relations not within the individual's repertoire at the time they are required; it may also be information that is presumed by the speaker to be shared by the speaker and the individual who is functioning as the listener. Consideration was given to the obvious sources of presupposition that might be encountered by the individual on entering community settings. Finally, the use of language and social skills required by conversation were discussed; of special concern was the value of conversation as a social act and the problems posed by prior institutional history.

A great deal remains to be discovered concerning the process of developing an effective communicator or communication recipient. It is undeniable, however, that the integration of developmentally disabled individuals into the community will dramatically increase the opportunity and necessity for the use of communication; if appropriate interventions are not undertaken, the very real possibility exists that disabled individuals will become isolated within the community because of insufficient preparation to interact or communicate with other members of that community.

Part IV
ADDITIONAL PERSPECTIVES TO DEINSTITUTIONALIZATION

Chapter 10
Evaluation of Residential Alternatives

Laird W. Heal and Thomas J. Laidlaw

Although the movement of handicapped individuals from institutions into the community has a compelling humanistic rationale, empirical evidence is critical in establishing which residential changes produce beneficial outcomes. As is the case with many social reforms, deinstitutionalization has occurred in advance of empirical undergirding. Unless empirical evidence is marshalled to refine the movement, it could easily degenerate, as did the state institutions that came before it. It seems imperative, therefore, that methodologies be developed for comparing the effectiveness of the various residential alternatives that have been developed for this population.

This chapter suggests a framework for the empirical comparison of residential alternatives for developmentally disabled individuals. In the analysis of the authors, six conceptually different clusters of variables reflect on the effectiveness of one placement vis-à-vis another: approximation to normalization, levels of individual and social competence, individuals' satisfaction with their placements, others' satisfaction with the placements, residential climate, and cost. These six clusters are discussed in turn, and instruments for the measurement of each are described and critiqued.

APPROXIMATION TO NORMALIZATION

Normalization has been defined by Wolfensberger (1972) as "ultilization of means which are as culturally normative as possible, in order to establish and/or maintain personal behaviors and characteristics which are as culturally normative as possible" (p. 28). Wolfensberger and Glenn (1975a, 1975b) have developed a measurement tool, the Program Analysis of Service Systems (PASS 3), that has become the operational definition of this quality of human services. Its 50 items consist of ratings that measure the extent to which an agency's clients and service programs are physically integrated into the community at large, are socially integrated into the community, are accorded age-appropriate and culture-appropriate "interpretations and structures," and are associated with enhancing symbolism and imagery (see Chapter 3).

Each of the 50 items of PASS 3 is scored independently by each member of an evaluation team immediately following their site visit to the human service agency that is being evaluated. Then, all team members meet to "reconcile" their differences on each of the 50 items. Each of the items is then weighted by its presumed importance, and the weighted sum of the items is taken as the total PASS score. The maximum attainable score is 1000; the "expected" level of service quality is 711; the "minimally acceptable" score is 0; and the lowest score possible is -947.

One of the distressing features of PASS 3 as an evaluation tool is the lack of normative data presented in its manual. Believing that they had almost axiomatic justification for their content, Wolfensberger and Glenn (1975a, 1975b) presented almost no data on empirical validity. Furthermore, because a single final score is established through "reconciliation" of a team of raters, the instrument developers have not published estimates of inter-rater or inter-team reliability. Finally, a number of practical considerations mitigate against gathering data for test-retest reliability (e.g., expense, reactiveness of the initial evaluation, and raters' likely recall of original ratings at the time of retest).

Fortunately, a number of studies have reported statistical data that reflect on the validity and reliability of the instrument. Flynn (1980) reported an alpha (generalized split-half reliability) coefficient of 0.91 based on 256 evaluations done in authorized PASS 3 evaluations and training workshops. Heal and Daniels (1978) reported an inter-rater reliability (correlation) of 0.46, based on nine natural homes, two group homes, and four apartments. Novak, Heal, Pilewski, and Laidlaw (1980) reported an unbiased generalized per-rater reliability (with rater bias counted as unreliability; see Winer, 1971, p. 293) of 0.678 based on ratings of 12 units of an apartment program, one rating of the overall program itself, and one of a 60-bed intermediate care facility. This reliability corrects, by the Spearman-Brown formula, to 0.808 for a team of two, 0.863 for a team of three, and 0.894 for a team of four. In view of these reliabilities, it might be tempting to establish an agency's PASS score by averaging individual team members' ratings rather than by reconciling them, as the PASS manual recommends, since reconciliation requires several hours. However, average scores, although reliable, consistently overestimate reconciled scores (Flynn & Heal, 1980) and should therefore be avoided when the absolute value of the PASS score is important.

In addition to reflecting on the reliability of PASS, several studies reflect on its validity. In terms of its concurrent discriminative validity, every study that has used PASS 3 to discriminate among service alternatives has revealed substantial differences among these alternatives. Berry, Andrews, and Elkins (1977) compared the average PASS ratings on a quota sample of special schools, sheltered workshops, residential programs, and activity centers in Australia. They found that their schools, with mean ratings at the "borderline and substandard" levels on only 3 of the 50 PASS items, were substantially more normalized than their workshops (13 borderline and substandard ratings) or residences (14 borderline and substandard ratings), which were in turn more normalized than activity centers (21 borderline and substandard ratings). In their study of developmentally disabled adults, Heal and Daniels (1978) found that the PASS 3 scores of group homes were significantly lower than those of either landlord-supervised apartments or natural homes. Flynn (1975), in his analysis of 102 PASS 2 evaluations, found a significant difference between community residential alternatives and "institutions." Finally, in his 1980 study of 256 PASS evaluations, Flynn found that community child development programs scored highest, followed by community residences, community education programs, community vocational programs, and public institutional residences (PRFs) in that order. Most differences between pairs of programs were statistically significant, although community child development programs did not differ significantly from community residences, and community education programs scored almost identically with community vocational services.

Factor-analytic Studies of PASS 3

Despite the notable internal consistency of PASS 3, implied by the alpha coefficient of 0.91, and the logical inconsistency of factor-analyzing an instrument that has an ideologically and rationally established construct structure, three studies have examined the factor-analytic characteristics of PASS 3. Using his sample of 256 agencies from five service types, Flynn (1980) extracted four factors: Normalization-Program (19 items), Normalization-Setting (12 items), Administration (8 items), and Proximity and Access (4 items). Although he used an orthogonal rotation to identify his original factors, Flynn's subsequent procedures permitted their inherent intercorrelations to surface. Having identified sets of items on each factor, Flynn treated each factor as a subscale and then correlated all items with all subscales in order to identify items that correlated with one and only one "factor." These item correlations were used to establish PASS subscales that corresponded approximately to the four factors that had been extracted. However, unlike the factors, the subscales were correlated with one another. For example, Normalization-Program and Normalization-Setting had a Pearson correlation of 0.53. Administration was correlated with Normalization-Program 0.42 and with Normalization-Setting 0.32. Other intercorrelations were all below 0.3, but all correlations except that between Administration and Proximity were statistically significant because of the large number (256) of cases on which they were based.

Nevertheless, the services had significantly different profiles on the four subscales. The most notable difference was a crossing of the Community Child Development and the Community Residential program profiles on the subscales of Normalization-Program and Normalization-Setting. Although the Community Residential Program (along with the other three services) had a Program score that was below its Setting score, the Child Development Program had a Program score that was substantially above its Setting score. Thus, it appears that those who provide community residential services concern themselves primarily with the normalized features of the residence and its setting, and neglect, perhaps justifiably, programming that would enhance normalization. On the other hand, providers of child development programs emphasize the training programs that will enhance normalized functioning, but have less concern regarding the setting in which these programs occur. However, more important than this particular result is the discovery that different human services can, in fact, have different profiles on the PASS subscales developed by Flynn, making it reasonable that the four subscales be used for getting the maximum information from this instrument.

Using a more homogeneous sample, Demaine, Wilson, Silverstein, and Mayeda (1978) factor-analyzed 98 PASS 3 scores from a variety of community residences, with an average of 2.5 clients each, in Southern California. Using a Varimax orthogonal rotation, Demaine et al. identified seven factors, six of which they labeled: Application of Normalization Principles (17 items), Administrative Policies (7 items), Environmental Blending of the Service with the Neighborhood (9 items), Ideology-related Administration (7 items), Location and Proximity of Service to Geographical and Population centers (4 items), and Comfort and Appearance of Service Setting (4 items). In a subsequent investigation, Eyman, Demaine, and Lei (1979) extended the study by Demaine et al. (1978) by examining the predictive validity of its six interpretable factors. Their approach was to correlate factor scores on these dimensions from the subjects' residences with subjects' average annual changes on the three AAMD Adaptive Behavior Scale (ABS) dimensions of Personal Self-Sufficiency, Community Self-Sufficiency, and Personal-Social Responsibility, which Nihira (1976) had found in a factor analysis of 3354 mentally retarded residents of 68 institutions in 39 states. Each of the three ABS gain factor scores was moderately but significantly associated with the PASS factor scores of (a) Service Location and (b) Service Comfort and Appearance, after covariance adjustments had been made for age, appropriate ABS pretest factor score, and IQ. In addition, Environment Blend was significantly correlated with Personal Self-Sufficiency, and Administrative Policies was correlated with Community Self-Sufficiency, both after covariance adjustments. Conspicuous by its absence was the correlation of Normalization with ABS change. Indeed, Ideology-Related Administration was *negatively* correlated with both Personal Self-Sufficiency and Personal-Social Responsibility after covariance adjustments for age, pretest, and IQ. Thus, location and environmental beauty appear to enhance adaptive growth, whereas the programmatic and administrative dimensions of normalization appear to have little effect.

PASS Short Form

Because the complete PASS is extremely time-consuming to administer, Flynn and Heal (1980) have explored the development of a more efficient version, by decreasing the number of items. The PASS Short Form, which was developed through factor-analytic and item analysis procedures, has very satisfactory validity and reliability, although it includes only 18 of the original 50 items.

INDIVIDUAL SKILL AND SOCIAL COMPETENCE

Although normalization ideology has great humanitarian appeal, the most compelling argument for deinstitutionalization has been that institutions appear to effect a degeneration in their residents' cognitive and adaptive abilities (see Chapter 2). Cognitive abilities are presumably measured by standardized intelligence tests, such as the Stanford Binet (Terman & Merrill, 1973) or the Wechsler Adult Intelligence Scale (WAIS; Wechsler, 1958). Although these instruments provide a general index to a person's intellectual functioning, studies have shown that IQ is not necessarily correlated with adaptation to independent living or vocational success (this literature is reviewed in Chapter 5 of this volume). Furthermore, personal and social functioning are much more amenable to intervention than is level of intellectual functioning. Therefore, it seems most useful to evaluate individual skill and social competence directly rather than indirectly with an intelligence test.

Two major types of evaluation measurements, norm referenced and criterion referenced, have been used in the area of skill assessment. Foster (1974) suggests that the two are distinguished by the needs they satisfy. Norm-referenced measures satisfy administrative and legislative requirements: they evaluate the individual in terms of various norms, so that general levels of functioning can be ascribed to members of a target population. Criterion-referenced measures address the individual's growth. The purpose of this type is to specify the skills on which the individual requires training. This objective is of extreme importance for habilitation planning, but creates some problems in that the program's benefits cannot be readily interpreted by legislators, administrators, and others who prefer convenient descriptions based on standardized, norm-based testing procedures. Consistent with Foster's analysis, these two types of measurement scales of adaptive behavior have dominated the measurement of residents' skills. Five of the more prominent scales are described briefly below.

The *Vineland Social Maturity Scale* (Doll, 1953, 1965) was developed to determine maturation of individuals in eight areas of social competence and social independence. An informant who knows the subject well responds to each item according to subjective, but very specific, criteria. This scale, which has only 117 items to determine Social Age scores that range from 0 to 25 years, is useful in determining the general level at which an individual is functioning, but is not of great assistance in terms of suggesting "fine-grained" training procedures. The Vineland has proven to be valid and reliable, and it has both the advantage of 40 years' use in the nation's public residential facilities (PRFs) and the disadvantage of some, although surprisingly little, obsolescence.

The *Adaptive Behavior Scale* (ABS) (Nihira, Foster, Shellhaas, & Leland, 1974) was developed because of the necessity of the American Association on Mental Deficiency to have a measure of adaptive behavior, since their definition of mental deficiency included "subnormal adaptive behavior" as well as "subnormal intelligence" (Grossman, 1973). It uses an informant procedure similar to that of the Vineland. The scale has two parts: the first 10 subtests (66 items) assess adaptive behaviors; the last 14 (44 items) evaluate maladaptive or pathological behaviors. The test is convenient in terms of administration and scoring and has satisfactory reliability and validity. Its greatest weakness is that it fails to specify the level that would be considered subnormal. Also, like the Vineland, it is too coarse to measure small variations in skills, so that it is best used for global evaluations, not individual programming.

The *Progress Assessment Charts* (PAC), developed by H. C. Gunzburg (1974), provide a means of recording the observed social behaviors of developmentally disabled individuals in four areas: Self-help, Communication, Socialization, and Vocation. In order to assess the progress made by an individual with this scale, charts are kept and compared over a period of time. Their primary function is to specify a sequence of skills for programmatic instruction. Although the PAC scales lack the psychometric elegance of most intelligence tests and the other measures of adaptive behavior reported here, they do provide a social competence index, which can be derived from the four areas named above.

The *Camelot Behavioral Checklist* (Foster, 1974) was designed to allow the evaluator to identify specific training objectives for an individual and also to provide a classification score that is directly based on the training objectives. In order to meet both of these demands, the scale consists of 399 behavioral descriptions, which are organized into 10 subscales. The respondent checks "yes" or "no" depending on whether or not the individual being scored can perform the task. Because items are not arranged in order of difficulty, several hours are required to complete one checklist, and it has limited value as a sequential training program. Its manual reports very satisfactory reliability and validity coefficients.

The Mid-Nebraska *Independent Living Screening Test* (Schalock, 1979a) is an instrument that combines the instructional focus of the PAC with psychometric characteristics that approach those of the Vineland, the ABS, and the Camelot. It features items in nine functional skill areas: Personal Maintenance, Clothing Care and Use, Home Maintenance, Food Preparation, Time Management, Social Behavior, Community Utilization, Communication, and Functional Academics. The instrument is completed by an observer, usually a trainer or home supervisor, who has had the opportunity to observe the subject closely for at least a 2-week period. The Mid-Nebraska has the advantage of several years of development in the context of preparing individuals who have been placed into the community from PRFs.

In their review of assessment instruments for mentally retarded individuals, Hill and Bruininks (1977) describe three additional instruments that appear to have some value for the evaluation of community residential alternatives: the Balthazar Scales of Adaptive Behavior (Balthazar, 1973, 1976), the Cain-Levine Social Competency Scale (Cain, Levine, & Elzey, 1963), and the Minnesota Developmental Programing System (Bock & Weatherman, 1976). The Balthazar scales focus on the functioning of severely and profoundly retarded individuals in a broad range of adaptive areas, and could become very useful as more and more severely handicapped individuals are placed into community residential alternatives. The Cain-Levine Scale is limited to the social competence of moderately retarded children, having been standardized on trainable students in the public elementary schools. It has four subscales: Self-help, Communication, Initiative, and Social Skills. The Minnesota Developmental Programing System has much the same purpose as the Mid-Nebraska Independent Screening Test—that of providing a refined assessment of the individual's competence in a variety of areas: toileting, grooming, dressing, eating, gross motor, fine motor, money, receptive language, expressive language, numbers, reading, writing, time, domestic behavior, and vocational behavior. Moreover, the Minnesota system, like the Mid-Nebraska, is "criterion referenced," providing a sequence of behaviors in each of its assessment areas. Given this sequence, the level achieved by a student in each area pinpoints the next subskill in that area to be trained. Characteristic of many criterion-referenced instruments, the Minnesota Scale lacks the norms of the Camelot, making guesswork of the empirical comparison of placement trainees with placement graduates.

CLIENT SATISFACTION

Clients' satisfaction with their living situations may be the most neglected outcome measure of residential placement, and yet is perhaps the most important. Indeed, our cultural values have affirmed the right of the individual to pursue happiness since at least 1776.

Various methods might be used to measure an individual's satisfaction. One such apporach (e.g., Edwards, 1957) is a standard attitude questionnaire, which could be designed to quantify a client's satisfaction with regard to his/her residential placement. The procedure would be to ask direct questions that are designed to elicit positive, negative, or neutral feelings from the respondent. The responses, in turn, could be scored on a 3- to 9-point scale.

Birenbaum and Seiffer (1976) used an adaptation of this method with residents of a large community residential facility (CRF) (Gatewood) who had been transferred from several public residential facilities (PRFs). Their method was to ask direct questions and record three types of responses: positive, neutral, or negative. The first question asked respondents to identify favorable or unfavorable aspects of their residential placements. At their initial interview, which occurred when the residents were still at their PRFs, 69 percent reported favorable aspects, and only 31 percent noted negative aspects of the PRFs. At the second interview, after 7 to 10 months at the CRF, 95 percent noted favorable features of their CRF, and only 5 percent reported negative aspects. Finally, after 16 to 20 months at Gatewood, 90 percent noted favorable aspects, and the remaining 10 percent listed negative aspects. The second item used to measure the residents' satisfaction requested them to express their attitudes toward Gatewood, which were then categorized as positive, neutral, or negative. The findings showed 60 percent positive attitudes, 38 percent neutral, and 2 percent negative on the first interview (at the PRF). In the second interview (the first at the CRF), 75 percent were positive, 15 percent neutral, and 10 percent negative. In the final interview (after 16 to 20 months at Gatewood) there was a large increase in neutral (34 percent) and negative (15 percent) attitudes, with a corresponding decrease in positive attitudes (51 percent). Birenbaum and Seiffer suggest that this shift in attitude appears to have been the result of residents' increasing aspirations to move from their mini-institution to a more independent living situation rather than a desire to return to a public residential facility. In a subsequent paper, Birenbaum and Re (1979) found that, after 40 to 44 months at Gatewood, 57 percent of the residents wanted to move elsewhere (26 percent to apartments, 21 percent to their parents' homes, 10 percent to foster homes).

In another study (Scheerenberger & Felsenthal, 1977), attitudes of the residents also tended to support a preference for community placement. The sample consisted of 18 developmentally disabled children and adolescents from foster homes, 32 adolescents and adults from group homes, and 25 adults (selected randomly from 64) from skilled and intermediate care nursing facilities. All facilities were located in Wisconsin. On questions comparing satisfaction levels of CRFs and PRFs, 88 percent, or 63 respondents, said they preferred their current placement in the community. Only 17 percent, or 12 respondents, wanted to return to "the institution." Only 74 percent of those in the nursing homes liked their placements, whereas all foster home residents were satisfied. Of the group home residents, 90 percent preferred their residence with the remaining 10 percent wishing to return to the institution. Seven residents of the nursing homes wished to return to the institution. Two residents of the foster homes wished to return to the institution, which is interesting since all of these residents had stated that they liked living in the foster homes.

In a study of deinstitutionalized individuals conducted by Edgerton and Bercovici (1976), 30 persons from Edgerton's original study, *The Cloak of Competence* (1967), were revisited and asked various questions on their experiences over the prior 10 years. Twenty-six of these individuals were asked to compare their current lives to their lives 10 years before. Twelve said they were happier, 7 said things were about the same, 6 said they were less happy, and 1 was not sure.

In another study, 10 institutions and 440 of their deinstitutionalized residents were examined (Wyngaarden, Freedman, & Gollay, 1976). The residents were asked several questions concerning their attitudes toward their current placements. Responses were rated to be either affirmative or negative. Of 334 people who had remained in the community, 94 percent liked their current living situation. Only 5 percent preferred the institution. More than a third said that they would prefer to live somewhere else in the community, such as their own home or apartment, or with their natural families. Of the 58 people who returned to the institutions after having been placed in the community, only about half indicated that they had been satisfied with their community residence. Forty percent said they would prefer another living arrangement, such as with their natural families or in a group home.

A somewhat different approach was employed by Novak et al. (1980) to measure the satisfaction of their subjects. Their Residential Satisfaction Scale consisted of 50 questions that probed each subject's satisfaction with his/her residence, its community setting, and its associated services. The scale featured eight subscales: General Satisfaction, Food, Leisure, Neighborhood, Services, Training, Rules and Supervision, and Money. Seventeen subjects from supervised apartments and an intermediate care facility for the developmentally disabled were questioned. The test-retest reliabilities (correlations between the series from different raters on the two occasions of measurement) were quite high: although the Neighborhood category had a reliability of 0.344, all other subscale reliabilities ranged from 0.615 (Rules) to 0.849 (General). The reliability of the weighted total score was 0.925. Resident satisfaction was significantly higher in the apartments than in the intermediate care facility.

The studies reviewed here indicate that residents who have been placed into the community can provide reliable information regarding their satisfaction with their residential placements. However, all of these studies have a common shortcoming. Most residents who have participated in these studies and in most community placements have been mildly and moderately retarded individuals with sufficient language skills to be interviewed. If all retarded citizens are to have a "voice" in their destiny, then methods of measurement must be developed to assess the satisfaction of individuals who lack language skills. Sigelman, Schoenrock, Spanhel, Hromas, Winer, Budd, and Martin (1980) have begun to investigate the problems of interviewing disabled persons, but much more needs to be done.

OTHERS' SATISFACTION WITH THE RESIDENT'S PLACEMENT

Another important, albeit neglected, domain of evaluation is that of others' satisfaction with a resident's placement. With society's increasing concern for ecological validity (e.g., Rusch, Schutz, & Heal, in press), it has become imperative that the neighbors, supervisors, employers, family, and friends of the individual consider the placement to be wholesome for him/her and for themselves. Given this imperative, Novak et al. (1980) developed three instruments to assess others' satisfaction with a placement: the Neighbors' Satisfaction Scale; the Employers' Satisfaction Scale; and the Prediction of Continued Placement Success, a scale to be completed by the resident's case worker. Other studies, most notably those of Baker, Seltzer, and Seltzer (1977) and Sigelman (1976), have evaluated the response of the neighborhood to the establishment of a community residence (this literature is reviewed in Chapter 7). All of the instruments used to assess others' satisfaction have been primitive questionnaires and interview schedules with no reliability estimates and only face validity. There is clearly a need for instrument development in this area.

CLASSIFICATION OF RESIDENTIAL CLIMATE

One of the difficulties of determining what effects, if any, are associated with various residential alternatives is that there are enormous differences among residences that have the same label. There are many definitions of the word "institution," which have been presented in a variety of contexts throughout this book, but the word remains open to the reader's personal interpretation. Size alone can range from under 50 to over 5000 residents. Similarly, some studies describe "group homes" that in actuality have up to 80 residents, so one can only hope that the reader will interpret reports carefully. Furthermore, other factors such as location, staff-resident ratio, types and numbers of programs, physical accommodations, and staff-resident relationships make it extremely difficult to control for a wide variety of such factors in any study of residential effects. A broad term to include most of the necessary variables might be "residential climate," the environment that includes most of the above factors of social milieu and interpersonal dispositions.

Several measures have been developed to classify residential climate. King, Raynes, and Tizard developed a Child Management Scale (1971) that indicates the use of a "child management" model instead of a "medical" model to rear children in congregated residential settings. Subscales include Rigidity, Block Treatment, Depersonalization, and Social Distance. This scale was adapted by McCormick, Bella, and Zigler (1975) in their cross-institutional, cross-cultural study to examine the differences between "institution oriented" and "resident oriented" care practices found among 19 mental retardation residential facilities in the northeastern United States and 11 such facilities in a Scandinavian country. Both of these studies indicated that the larger institutions were indeed more institution-oriented than the smaller, community-based residences.

Eyman, Silverstein, McLain, and Miller (1977) described two instruments used to assess the effects of different residential settings on the persons living there: the Characteristics of the Treatment Environment (CTE; Jackson, 1969), and the Residential Management Survey (RMS), a questionnaire version of the Revised Child Management Scale (King et al., 1971). They found an association between ABS gains and residential climate, but no data were presented to show which climates predisposed subjects to improvement and which did not.

Perhaps the most comprehensive effort to classify institutional and family environments has been made by Moos (1975). Three scales may be of particular value to distinguish among variations within individual residence types: the Correctional Institutions Environment Scale (CIES) has been found to discriminate among different types of prison environments and could be easily adapted to classify institutions for developmentally disabled citizens; the Community-Oriented Programs Environment Scale (COPES) discriminates among the climates of community service programs, including group homes and other group living arrangements; and the Family Environment Scale (FES) distinguishes among different family types. The procedure used on all Moos scales is to have program participants complete a questionnaire of about 100 true-false items falling into approximately 10 environmental climate categories. For example, the Family Environment Scale has nine Cohesion items, nine Expressiveness items, 10 Conflict items, nine Independency items, nine Achievement Orientation items, nine Intellectual-Cultural Orientation items, nine Active Recreational Orientation items, nine Moral-Religious Emphasis items, nine Organization items, and nine Control items. The responses of all family members are averaged to provide a subscale score in each of these climate categories. Then a profile is plotted from these scores. For example, Moos has found that families tend to fall into one of several types, such as "high relationship and low control," "achievement orientation," and "high conflict."

In their research on (foster) family care and natural family placements in New York State, Intagliata (1978) and Willer (1978) found a number of interesting relationships between family type and other measures related to deinstitutionalized residents' placements. Basing his analysis on the Moos and Moos taxonomy (1976) of six types of family environments, Intagliata (1978) found that 85 percent of family-care families had a highly structured home environment (i.e., scored high on Moos' subscales of organization and control). Willer (1978) found that only 50 percent of natural families accepting a retarded person back into the home were "structure-oriented." He also found that home placement families were more "independence-oriented" (i.e., were highly oriented to autonomy and family members' independence), and less "achievement-oriented" than other community placement families. The latter difference suggests that a retarded person is more likely to be perceived as a burden by a family that is upwardly mobile and oriented to high achievement.

Finally, PASS-3 can be seen as a measure of residential climate, although it ranges beyond the residence itself for much information. Furthermore, PASS assesses only the normalization of the setting, program, and administrative philosophy of a human service; it was not designed to provide a multidimensional measure of a residence and its physical and social climate.

COST OF SERVICES

In addition to comparing the normalization, achievements, and satisfactions associated with various residential alternatives, it is important to compare their costs. The purpose of focusing on costs in this section is not to legitimize community placement only because it has less impact on the public treasury. The other clusters of variables are of greater importance from a humanitarian viewpoint. Nevertheless, the problem of cost arises because there are limited resources available to support the public welfare. It would be beneficial to demonstrate through valid accounting and budgeting procedures that providing services to developmentally disabled citizens in the community consumes less of society's resources than the placement of these individuals in large and isolated institutions. For the skeptic who is not impressed with ideological arguments, lower costs could provide a rationale for the demise of these institutions.

Cost Studies of Residential Alternatives for Developmentally Disabled Citizens

Perhaps the most difficult area to evaluate is that of residential service costs. Because of their poor quality, cost data were eliminated from the analyses of both Gollay et al. (1976) and O'Connor (1976). The poor quality of cost data poses a dilemma for decision makers, because one of their most important considerations is a program's costs. Because of their importance, several studies assessing the costs of institutional and community placements are reported here, but the reader is advised to interpret them with greatest caution. The data from these studies are presented in Table 10.1.

Baker et al. (1977) reported that the average annual budget of their community alteratives respondents in 1973 was about $4680. The costs varied from model to model. At $5690 per year the small group home was more than twice as expensive as the large group home. At $5200 per year the sheltered village was about as expensive as the small group home and semi-independent apartment living ($5440). These figures compare very favorably with the average operating budget ($8717) of the nation's public residential facilities (PRFs) in fiscal year 1973–1974 as reported by Scheerenberger (1976b).

PRF and CRF costs are not calculated on the same basis; the PRF budget typically includes nonresidential program costs and excludes capital costs. Mayeda and Wai (1975) found that residential costs accounted for about 75 percent of total PRF costs in two widely separated institutions. Conley (1973) estimated capitalization costs at $1000 per resident per year in 1968, a figure that can be reasonably augmented by 10 percent per year to adjust for inflation in the building industry. Thus, a reasonable formula for adjusting Scheerenberger's budget figures so that they are comparable to those of CRF budgets is:

$$APB = (0.75)(PRF\ budget) + (0.1Y + 1.0)(\$1000)$$

where APB is the "Adjusted PRF Budget" per resident per year, and Y is the number of years since 1968. The 0.1 multiplier is used to account approximately for an annual inflation rate of 10 percent. Using this formula, the APB of 1973–1974 is $7664, which is about 1.4 times the cost of a small group home as reported by Baker et al. (1977).

In their cost analysis of the residences of 29 developmentally disabled adults in 1977, Heal and Daniels (1978) found that the average annual societal costs (i.e., costs not borne by the residents themselves) of natural homes, group homes, and independent apartments were $4602, $5361, and $1834, respectively. Marginal societal costs of adding a developmentally disabled individual to a natural home were calculated at $2525 per resident per year, since approximately $2077 of the average cost was for domiciliary requirements that would presumably have been paid regardless of whether or not the handicapped adult was in the residence. The national average PRF cost in the same year (1977) was $16,144, which gives an APB of $14,008.

Table 10.1. Cost estimates of public (PRF) and community (CRF) residential alternatives for developmentally disabled citizens (in dollars)

Residence type	Study and sample	1968	1970	1973	1974	1975	1976	1977
Public residential facilities (PRFs)[a]	Conley (1973) USA	3625	4650					
	Scheerenberger (1976b, 1978) USA				7664		11,598	14,008
Group home for 10 or fewer	Baker, Seltzer, & Seltzer (1977) USA			5690				
	Gardner (1977) OH					6403		
	Intagliata, Willer, & Cooley (1979) NY							10,128
	Heal & Daniels (1978) WI							5361
	Peat, Marwick, Mitchell, & Company (1977) IL						9519	
	Jones & Jones (1976b) MA						6060	
Group home for 11–20	Baker, Seltzer, & Seltzer (1977) USA			4080				
Group home for 21–40	Baker, Seltzer, & Seltzer (1977) USA			3380				
Foster family care	Baker, Seltzer, & Seltzer (1977) USA			2240				
Sheltered village	Baker, Seltzer, & Seltzer (1977) USA			5200				
Workshop dormitory	Baker, Seltzer, & Seltzer (1977) USA			3450				
Visiting professional apartment	Baker, Seltzer, & Seltzer (1977) USA			5440[b]				
	Heal & Daniels (1978) WI			1834				

[a] All PRF figures are adjusted to include estimated capital cost and exclude program costs, referred to as adjusted PRF budget (APB) in text.
[b] This figure includes the contribution by the resident.

In another cost comparison study, annual costs in Ohio group homes described by Gardner (1977) ranged from $3729 to $4851 plus $2310 for administrative overhead in 1975-1976. The average of $6403 was less than half the cost of his state's institutions.

Intagliata, Willer, and Cooley (1979) compared an institution, group homes, family care (foster) homes, and natural homes, all in New York State. Their annual rates were based on Bureau of Labor Statistics figures for natural homes, on an accounting of state and federal subsidies for the group and family care homes, and on the estimated domiciliary portion of operating costs for the institution. The annual cost per resident was found to be $14,630 in the institution, $9255 to $11,000 in the group homes, $3130 in family care, and $2108 in the natural family. These latter two figures should probably be seen as marginal, not average, costs. Although the date to which these costs apply was not provided, it was presumably about 1977, making it reasonable to add $2000 capitalization cost to the institution's figure.

At least two other studies (Jones & Jones, 1976a; Murphy & Datel, 1976) have concluded that community residential placement is far less expensive than institutional placement. In sum, all of the studies that have attempted to compare institutions and community living alternatives have found that it is less expensive to place developmentally disabled individuals into the community, especially into natural or foster homes. However, several arguments have been advanced to suggest that PRF and CRF costs are only apparently different, and may in actuality be very similar.

Peat, Marwick, Mitchell, and Company (1977) examined CRF requirements and projected CRF costs for the State of Illinois, assuming that professionals and paraprofessionals were paid at competitive rates. Based on 100 percent occupancy, they estimated that the average annual cost per resident in a group home would range between $9519 and $15,323 in 1976 dollars, depending on the extent of disability. This figure included rent but excluded training and many other service costs that are included in PRF cost figures. Scheerenberger's (1976b) fiscal year 1975-1976 figure for average annual PRF budget was $13,129 per resident. The APB for this figure is $11,598, which compares favorably with the Peat, Marwick, Mitchell, and Company estimates just cited. However, this projection stands in contrast not only to the data reported above, but also to the "ideal" group home costs of $6060 estimated in a systematic study by Jones and Jones (1976b).

In what appears to be the most careful cost comparison of residential alternatives to date, Mayeda and Wai (1975) reported that the total accountable service costs for a 6-month period in 1974 and 1975 were $638 and $6247 for community and institution residents, respectively. Pointing out that the average cost for a service actually used was about the same in the community and in the institution, Mayeda and Wai concluded that community placement was not less expensive than institutional placement, but that the community was lacking a full array of needed services! It is just as reasonable to assert that the institution renders services to its residents that they or their advocates would not seek if they were left to their own choosing.

Quite apart from any controversy regarding the utilization of services, the long-range picture is certain to show a smaller difference between CRF and PRF costs. One of the reasons for the acceleration of PRF costs has been the decline in their populations. The loss of the higher-functioning clients has removed from the PRF a major pool of productive laborers whose replacements command much higher wages. In addition, many of the PRF costs are fixed in the short run, and cannot be immediately reduced as the population decreases. In time some of these fixed costs may be reduced. On the other hand, CRFs have typically underpaid their professional and paraprofessional staffs, a situation that is likely to be corrected as the newness and glamour of the movement dissipates. It may well be that the costs will, in time, be similar in PRF and community placements.

Residential costs have the potential of providing a universal scale of effort, one that can be used to compare services regardless of their content. Given its potential and the fact that most CRFs are supported by public funds, it seems irresponsible that no uniform accounting procedures have been adopted to provide for uniform cost accounting in CRFs and other human services.

Uniform Functional Cost Accounting in Human Services

The comparison of costs between PRFs and CRFs has been hampered by the absence of uniform accounting procedures (Conley, 1973; Intagliata, Willer, & Cooley, 1979; Sipe, 1976). Although this shortcoming is mandated in part by the diversity of funding systems for CRFs (National Association for Retarded Citizens, 1976), it would be beneficial for all organizations serving developmentally disabled individuals to provide a line budget for each functional program within the agency instead of a simple line budget for each category of expenditure, which tends to obscure costs of different programs. By providing line budgets for each program of service within the agency, the costs of various programs could be associated with the effects they have on certain areas, such as levels of competence, normalization, and client satisfaction. Figure 10.1 presents a system of budgeting that could be universally applied to human services and would permit the comparative cost analysis of human service programs. This figure features four dimensions of cost categories, each of which has three levels. The *Activity* dimension includes the levels of Domestic, Production, and Leisure. A second dimension is the *Recipient* of the expenditure. The Recipient can be the Client, the Administration of the agency, or the "Buildings," that is, the physical plant and capital equipment. A third dimension is the *Purpose* of the expenditure. The expenditure can be for Operation, for investment in Renewal, or for procurement of Funding. Renewal is seen to be any activity whose purpose is to increase the competence and/or value of any of the three Recipients. Funding refers to expenditures that are necessary to raise or maintain the financial support for any of the three Recipients. Expenditures that cannot be explicitly assigned should be proportionately distributed across the relevant levels of Activity and

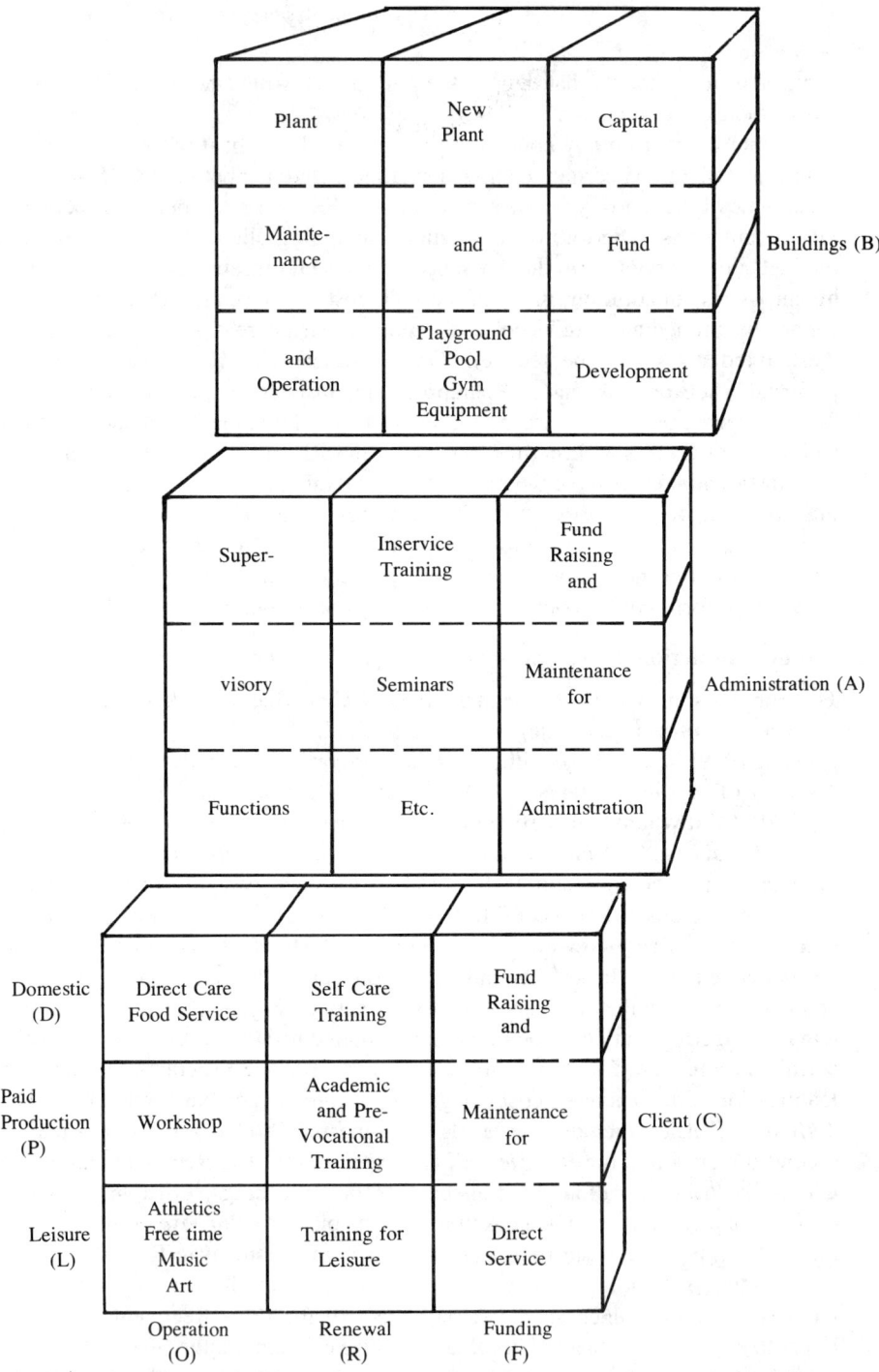

Figure 10.1. Cost accounting system for human services. A fourth dimension is Personnel, Supplies, and Intangibles.

Recipient. Operation is most easily seen as the residual Purpose category: it includes all expenditures for the maintenance and operation of a program that cannot be attributed to Renewal or Funding purposes. The fourth dimension, which has almost no programmatic relevance, is the *Accounting* dimension, which has the levels of Personnel, Supplies, and Intangibles. Refinements could undoubtedly be made in the Client slice of this cube, especially in the Renewal column. It is in this column that expenditures are expected to relate most closely to increased competence. An excellent cost accounting manual for community residences that could easily be adapted to Figure 10.1 has been developed by Sipe (1976).

Determining Cost of Residential Services

Turning to residential or domiciliary (domestic) costs themselves, current accounting practices tend to make it difficult to compare one service or type of service with another. Five problems stand out:

1. Capital costs are inconsistently separated from operating costs.
2. Costs of domiciliary services are ordinarily not separated from those of other services.
3. The economic benefits of gifts and volunteer labor are seldom taken into account.
4. The contribution made by residents to their own domiciliary service is not usually separated from that made by society.
5. The economic benefits of resident labor are seldom taken into account.

These problems are explained more fully in the next five sections.

Separation of Capital and Operating Costs When public residential facilities (PRFs) report their annual or daily costs, they report only their operating budget. Their physical plant, which has ordinarily been funded by a bond issue, is excluded. Community residential facilities (CRFs), on the other hand, nearly always include their rent as a major item. To complicate matters further, many CRF rents (e.g., apartments) include utilities and maintenance, which would be included as operating items by the PRFs. In order to assure comparable cost estimation, it seems crucial that capital cost be included in estimates of total human services costs. When rent is paid, it should be included. When rent is not paid, it should be estimated, either directly or by estimating the value of the buildings and grounds, and using, as a proxy for rent, the amount that would be earned were these assets to be sold and the money invested in AA bonds at the current rates of interest. When furnishings are owned, they should be included as capital items, with rental estimates that are similar to those of buildings and grounds. (As its estimate of the value of a home's furnishings the home insurance industry uses 50 percent of the value of the home itself.)

Separation of Domiciliary and Other Services The commingling of domiciliary funds with those of other programs greatly distorts the estimates of residential costs. For example, the operating budget of the PRF includes the costs of all day services, all health services, and nearly all administrative services in addition to domiciliary services. On the other hand, CRF budgets rarely include the costs of daytime programs or administrative overhead, which typically approach the residential costs themselves. Mayeda and Wai (1975) found that institution day programs accounted for nearly 25 percent of the total operating budgets of two PRFs in California and Florida.

Economic Value of Gifts and Volunteer Labor Both PRFs and CRFs are the recipients of charity, and both should account for any gift that they receive if their costs are to be reasonably compared. In the case of tangible gifts, the market value should be included in the capital value of the residence on the assumption that the residence could always sell the gift and invest the money if it chose. In the case of volunteer labor, a reasonable hourly rate should be established for each volunteer. From the total annual contribution of such labor, the residence must subtract the total cost of recruiting, training, and managing its volunteer program. In natural and foster homes, parents' labor must be accounted for like that of any other volunteer.

Residents' Contributions to Their Own Domicile Residences vary greatly with regard to the contribution that the residents make to their own domiciliary service. This cost is theoretically very different from the cost borne by society, although the two tend to be negatively correlated (Heal & Daniels, 1978; Novak et al., 1980). Cost to society provides an index that society would like to minimize, other things being equal, so that an individual's financial burden on society is the least possible. The individual's cost, on the other hand, provides a proxy for the individual's talent. The more an individual is able to contribute to his/her own residential service, the greater ability he or she is assumed to have. Thus, when residential alternatives are compared, it is important to use individual cost as a control variable, holding it constant while the societal costs of various residential alternatives are compared.

Economic Benefit of Residents' Labor The individuals' cost consists not only of their monetary contributions to their residential services, but also their in-kind contributions. If the residents didn't make their own beds, clean their own rooms, or do their own laundry, then staff would have to be employed to do these chores. For example, when comparisons are made in which some of the services require employees to feed residents, then the self-feeders' contribution should include an estimate of the value of this service.

This cost must be the net difference between the value of the residents' labor and the cost of training and supervision required in order to utilize it. The calculation of this net is complicated by the fact that self-care, room maintenance, cooking, and other skills are often a part of the regular residence curriculum. If training costs are deducted from residents' in-kind contributions, they cannot, of course, be included as training costs elsewhere in the cost analysis.

Estimating Comparable Domiciliary Costs Given the preceding considerations, it appears that the following items are essential for a minimum cost comparison of residential alternatives. These should be estimated on an *annual,* *per-resident* basis in order to avoid size and seasonal distortions (e.g., higher heating costs in the winter).

1. Annual rent, and/or annual return on the alternative investment of the funds that would result from the sale of the capital assets of the residence at their current market value.
2. Annual operating budget *for domiciliary services only,* including the cost of administrative overhead (prorated share of general agency costs).
3. Annual value of volunteer labor, less the cost of recruitment, training, and management.
4. Annual monetary contribution of the residents to their own domiciliary services.
5. Annual value of residents' unpaid labor, less the cost of training and supervision.

Any of these costs that are borne by someone other than the individual should be called "societal costs"; any that are borne by the individual should be called "individual costs." These two indices can be realistically estimated for any residence and permit, we feel, the most valid cost comparisons among public and community residential alternatives for developmentally disabled individuals.

Average and Marginal Costs

In order to obtain a clear picture of costs it is necessary to differentiate between average and marginal costs. Marginal costs refer to changes in costs that occur when the services provided by a program are increased by one unit (e.g., by one resident). As a rule, marginal costs are less than average costs because of "economy of scale." Similarly, marginal benefits (dollar value of benefits resulting from a unit increase in costs) usually surpass average benefits (Conley, 1973). In the case of adding another member to a natural home or a group home, marginal costs must be considered. In a case of this nature, the marginal costs are usually less than the average costs, while the benefits remain approximately the same as for all other residents. That is, the costs for rent and utilities remain nearly fixed, regardless of whether or not a resident is added, but the new resident receives nearly the same benefits that the other residents received prior to his/her arrival. However, this pattern of marginal benefits and costs in community services can be reversed when the most promising clients enter the program initially and, as the program expands, the more difficult cases are selected: marginal costs rise, which pulls up average costs, and marginal benefits drop, which brings about a decline in the average benefits produced by the service.

COST-EFFECTIVENESS ANALYSIS

Cost-benefit and cost-effectiveness analysis have attracted considerable attention in the social sciences (Bernard, 1979; Cohen, Butter, Deline, & Nutter, undated; Conley, 1973; Layard, 1972; Levin, 1975). Although there are many variations that could be applied to residential services, we believe that the research by Heal and Daniels (1978) represents a prototypical study in this area, and present it in considerable detail.

The general method of this study was to interview 29 developmentally disabled individuals and their residential supervisors. These subjects were seen to be representative of the developmentally disabled adults in three Northern Wisconsin counties who resided in two group homes, in their natural homes, or in landlord-supervised apartments. During the interviews several scales and schedules were completed, which were the bases for the six indices that were calculated for every subject: Wolfensberger and Glenn's (1975a, 1975b) Program Analysis of Service Systems (PASS 3); the Client's Residential Satisfaction Scale (CRSS, developed by the authors); the contribution in labor and money of the individual to his/her own residential service (INDCOST); the contribution in labor and money of society and family to the residential service (SOCCOST); and Parts I and II of the AAMD Adaptive Behavior Scale (Nihira et al., 1975). The three residence types were compared on the six indices using both univariate and multivariate analyses.

Cost estimates were made as follows. All residential costs were divided into two categories: the individual's contribution to his/her own residential service (INDCOST) and society's contribution to the residential service (SOCCOST). The latter included the family's contribution. Every effort was made to determine costs comprehensively. The total cost of residential service took into account the dollar value of both the residents' and supervisors' (including parents') labor: anticipated investment return on household capitalization, including household furnishings: and all other domiciliary costs.

In the estimate of labor costs, a careful analysis was done of the services and pay of the group home parents. Their required hours on duty were carefully estimated (sleeping hours were arbitrarily counted as one person working half-time), and then their total pay was calculated. This figure included an equal per-person share of the home's food and household supplies budget, an estimate of the value of the housing furnished for them, half their inservice training allowance, an equal per-person share of the telephone and other miscellaneous household expenses (unless they maintained their own residence nearby), and their nominal salary and benefits. The total pay of the regular house parents of the group homes was divided by the total hours required of both in order to get a weighted average hourly rate of pay. This rate ($1.67 per hour) was used as the par value for parents' and others' supervisory duties relating to the subjects in their natural homes. Par value of residents' labor rendered in support of their own residence was also taken at $1.67 per hour. The basic capital cost per year was taken as the annual rent per resident. In nonrental residences 12 percent (1 percent per month) of the estimated market value of the residence, divided by the number in the household, was used as the annual capital cost of the residential structure. Household furnishings were taken to be half the value of the residence, a standard figure for home insurance calculation. This value, divided by the number in the household, was multiplied by 0.0796, the August, 1977, rate of return on grade AA bonds, in order to estimate the annual foregone earnings on the capital investment in the residential furnishings. Taxes, when not included in the rent, were obtainable on only four of the nine natural homes. They averaged $200 per person for these four. This figure was used for all individuals, including the eight living in a group home that was tax exempt. This unpaid tax was included in "societal cost" on the assumption that society at large must necessarily pay the "tax" on tax-exempt facilities. Food, household expenses, utilities, transportation, entertainment, clothes, and special costs were all estimated for each resident on the basis of interviews with the residents and/or their supervisors or parents.

These costs were then separated into the two categories mentioned above: the individual client's cost (INDCOST) and society's (including family's) cost (SOCCOST). Furthermore, two SOCCOST figures were used. Average SOCCOST (SOCCOSTA) was the total family and societal cost of owning and operating a residence divided by the number of residents. Marginal SOCCOST (SOCCOSTM) was family and societal cost of adding a disabled resident to an already existing domicile. SOCCOSTA and SOCCOSTM were taken to be the same for apartments and group homes, since they existed solely for the residential placement of their inhabitants. However, the natural home would presumably have existed regardless of whether or not it housed a disabled resident, and the true cost to society would undoubtedly have been exaggerated by including the cost of real estate, utilities, heat, taxes, and household maintenance. Thus these were excluded from the Marginal SOCCOST of natural homes. SOCCOST, Average or Marginal, was obviously the crucial measure of residential cost. INDCOST, on the other hand, was used as a control variable, to proxy for individual differences in economically valued production.

An obvious weakness in this study was the absence of evidence of reliability or validity of the cost data. All information on hours worked by the subjects and residential supervisors were estimates, and nearly all cost estimates of the natural homes and apartments were based on interview responses that had very little documentation other than verification with income. Nevertheless, costs discriminated among the residential alternatives and correlated significantly with other variables in the study.

Despite the small number of experimental units, home types differed significantly on all seven of the dependent variables. The prevalent pattern, for five of the seven dependent variables (INDCOST, ABS-I, ABS-II, PASS, SOCCOSTA), was that the apartments had the most cost-effective scores (lower SOCCOSTA, higher scores on other variables) of the three residential alternatives, the other two being similar to each other. Only marginal costs (SOCCOSTM) and residential satisfaction (CRSS) varied from this pattern. For these two variables, the group homes had significantly less desirable scores than either the natural homes or the apartments, which did not differ from each other. A discriminant analysis supported the significant discrimination among residence types on PASS, CRSS, and SOCCOSTA or SOCCOSTM, after covariance adjustments had been made to equate residents on INDCOST, ABS-I, and ABS-II. Based on these data, Heal and Daniels concluded that the natural home and the landlord-supervised apartment were more desirable residential alternatives for developmentally disabled adults than was the group home.

Although its region and number of cases was limited, this study is recommended as a methodological model for more ambitious cost effectiveness comparisons of residential alternatives. It presents the major variables that must be included in such comparisons; it provides a rationale for most of the cost accounting decisions that are required in this area of research; and it demonstrates the use of statistical control to equate subjects so that ability differences from one residence type to another are minimized.

CONCLUSIONS

This review of the measures available for the empirical evaluation of residential alternatives for developmentally disabled individuals has revealed an impressive evaluation technology. Measures exist or can be readily constructed in all six areas that were seen to be important for residence comparisons: normalization, adaptive behavior, residents' satisfaction, others' satisfaction, residential climate, and cost. Optimal matching of clients to particular settings can be measured on several different continua. Additionally, analysis of "successful" placement can be made using more than one measure. Finally it seems that the technology for the evaluation of residential alternatives provides policymakers with the opportunity to provide empirical evidence in support of the allocation of society's resources to one particular combination of residential alternatives or another.

Chapter 11
Legislative Constraints and Facilitations for Community Integration

Cheryl Hanley-Maxwell and Laird W. Heal

Federal, state, and local legislatures can facilitate or constrain the integration of developmentally disabled individuals into the community. This chapter reviews legislation at these three levels of government in order to assess its potential impact on policy and service delivery. First, federal legislative history affecting the funding, planning, and regulation of community residential services is reviewed. This is followed by a report on a survey conducted by Hanley-Maxwell that investigated state statutes and licensing regulations affecting community residential facilities. Finally, the effect of zoning ordinances at the local policy-making level is analyzed.

FEDERAL LEGISLATION

The history of federal legislation on deinstitutionalization has been reviewed in detail by others (Boggs, 1971a, 1971b, 1972; Bradley, 1978; Comptroller General, 1977; Department of Health, Education, and Welfare, 1968; Soloyanis, 1972; Soloyanis & Yoder, 1973, 1975), and is only summarized briefly here. Prior to 1963, decisions and legislation dealt almost exclusively with mentally ill citizens; inclusion of mentally retarded citizens was tacit or assumed. However, since 1963 a series of Presidential messages (in 1963, 1966, 1971, and 1974) to Congress have reflected the growing awareness of the need for the development of comprehensive community-based services for mentally retarded citizens as well as the mentally ill.

Following the report of the President's Panel on Mental Retardation (1962), Congressional action provided for the development of community-based mental health centers and services. Funds for the development of such facilities were provided through the HEW appropriations act for fiscal year 1963 and the Mental Retardation Facilities and Community Mental Helath Centers Construction Act of 1963 (PL 88-164). Additionally, a staffing grant for community mental health centers was provided by the 1965 Amendments to the Mental Retardation Facilities and Community Mental Health Centers Construction Act (PL 89-105). Funding for community mental health services was also provided for by the Comprehensive Health Planning and Public Health Services Amendments of 1966 (PL 89-749) and the Partnership for Health Amendments of 1967 (PL 90-174).

Construction for some community residences for retarded individuals was authorized by the Vocational Rehabilitation Amendments of 1965 (PL 89-333). Additionally, funds for staffing community facilities for retarded individuals were provided through the Mental Retardation Amendments of 1967 (PL 90-170).

Starting in 1970, Congress took a more direct approach to the provision of community living facilities. The Developmental Disabilities Services and Facilities Construction Act of 1970 (PL 91-517) provided formula grants to states for planning and delivery of services, and for construction of facilities for developmentally disabled individuals. The Housing and Urban Development Act of 1970 (PL 91-152) requested community care housing for those not in need of institutional care. Then, in 1971, through a Presidential Statement on Mental Retardation, the Department of Housing and Urban Development (HUD) was directed to help develop housing for independent living facilities for retarded individuals. Furthermore, through the Housing and Community Development Act of 1974 (PL 93-383), the definition of handicap for HUD programs was changed to specifically include persons with developmental disabilities.

Two Social Security amendments provided monetary facilitation for deinstitutionalization. In 1971 amendments to the Social Security Act (PL 92-223) provided Medicaid money for the care of retarded individuals in intermediate care facilities. Through the Social Security Amendments of 1972 (PL 92-603), the Supplemental Security Income program was federalized and standardized to provide federally subsidized income maintenance programs for individuals who were aged, blind, or disabled (including those who were mentally retarded). Additionally, through this Act financial penalties were applied to states "overusing" institutions.

The development of community services to help prevent institutional placement was supported through the Special Health Revenue Sharing Act of 1975 (PL 94-63) and the Developmentally Disabled Assistance and Bill of Rights Act, 1975 (PL 94-103). PL 94-63 not only supported community services for mentally ill individuals (again, tacitly including those with mental retardation), but also strengthened program requirements to help reduce inappropriate institutional placements. Services provided in a setting that is least restrictive of the person's liberty were provided through PL 94-103. According to this Act, the facilities must not only be the least restrictive, but must also meet fire and safety regulations and other requirements to qualify for federal money. States receiving money under the formula grant (PL 91-517) must prepare plans to establish community programs as alternatives to institutional placement. Thus, "appropriate" placements are presumably assured. The Rehabilitation Act of 1973 (PL 93-112) and its 1978 amendments (PL 95-602) allow grant money to states for the integration of vocational training with training for living independently in the community; to qualify, states must submit 3-year plans describing proposed comprehensive services for independent living for severely handicapped individuals.

In 1976 the federal government began to focus on the personal monetary needs of individuals placed in community residences. Through the Unemployment Compensation Amendments of 1976 (PL 94-566), Title XVI of the Social Security Act was amended. Supplemental Security Income (SSI) payments were authorized to eligible persons living in publicly operated community living facilities serving 15 or fewer persons. The amendment also stated that as of October 1, 1977, all group living facilities housing or likely to house a significant number of SSI payees must have standards that have been established and enforced by state legislatures.

It appears that the development of the majority of states' community residential facilities were in direct response to the Federal Developmental Disabilities Services and Construction Act (PL 91-517) as amended by the Developmentally Disabled Assistance and Bill of Rights Act of 1975 (PL 94-103). These acts mandated the establishment of state and local Disabilities Councils to develop and implement the state and local plans for services.

In summary, federal legislation has shown an increasing disposition to support and, indeed, to mandate the integration of developmentally disabled citizens into normalized community housing. However, as we shall see, state and local legislation has not always followed the federal lead.

STATE STATUTES RELATED TO DEINSTITUTIONALIZATION

In the spring of 1978, a review of state statutes pertaining to community residential facilities was conducted via a search through the most recent statutes available at the law library of the University of Illinois. Of the 50 states, the statutes of 38 explicitly mentioned community residential alternatives to institutions, 11 states alluded to such alternatives, and only one state, New Mexico, neither mentioned nor alluded to community placements.

Forty-seven states had comprehensive statutes for commitment and admission to their state institutions. The other three alluded to the topic. The statutes of all but five states provided detailed legislation for review of placement, discharge, or transfer from their state institutions. Only 19 states dealt with staffing requirements. The remaining 31 states mentioned such requirements only vaguely or not at all. Programming specifications were found in half the state statutes, invariably stated in global terms. It appeared that staffing and programming requirements were specified, if at all, by licensing regulations.

State Licensing Regulations for Residential Facilities for Developmentally Disabled Individuals

Although the general picture of a state's legislative posture is provided by its statutes, the final interpretation of these statutes for implementation with specific residential alternatives is ordinarily embodied in state licensing regulations. In order to inquire about the actual "state of the system" regarding these regulations, a letter was sent to the Coordinator for community residential services for developmentally disabled persons in each of the 50 states. Addresses were obtained from The Council for Exceptional Children's *Handicapped Children in Head Start Series* (1974). The states were requested to send the following information:

1. State licensing regulations covering structures, personnel, and programming for community living facilities for developmentally disabled adults. These facilities would include group homes, foster homes, intermediate care (nursing) facilities, halfway houses, supervised apartments, nursing homes, and so on.
2. Legislative mandates, including sections of the statutes, relating to the transfer of developmentally disabled adults from large, public, residential facilities to smaller, community-based facilities.

Of the responding 42 states, all but six sent some information on their licensing regulations for community residential services. The type of home to which various regulations applied was classified according to the system developed by Baker, Seltzer, and Seltzer (1977). To complete the typology, two additional types of facilities were included: boarding homes and intermediate care facilities.

Only 13 of the 42 responding states licensed semi-independent units; 34 licensed boarding homes; 22 licensed group homes; 25 licensed intermediate care facilities; 21 licensed elderly nursing homes; 16 licensed foster-family care; and none licensed sheltered villages or workshop dormitories. Two responding states sent licensing information that did not specify the types of facilities licensed. Additionally, from many state definitions it was difficult to determine the categories into which their facilities fell. Finally, many facilities fell into more than one category.

Of the 42 responding states, 35 indicated regulations that related to one or more specific facility types. The content analysis of these regulations is summarized in Table 11.1. This table features 19 categories and subcategories of regulation as rows and six types of community residential facilities (CRFs) as major columns. Within each major column, three classes of responses are distinguished:

NO: no mention was made of this class or regulation in the materials that were received.

Local or NS: some mention was made of the regulatory category, but no specific requirement was indicated.

S: specific rules exist for at least one aspect of this category of regulation.

Table 11.1. Summary of state requirements for community residential facilities for the developmentally disabled

	Semi-independent (N = 7)			Group homes (N = 30)			Boarding homes (N = 16)			ICF (N = 14)			Elderly/nursing (N = 11)			Foster family (N = 6)			Total (N = 84)		
	NO	Local or NS	S	NO	Local or NS	S	NO	Local or NS	S	NO	Local or NS	S	NO	Local or NS	S	NO	Local or NS	S	NO	Local or NS	S
1. Zoning ordinance	4	3	0	12	18	0	6	10	0	5	9	0	3	8	0	3	3	0	33	51	0
2. Structural	2	0	5	2	0	28	1	0	15	0	0	14	0	0	11	0	1	5	5	1	78
3. Electrical	3	3	1	6	22	2	3	11	2	2	9	3	2	6	3	1	5	0	17	56	11
4. Plumbing	4	3	0	4	26	0	2	14	0	2	11	1	0	8	3	0	6	0	10	68	6
5. Health	2	5	0	4	25	1	2	14	0	0	11	3	0	9	2	1	5	0	10	69	5
6. Fire	1	5	1	1	15	14	1	11	4	1	6	8	0	4	7	2	2	3	4	43	37
7. Dietary	3	3	1	3	12	15	2	4	10	0	6	8	0	0	11	0	3	3	8	22	54
8. Medical/dental	3	2	2	3	10	17	3	4	9	0	0	14	0	2	9	0	2	4	9	21	54
9. Program	0	5	2	6	13	11	2	6	8	0	4	13	2	4	5	1	3	2	15	35	34
10. Fiscal management	1	3	3	15	10	5	7	5	4	5	3	4	5	2	4	2	1	3	37	24	23
11. Personnel																					
a. Administrative	1	3	3	3	11	16	2	6	8	0	6	8	0	3	8	0	1	5	6	30	48
b. Other	1	6	0	4	19	7	2	10	4	1	7	6	0	6	5	0	1	5	8	49	27
12. Credentials																					
a. Administrative	3	3	1	6	11	13	3	7	6	3	1	10	3	1	7	1	2	3	19	25	40
b. Other	3	3	1	8	13	9	3	7	6	5	2	7	4	1	6	1	2	3	24	28	32
13. Duties																					
a. Administrative	3	3	1	13	6	11	7	4	5	2	2	10	1	1	9	1	3	2	27	19	38
b. Other	3	4	0	14	12	4	8	5	3	4	4	6	2	2	7	1	3	2	32	30	22
14. Size	3	1	3	6	1	23	1	1	14	7	0	7	6	0	5	0	0	6	23	3	58
15. Admissions	1	2	4	4	11	15	2	3	11	2	3	9	1	1	9	2	3	1	12	23	49
16. Discharge/transfer policy	5	0	2	18	8	4	11	1	4	7	3	4	5	2	4	4	0	2	50	14	20
TOTAL	46	57	30	132	243	195	68	123	113	50	82	134	34	60	115	19	46	49	349	611	636
		133			570			304			266			209			114			1596	

In constructing Table 11.1, a tally was made for each state in one or another of these subcolumns under every residence type to which that state's regulations applied. The N shown for each column is a count of the states that had regulations relating to that column's residence type. Thus, table entries are the number of states whose regulations were classified into each of these subcolumns for each of the 19 regulatory subcategories. A total of 84 facility types were regulated by one state or another; the total number of tallies in the table is 19×84 or 1596.

Pattern of Licensing Regulations

The pattern of regulations is strikingly similar across facilities. There is a disposition to take zoning (#1) and building codes (#3, #4, #6) for granted, but to make specific structural requirements (#2). Few facilities have general health (#5) regulations, but many have dietary (#7) and medical (#8) requirements. Fiscal standards (#10) are ordinarily not specified, presumably because funding is usually not done by the licensing agency. Aside from the requirements for the residence administrator, program standards (#9) and staff competencies (#11, #12, #13) are usually left to chance. Facility size (#14) is ordinarily specified, although a surprising number of facility types have no maximum in some states. Only about 58 percent of all facilities have specific admissions policies (#15) and even fewer (24 percent) have specified discharge and transfer policies (#16).

The total number of specific regulations was 636 of the total 1596 regulations that could have possibly been specified. Almost half of these occurred in the areas of Structure (78), Diet (54), Medicine (54), Size (58), and Admissions (49).

The overriding concern in nearly all of the states' regulations appears to be the physical plant. Pennsylvania and Utah were notable exceptions in the 35 states who submitted regulations. All but a few residence licensing regulations mention electrical and plumbing codes with which the residence must comply. Additionally, specified health and safety standards must typically be met. Fire regulations were especially pervasive and detailed. These results are consistent with those of O'Connor (1976), who found that 76 percent of 611 community residential facilities surveyed required at least one state license or certificate, the most common being fire, health, and building codes. More than one license of the same type (e.g., fire or health) had to be obtained from different agencies in 22 percent of the facilities in her study.

Perhaps the most important implication of these results for deinstitutionalization relates to their probable effect on the policies of the facility. Dietary and medical requirements in combination with physical plant specifications seem to mandate a preoccupation with custodial care (i.e., meeting daily living needs). Often regulations for specific dietary and medical requirements, and specific and stringent physical plant requirements, lack any degree of structured programming and staff requirements. Frequently, when this combination is found, admissions policies are mentioned either specifically or generally, but transfer and discharge policies are conspicuously lacking. Regardless of the dietary and medical policies, transfer and discharge policies are required by the principle of least restrictive alternative, i.e., movement along a continuum toward greater independence implied by the tenets of normalization and egalitarianism.

Of the reviewed regulations relating to all 84 licensed alternatives in responding states, 72 had admissions procedures (49 specifically stated; 23 generally stated), whereas only 34 had discharge or transfer policies (20 specific; 14 general). It would appear that constraints on community integration are applied through this asymmetry. That is, the asymmetry of admission and discharge regulations anticipates the neglect of training for transfer to less (or more) restrictive settings. Conversely, symmetry of regulation would anticipate continuity of programming across facility types, encouraging the development and practice of skills in order to maximize progressive independence. State regulations presently tend to deal with program requirements in only a general way; often they suggest areas for skill development, but rarely is there mention of training for transfer across types of facilities.

Since regulations tend not to specify programming, it is not surprising that credentials and duties of personnel are usually elusive. A few states specify credentials, but vaguely indicate that staff should be "qualified mental retardation personnel." Occasionally, specific standards for employment at a residence are set; but even when positions require specific credentials, duties are rarely designated. The residence's administrator is usually the only staff member, if any, with both specified duties and specified credentials.

There are, of course, certain imperfections in the data reported in Table 11.1. First, the response rate is less than optimal, with only 42 of 50 states (84 percent) responding. Even this figure is misleading, since only 35 of the 42 provided state licensing information. It is possible that the seven who responded but sent no licensing information had none to send. However, it is more likely that the information exists, but was not sent for one reason or another: perhaps it was not economical; perhaps other agencies coordinate licensing information; or perhaps the letter of inquiry was misunderstood. In addition to the sampling imperfections, the content analysis might be quesitoned. Our system of regulatory categories might be idiosyncratic, and our distinction between a specific (S) and nonspecific (NS) regulation may be unreliable. Nevertheless, the patterns of results were very consistent across the states that did respond, and there is no reason to believe that the nonrespondents were atypical. Instead, it is probable that they lagged behind the respondents in preparation and dissemination of their regulations. Finally, with the possible exception of discharge policies, these data are consistent with the state statutes, which are universally available. Thus, there is every reason to believe that, although present data are imperfect and incomplete, they present an unbiased picture of the current status of state licensing regulations that impinge on community residential facilities for developmentally disabled citizens.

In summary, state legislation and regulations are both facilitative and inhibitory with regard to the implementation of the federal mandate that least restrictive residential alternatives be sought for developmentally disabled citizens. Although states have provided for many residential alternatives, they tend to stress architectural rather than programmatic standards. Thus, client health and safety are emphasized at the regulatory level, at the expense of mandating client progress and normalized integration into the community (Wolfensberger, 1972).

LOCAL ZONING ORDINANCES

Local zoning ordinances complete the trilogy of the legislative regulations confronted by community residential facilities. Compliance with zoning regulations is ordinarily the first requirement mentioned in state regulations, being couched most often in terms of residents' health and safety.

Zoning regulations are intended to improve the general welfare of the community by placing restrictions on the full range of possible uses of an owner's property. Since 1928 every state has had enabling legislation or constitutional provisions that give zoning power to counties or cities, or other local units. Generally, these statutes or provisions require only that ordinances safeguard against those things that are harmful to health, morals, safety, or welfare, and they give each unit wide discretion as to the exact requirements of their ordinances. This policy gives rise to a large number of agencies that exercise zoning authority (Chandler & Ross, 1976).

The zoning application procedure is fairly standard from state to state. Generally, once the application has been made it is reviewed by a regional (usually county) planning administrator. The planning administrator forwards it to the planning commission with his/her recommendations. Formal recommendations are made by the planning commission in an open hearing for residents within a certain radius of the proposed facility. Ideally, the limitations that must be imposed on the facility to achieve compliance are to be determined through the information gathered at this meeting. In reality, the entire procedure is an administrative reevaluation of whether the use is appropriate for the zone in question. In essence, the commission amends the standing ordinance. Appeal of the planning commission's decision may be made to the city council or the zoning board of appeals (Chandler & Ross, 1976). Most communities treat family and group care facilities as special or conditional uses within the zoning district. Family and group care facilities may be located in the district once it has been shown to the planning commission that the spirit of the ordinance is met by the facility in question (Lauber & Bangs, 1974).

Zones are labeled according to the type of structures permitted. "R-1" is a zone restricted to single-family dwellings. These are dwellings that are for one family and for residential use only. "R-2" allows single and two-family dwellings that are again restricted for residential use. "R-3," "R-4," and "R-5" permit multiple dwellings and apartment houses that are for residential use only (Chandler & Ross, 1976).

Usually the legal basis for exclusion of family and group care facilities for developmentally disabled citizens is the restriction of a residential zone to "family unit." Critical to the zoning issue is the definition of "family." Definitions within local ordinances vary radically, but they can usually be put into four major categories: 1) no definition of family; 2) definition of family, in broad terms, as a housekeeping unit; 3) definition of family according to traditional terms (related by blood, marriage, or adoption), or limit on the number of unrelated persons; or 4) restriction of family exclusively to traditional terms (Hopperton, 1975b).

Since family care, foster, and group homes are fairly new phenomena, there are at present few provisions for such facilities in the majority of zoning ordinances. In many cases, a local zoning commission may view these smaller facilities as boarding, rooming, or lodging houses. On the surface, group homes may resemble such dwellings, but in reality residents' social needs are much different. In contrast to the rooming house, the group home consists of individuals whose daily lives are, to some degree, dependent on each other and on the "family" that they comprise. In order to accomplish the goal of normalized lives for its residents, the group home must be based on homelike surroundings and atmosphere (Lauber & Bangs, 1974).

Because foster and group homes are often licensed and supported by the state, and because municipal and county planning bodies often see state support and licensing as a business use of property, they often limit these homes to commercial and industrial zones. Similarly, some zoning agencies restrict the location of homes that require some medical supervision to zones where municipal hospitals, nursing homes, or convalescent hospitals are allowed (Chandler & Ross, 1976).

Of 400 planning department directors surveyed by the American Society of Planning Officials (Lauber & Bangs, 1974), about 40 percent reported that family care facilities (serving seven or fewer residents) were allowed in single-family districts. Larger facilities (serving eight or more residents) were allowed in 34 percent of the single-family districts and more than 40 percent of the commerical districts.

Lauber and Bangs (1974) and Hopperton (1975b) recommend that family care homes be permitted in all residential areas, whereas group homes should be allowed in all multifamily districts through special use permit only. This recommendation is based on the belief that case-by-case review would require systematic planning of site location, and would prevent saturation of one or two districts.

It is through zoning ordinances that communities can express their opposition to a proposed community residential facility for developmentally disabled citizens. According to Lauber and Bangs (1974) neighboring residents are often alarmed about the "negative effects" that a facility might have on the neighborhood. Possible decrease in property values, rise in crime rate, sexual deviancy, violent behavior, aesthetically unattractive residents, noise level, traffic volume, and parking demands have all been raised as concerns of the community. Field studies done by the California Department of Helath in cities where community living facilities exist have shown that most of the negative attitudes and fears expressed are the result of a "lack of knowledge concerning the program objectives and fear of the stereotyped images of people in these facilities" (Lauber & Bangs, 1974). Existing evidence shows that, once exposed to a community residential facility and its residents, the majority of skeptical individuals become more supportive of them (Heal, Sigelman, & Switzky, 1978; Kastner, Reppucci, & Pezzoli, 1979; Lauber & Bangs, 1974; Sigelman, 1976; see also chapter 7 of this volume). Additionally, Wolpert (1978) has shown that property values in areas with group homes neither increase nor decrease compared to matched control areas. Proximity to group homes does not affect a property's market value, nor does the existence of group homes generate a higher degree of neighborhood property turnover. Additionally, the exterior maintenance of the group homes in their study was generally better than that of the surrounding properties.

CONCLUSIONS

This paper presented an overview of the status of legislative facilitations and constraints relating to community residential facilities (CRFs) for developmentally disabled citizens. Federal legislation was seen to be a global but primary force in mobilizing state and local governments. The state legislation must be seen as implementative, but preoccupied with health, safety, and building design; although considerable freedom is thereby allowed to local agencies in planning programs for their clients, the absence of any standards for client progress or integration might be focusing agency attention in ways that are detrimental to client progress. Finally, local restrictions are apparently inhibitory, bureaucratic zoning crises being prerequisite to providing handicapped individuals with any community living arrangements besides their natural homes.

Thus, if state licensing regulations have a tendency to segregate developmentally disabled citizens, local zoning codes do so with certainty. Segregation of this minority, like any minority, is tantamount to stigmatization, devaluation, and denial of constitutional rights. We would urge that this tendency be reversed as these licensing regulations are revised and implemented.

Chapter 12
Litigation Concerning Community Integration

Nancy Emmel

The principle of deinstitutionalization has been firmly established throughout the United States. Developmentally disabled persons are returning from large, state-operated institutions to smaller, community-based facilities, group homes, sheltered care homes, and individual apartments. Although the concept of deinstitutionalization has received judicial support, legal barriers and community opposition still preclude absorption of developmentally disabled persons into our residential communities. This chapter examines the case law foundations for deinstitutionalization and selected litigation concerning various zoning barriers, to provide the reader with an introduction to some of the legal issues involved in integration of developmentally disabled citizens into the community.

CASE LAW FOUNDATIONS FOR COMMUNITY INTEGRATION

A brief look at the status of citizens with mental handicaps in past judicial decisions is useful. The courts have been a forum frequently utilized to make public several societal inequalities toward minority groups. The late 1950s and the 1960s saw many legal challenges establishing, "in the eyes of the law," the civil rights of racial and cultural minorities. Similarly, in the 1970s the courts have been the center for identifying and verifying the rights of handicapped persons. Litigation has occurred in a variety of areas relating to handicapped persons, including treatment, education, architectural barriers, employment, and housing.

For the developmentally disabled adult, however, the establishment of the right to treatment has been particularly significant. The landmark case of *Wyatt v. Stickney* (1972) established that mentally retarded persons involuntarily confined to a state institution had a constitutional right to habilitation. The court developed specific standards for that state institution that revolved around four principles: a humane psychological and physical environment, an individual habilitation and training plan for each resident, qualified staff to provide individual programming, and habilitation in the least restrictive setting. Although this is considered to be the landmark right-to-treatment case for developmentally disabled persons, more recently the plaintiffs are making efforts to obtain relief because of lack of compliance with the original order (*Wyatt v. Hardin*, 1975).

Judicial decisions concerning the right to treatment for mentally retarded and handicapped citizens have been made in several states. The most profound of these is the recent Pennhurst decision (*Halderman v. Pennhurst State School and Hospital*, 1978) in which several current and former residents of this Pennsylvania state facility filed a petition against the facility administration and the State and County alleging that the constitutional and statutory rights of the residents were being violated. Among the conclusions of the federal district court were that, when a state institutionalizes individuals because of mental retardation, regardless of the voluntariness of the admission, the U.S. Constitution and the laws of the State of Pennsylvania:

> require the state to provide such minimally adequate habilitation as will afford a reasonable opportunity for them to acquire and maintain such life skills as are necessary to enable them to cope as effectively as their capacities permit; that the Rehabilitation Act of 1973 (Section 504) provides rights to handicapped persons, including residents at Pennhurst and that these rights have been and are being violated; and that Pennhurst residents do not receive minimally adequate habilitation because Pennhurst does not provide an atmosphere conducive to normalization which the experts agree is vital to the minimally adequate habilitation of the retarded. (*Halderman v. Pennhurst*, Memorandum at pp. 1 and 2)

Given these conclusions, the court ordered the Commonwealth and County defendants to:

> provide suitable community living arrangements for the residents of Pennhurst and those retarded persons on its waiting list, together with such community services as are necessary to provide them with minimally adequate habilitation until such time as the retarded individual is not longer in need of such living arrangement and or community service. (*Halderman v. Pennhurst*, Order at p.1)

The court also required the appointment of a Special Master to organize, supervise, and monitor the court order. For this discussion of community integration of developmentally disabled citizens, the determination that an institution such as Pennhurst could not provide minimally adequate habilitation simply because it *was* an institution, and the subsequent order for the defendants to provide community living arrangements, is particularly important. (See note on p. 8.)

The principle of the least restrictive alternative has also been used to create a basis for the development of residential living alternatives for handicapped citizens. The least restrictive alternative as a legal concept is defined as follows:

> Even though the governmental purpose be legitimate and substantial, that purpose cannot be pursued by means that broadly stifle personal liberties when the end can be more narrowly achieved. (*Shelton v. Tucker*, 1960)

This concept has been used to condemn the placement of handicapped persons in large residential institutions in favor of community-based living situations that are, according to the tenets of normalization, less restrictive to the personal liberty of developmentally disabled residents. This concept was applied in *Welsch v. Likens* (1977), in which the court determined that mentally retarded residents of an institution should be placed into a residence that least restricted their personal liberties. In this case and in *Dixon v. Weinberger* (1975), the court required the state to create specific living alternatives when the need of developmentally disabled clients was not met by existing facilities.

Thus, the development and implementation of the concepts of the right to treatment, minimally adequate habilitation, and the least restrictive alternative have created a foundation in case law for community integration of developmentally disabled citizens.

LEGAL BARRIERS TO COMMUNITY INTEGRATION

Notwithstanding this strong judicial basis for moving developmentally disabled persons from large residential facilities into smaller community-based facilities, group homes, sheltered care homes, and individual apartments, there are many barriers to successful integration. Such barriers include legislative ones, such as restrictive zoning ordinances, discrimination in public and private housing, and general community opposition. As with the institutional environment, case law intervention has sought to ameliorate these problems. An examination of selected litigation concerning zoning and housing discrimination follows.

First, a brief definition of zoning is necessary. Zoning is defined by Hopperton as:

> Systematic regulation of the use and development of real property. Zoning restricts the ways in which a private owner can use his property by dividing a city into districts and then prescribing the uses to which real property within those districts can be put. This systematic regulation of land is designed to promote orderly and healthy community development through a comprehensive zoning plan which prohibits that which is harmful to health, morals, safety or welfare. (Hopperton, 1975b, p. 3)

Thus, zoning serves to divide a municipality into districts or zones for various land functions, thereby controlling and restricting the uses of land within that community. As stated in the foregoing description, zoning is intended to maintain the welfare of the community. Unfortunately, zoning has excluded not only industry and certain businesses from residential districts, but has been used to exclude certain people, such as members of racial minorities and handicapped persons, from some residential areas.

Generally, it is thought that a municipality is justified in exercising control over its composition and land use. Municipalities get their "zoning power" from one of two sources: a state zoning statute, which provides specific municipal authority over land regulation; or a state constitutional home-rule law, which allows the community sovereignty over many or all functions relating to the locality, including zoning. Thus, a municipality has the right to zone, and it may choose to do so in many ways. The following discussion concerns those types of zoning ordinances that may exclude special homes for developmentally disabled persons.

The most discriminating zoning ordinances in regard to handicapped citizens are those that exclude specific types of residents. An example of such a restriction may be found in Sedalia, Missouri, where an ordinance excluded homes for alcoholics, drug addicts, and insane and feeble-minded persons in certain residential areas in that city.

Another type of zoning barrier is found in ordinances that provide a narrow definition of "family." One such definition is:

> Family is either an individual or two or more persons related by blood, marriage, or adoption who live together in one dwelling unit and maintain a common household. (Hopperton, 1975b, p. 3)

Although not as restrictive as this definition, the following definition is still exclusionary:

> Family is any number of individuals living and cooking together on the premises as a single housekeeping unit, but it shall not include more than three individuals not related by blood, marriage or adoption. (Hopperton, 1975b, p. 3)

Still another type of ordinance defines family more broadly:

> Family is one or more persons occupying the premises and living as a single housekeeping unit. It is distinguished from a group occupying a boarding house, lodging house, club, fraternity or hotel. (Hopperton, 1975b, p. 3)

Finally, the following does not define family but rather describes a "single family dwelling":

> Single family dwelling is a residential building arranged, intended or designed for one family. (Hopperton, 1975b, p. 3)

By providing a definition of what is considered to constitute a family, a municipality can control the number of persons, especially unrelated persons, living in a residential unit. The logical intent of such a definition is to restrict the composition of residential areas largely to traditional families and thereby maintain the perceived character, integrity, and continuity of the community.

Traditionally, courts have supported the community's right to regulate the use of its property through zoning ordinances containing a definition of family. The following three cases are examples of that support.

In interpreting a local ordinance that called for one family per lot in a residential section, the Connecticut State Supreme Court, in *Planning and Zoning Commission of the Town of Westport v. Synanon Foundation, Inc.* (1966), stated that the word "family" must relate to and be consistent with the context in which the word is found and that the regulation's purpose was relevant to determining the meaning of the word. The court found that the purpose of the regulation in question was to restrict the use of property in accordance with a plan to promote the community welfare. The programs of the Synanon group, a group involved in the rehabilitation of persons with drug problems, did not come within the context of a "reasonable judicial construction" of the word "family" found in the regulation, and thus the court overruled a lower court decision in favor of Westport.

Similarly, in California, a district court judge found that the use of the terms "single family residential" and "family," which was defined as "one person living alone, or two or more persons related by blood, marriage or legal adoption, or a group not exceeding four persons living as a single housekeeping unit," did not infringe on the plaintiffs' (members of communal living groups) constitutional right to freedom of association. The court went on to claim that the ordinances were "rational in the meaning of the equal protection and due process clauses of the 14th Amendment" (*Palo Alto Tenants Union v. Morgan*, 1970). The judge further supported the ordinances by saying that courts had long recognized the value of the traditional family. The court claimed that the communal family was not like the traditional family in that its membership was fluctuating and voluntary. Finally, it held that the state has an interest in preserving the traditional family.

In still another instance, *Village of Belle Terre v. Borras* (1974), the U.S. Supreme Court upheld the constitutionality of a zoning ordinance that restricted particular land use to single-family dwellings. In this case, "family" was defined as:

> One or more persons related by blood, adoption or marriage, living and cooking together in a single housekeeping unit exclusive of household servants. A number of persons but not exceeding two (2) living and cooking together as a single housekeeping unit though not related by blood, adoption, or marriage shall be deemed to constitute a family. (416 U.S. at 2)

The court claimed that the plaintiffs, six unrelated college students living together, were unsupported in their contention that the ordinance violated their constitutional rights of association, travel, and privacy. Rather, the court found these rights unviolated and held that the ordinance bore a rational relationship to a permissible state objective. Also, no violation of equal protection was found. Although the *Belle Terre* case has been interpreted as an obstacle to challenging such zoning ordinances, its applicability to homes for developmentally disabled and handicapped citizens is somewhat unfounded due to the differences between college students and handicapped persons, specific circumstances, and the purpose of community residences for developmentally disabled individuals.

Although the litigation cited here that has sought to challenge zoning ordinances with restrictive definitions of "family" has been rather unsuccessful for college students, commune members, and drug addicts, litigation that has attempted to clarify similar definitions for the purpose of establishing and maintaining group homes and other residential facilities for mentally retarded and handicapped persons has been more promising. For example, in the Ohio case of *Driscoll v. Goldberg* (1970), the Court of Appeals held in favor of the defendants, who attempted to establish a group home for mentally retarded children in a residential area. The defendants were found not in violation of a local zoning ordinance that restricted the use of that area to single-family dwellings. The court claimed that the ordinance defined "family" to be a group living as a "single housekeeping unit," and that the group home that the defendants sought to establish would function much like a traditional family and was thus permissible.

In *City of White Plains v. Ferraioli* (1974), the New York Court of Appeals found that a group home for 10 foster children did not violate an ordinance that called for single-family dwellings in a residential area. The court said:

> So long as the group home bears the generic character of a family unit and is not a framework for transients or transient living, it conforms to the purpose of the ordinance.

The fact that the court looked at whether the group home had the character of a family unit rather than at the number of persons present in the residence or at biological relationships is an important step toward acknowledging the important normalizing function of community-based living alternatives.

The court in *Little Neck Community Association v. Working Organization for Retarded Children (WORC)* (1976) applied reasoning similar to that found in *City of White Plains v. Ferraioli*. It claimed that a group home for mentally retarded children constituted a "family" within the meaning of the applicable single-family dwelling ordinance. What is particularly significant about this decision is that the judge, in addressing the community's fear of the establishment of an institution in a residential area, identified the trend toward the development of community residences for mentally retarded citizens that focus on providing domiciliary services and social contacts in a noninstitutionalized environment. In addition, the court pointed to the advantage of a group home in the residential community:

> It will provide retarded children with a stable environment in a setting in which they will have a real opportunity to develop their full potential.

The cases of *Driscoll v. Goldberg, City of White Plains v. Ferraioli* and *Little Neck Community Association v. WORC* are examples of litigation that successfully challenged local zoning ordinances. Although these cases dealt with mentally retarded children, their findings have major implications for the adult developmentally disabled population. First, the court in each of these cases looked to the function and character of the group residence in determining the appropriateness of the facility in a residential area. Second, the courts in *White Plains* and *Little Neck* identified the importance of a normalized environment for the development of disabled clients. Similar logic is applicable when considering a small group facility for handicapped adults, since adults also require a normalized environment and familylike settings for appropriate habilitation.[1]

LEGISLATIVE AVENUES TO AID COMMUNITY INTEGRATION

Even though litigation has been useful as a tactic for eliminating zoning barriers, there is some agreement among legal and other professionals that seeking specific legislation that prohibits restrictive zoning ordinances is preferable. State-level legislation can preempt local zoning authorities to assure that municipalities will not restrict facilities for developmentally disabled citizens from residential areas. Such legislation currently exists in at least 11 states and several others have proposed similar statutes.

One example of such legislation is Ohio's series of amendments to the state civil rights law. It prohibits discrimination on the basis of handicap in employment, access to public transportation, accommodation, housing, housing loans, and insurance. In regard to housing, the legislation forbids discrimination in housing sale or rental. It also provides that the state housing development board must verify that one in 20 state-supported housing developments is accessible to the handicapped. The law does not require owners of private residences to make similar accommodations.

Recently, several suits have been filed claiming that handicapped individuals have been discriminated against in public housing and admission to training programs, on the basis of federal regulations in Section 504 of the Rehabilitation Act of 1973. In *Cotten v. Evangelist Temple Homes, Inc.*, (1974), a blind woman claimed she had been denied residence in a federally subsidized housing project on the basis of her handicap, and that she had suffered economic and emotional hardship because she was refused such housing. She claimed that the U.S. Department of Housing and Urban Development (HUD) had failed to implement Section 504 and had thus violated the Act. In *Southeastern Community College v. Davis* (1979), a hearing-impaired woman who had sought admission to a nursing education program brought to the forefront the interpretation of "otherwise qualified" in the Section 504 regulations. As the first Supreme Court decision based on action sought under 504, *Davis* is a very narrow decision, offering little guidance to employers on making the distinction between mandatory affirmative action and illegal discrimination. The adequacy of Section 504

---

[1]For a more thorough discussion of such cases the reader is referred to: "Zoning for Community Residences," *Mental Disability Law Reporter*, Sept.-Dec. 1977, pp. 315–327; "*Community Living: Zoning Obstacles and Legal Remedies,*" National Center for Law and the Handicapped, Dec. 1977; "Zoning Restrictions and the Right to Live in the Community," in M. Kindred, J. Cohen, D. Penrod, & T. Shaffer (Eds.), *The Mentally Retarded Citizen and the Law*, 1976; "Housing and Zoning Restrictions," in R. L. Burgdorf (Ed.), *The Legal Rights of Handicapped Persons: Cases, Materials, and Texts*, 1980, pp. 703–752; and "A Sanctuary for People: Strategies for Overcoming Zoning Restrictions on Community Homes for Retarded Persons," Marcia K. Lippincott, *Stanford Law Review*, April 1979, pp. 767–783.

for litigation seeking equal housing and community service opportunities for handicapped persons remains an issue that will be subjected to much doubt, haggling, questioning, and legal interpretations in the years to come.

SUMMARY

This chapter has analyzed the case law basis for deinstitutionalization, including the concepts of the right to treatment, minimally adequate habilitation, and the least restrictive alternative. Various zoning barriers were described, and selected litigation demonstrated how specific zoning ordinances could be interpreted to prevent or allow residences for handicapped citizens. Legislation that may prohibit housing and other such discrimination against handicapped citizens was discussed. Although there are both case law and legislative bases for the return of developmentally disabled citizens to our communities, legal and other community opposition also exists. Such opposition will be challenged in our courts and in our legislatures until the right to live in a normal, healthy environment is available to all.

Chapter 13
Backlash to the Deinstitutionalization Movement

Angela R. Novak

The deinstitutionalization movement has contributed to widespread relocation in recent years of a large number of developmentally disabled individuals. Many of these individuals have been moved from large public residential facilities into smaller institutions, group homes, foster care homes, and their natural homes—ostensibly with more direct ties to community life. Several research trends, however, indicate the actual and potential formation of a "backlash" to counteract this movement into the community. Recent literature indicates serious problems in four particular areas: extreme reactions to relocation in specific individuals, negative parent reactions, evidence that community facilities are no better and sometimes worse than institutional facilities, and possible testimony to the failure of the movement by the high rates of readmission to institutions.

RELOCATION REACTIONS

The existence of anxiety reactions to relocation has been known for a number of years. Coffman and Harris (1978) summarized the "transition shock" and "culture shock" symptoms of anxieties, depression, and loneliness experienced by Peace Corps volunteers moving to foreign environments, by prisoners released from comfortable and well-known prison surroundings into the threatening and unfamiliar community, by persons experiencing loss of emotional stability when undergoing a divorce, and by long-term overseas sojourners and foreign students. They also list other instances of major changes in life situations where transition shock and difficult processes of adjustment are manifested: changes in school, job, and career; marriage, separation, and divorce; transition from civilian to military to civilian life; and retirement. The anxieties of transition include reactions of anger and hostility, nostalgia for things back home (or the "good old days"), low levels of tolerance for minor pains or irritations, problems with eating and sleeping, and despair of ever "fitting in."

The deleterious effects of relocation for persons who are elderly have often been recounted; a policy of frequently moving individuals from one institution to another often results in an increase in mortality rates. Aldrich and Mendkoff (1963), expecting an annual mortality rate of 19 percent among elderly institutionalized citizens, reported instead a 32 percent rate within 1 year following relocation. Bourestrom and Tars (1974) described characteristics frequently occurring among relocated elderly persons: increased pessimism about personal health, decreased psychological functioning, decreased physical and mental health, and decreased self-care and social capacities. Miller and Lieberman (1965) also reported declines in psychological functioning in more than half of the relocated elderly persons in their study.

Cochran, Sran, and Varano (1977) cited several studies of the severe depression of "relocation syndrome" in elderly persons reported by health personnel working with them. They liken this "transition shock" to the severe depression they found in a few mentally retarded residents moved to a group home. The youngest person in their study, who was only 19 years old, contracted pneumonia and died shortly after being moved, although it appeared that the seriousness of the illness was not sufficient in itself to cause death. Coffman and Harris (1978) also compared the "transition shock" symptoms they described in nonhandicapped persons undergoing major life changes to those experienced by deinstitutionalized retarded persons. When undergoing the move from the institution, these persons are subject to the same "transition shock" manifestations of severe depression, arising from the loss of the equivalent of a "family" and from the loss of emotional ties and customary habits.

Rago (1976) warned that the mortality rate of profoundly retarded individuals transferred from a state hospital to a convalescent hospital was double that of those who remained in the state hospital. Although the average life span of profoundly mentally retarded persons is increasing, their mortality rate peaks during the initial year of institutionalization. Rago postulated a form of "cultural shock" experience by profoundly retarded individuals, who have a precarious ability to survive. When relocated, they experience much stress on their ability to adapt to new situations.

Cohen, Conroy, Frazer, Snelbecker, and Sprent (1977) delineate the specific pressures and complex interactions of stress involved in transfer from one institution to another, especially for individuals with poor coping skills. These include separation from loved ones, pressure to adjust to a new physical and interpersonal environment, confusion and resentment regarding helplessness, and anxiety about the future—all leading to decreased functioning, depression, withdrawal, anger, and fear. Of the individuals in their study who were transferred from a large state institution to a smaller community living facility, the higher-functioning residents showed a pattern of lowered functioning and withdrawal following relocation. Even after 8 weeks, they remained withdrawn and were still suffering setbacks in language development. The lower-functioning residents showed increased levels of both adaptive and acting-out behavior.

Cohen et al. applied Parkes' (1971) theory of psychosocial transition to their results. Parkes had theorized that individuals with poor coping skills would be the most vulnerable to the adverse effects of relocation, and would be more likely to exhibit depression, withdrawal, anger, fear, and decreased functioning. Although Parkes had not specifically mentioned mentally retarded persons, Cohen et al. found his theory certainly applicable to the higher-functioning residents of their study.

Those reporting these severe reactions to relocation have also made suggestions for easing the stresses of transition experienced by vulnerable mentally retarded and other developmentally disabled persons. When intra-institutional transfer is being considered, Cochran et al. (1977) and Cohen et al. list specific suggestions for easing the transfer stress, including preparatory site visits to the new facility, involvement of the client in the actual move, involvement of the family, and close concern by a personal advocate.

Seevers (1975) has pointed out many interactions between individual personalities and the varying environments of community placements (e.g., group homes compared to apartment settings). He concluded that it is not enough to measure increases in skills as the test for the success of community living alternatives; more concern for the affective domain must be extended by those responsible for transferring individuals from one setting to another.

Coffman and Harris (1978) postulate that the adjustment period of deinstitutionalized individuals follows the same U-shape curve as that of adjustment to living in a foreign country: (a) a "honeymoon" period, (b) disillusionment, and (c) resolution. They provide specific "guideposts for programming" to aid adjustment in each of these phases, and also admit that much more research is needed about what kinds of individuals follow what stages of adjustment, and about how that adjustment can be facilitated.

PARENT COUNTERREACTIONS

A second form of backlash is arising on the part of parents of handicapped individuals who have been returned to the community or who have been considered for return. Payne (1976) has warned of the development of a substantial movement, that parents are coalescing to support the continuation of large institutions and to restrict money being spent on the development of small group homes. Evidence of this parent backlash is embodied in the parents' briefs filed in deinstitutionalization law suits, when courts have ordered or are considering ordering that institutions be closed and that residents be moved to community programs. The parents in the *Halderman v. Pennhurst* (1978) appeal were particularly concerned about their children who had lived in the Pennsylvania institution for so long that their abilities had significantly regressed, or who were so old that their parents opposed their being subjected to the major life transition of being integrated into the community (Gilhool, 1979). Similarly, parents in the *Connecticut Association for Retarded Citizens v. Mansfield Training School* case

(1979) have expressed fears about their children being thrust into group homes in the community without close supervision and constant care; these parents feel that only the institution can provide the structure and protection they feel their children need. It is ironic that deinstitutionalization suits that are initiated by some parents result in opposition to the suit by other parents.

Among parents' reasons for support for institutional settings is the belief that large institutions are better for their retarded and disabled children—there are more experts concentrated there; retarded residents can be with their own kind; they can be protected from the stresses of living in the community; and this is the tried and true method for caring for retarded persons. However, the primary area of concern seems to stem from parents' desire to be assured that the institution will continue to exist as an option for them—that the institution will remain available as one of their choices for a permanent solution to the problems of caring for their retarded children when they become too old to provide the care, or after they die.

These are the parents who fall at the extreme end of the continuum of parental opinion against deinstitutionalization. Turnbull and Turnbull (1978), in their analysis of parental attitudes toward "least restrictive" policies, have pointed out that many parents placed their children into institutions years ago on the advice of professionals. After years of agonizing over the decision, of maintaining only minimal contact with the child, and of developing a "new life" for themselves that has to be substantially modified when a retarded child is returned to them, many of these parents strongly oppose state deinstitutionalization plans. Furthermore, they are acutely aware that community services and public school programs still have severe limitations, and they don't want to expose their children to greater safety hazards, insecurity, and to teasing and rejection by nonhandicapped persons. Ferrara (1979) also found resistance at the "grass roots" level, in that parents of handicapped children in her survey expressed positive attitudes toward the general principle of normalization, but not when it was applied specifically to their own children; parents of more severely handicapped children were more positive toward normalization, possibly because their children had not been as exposed to normalization activities and, therefore, the principle remained theoretical and less of a "risk" to these children and their parents.

Sentiments for the continuation of institutions were also expressed by the parents of children that Ellis, Moore, Taylor, and Bostick (1978) studied. Between the two residential extremes of total home care or long-term institutionalization, these authors evaluated an intermediate alternative: short-term institutionalization of severely and profoundly retarded children for the purpose of intensive training. This residential training program had the express goal of minimizing the likelihood of long-term institutional placement, of trying to assure that a child would be kept in the natural home once s/he had been returned there after the training. The plan in a sense backfired. Since the care and training provided during the short-term institutionalization (mainly in life skills like toileting, eating, and dressing) was of such a high quality, parents indicated that their attitudes to institutions had changed favorably as a result of the program. Of the 100 families, 65 percent reported that they would place their child permanently in an institution like the one Ellis et al. studied if it were available. Their experience with this institution made some parents aware of the positive benefits of an institutional program, both for the good of the child and the good of the family. Many parents appreciated the new-found "freedom" of having the child out of the home for the first time.

Ellis et al. found that, despite the training program, reinstitutionalization was highly related to whether the parents' long-range plans and initial intentions for their child had been long-term institutionalization or home care. Seventy-five percent of those who had originally intended institutionalization, and 35 percent of those who had intended home care, would eventually institutionalize their children, according to their rates of projection. Nevertheless, the short-term training did postpone placement up to 2 or 3 years for some of the children whose parents had initially intended to institutionalize them immediately.

Townsend and Flanagan (1976) intervened in the home situation, training parents to handle objectionable child behavior and providing counseling to the family. Even after these interventions, they too found that the initial intentions of parents to institutionalize a child were highly associated with the eventual outcome for the child, i.e., whether s/he remained at home or was placed in an institution.

Of Ellis et al.'s parents, 96 percent were opposed to phasing out institutions for severely and profoundly retarded children. Payne (1976) compares this sort of opposition to what Klaber (1969) found: that parents of persons in institutions were "convinced of the excellence of the facilities in which their children were placed" and that "the praise lavished on the institutions was so extravagant as to suggest severe distortions in reality in this area" (p. 180).

"DUMPING"

Pressure from the courts, the public, and state and federal governments to reduce the population of large institutions, to close down the "warehouses," to return the people living in institutions to useful lives in the community (President's Panel on Mental Retardation, 1962), has resulted in thousands of unprepared, untrained, handicapped individuals simply being moved out, as quickly as possible, without any existing support systems. This extremely serious situation of "dumping," existing in many communities, is a potential root for professional and public rejection of the deinstitutionalization movement. New facilities accepting disabled persons are usually smaller, but sometimes are indeed "institutions" in terms of the amount of authority and control exerted over residents' lives (Goffman, 1961), the amount of care provided, the amount of training scheduled, the number of restrictions and barriers existing, or the pleasantness of the immediate environment.

The possibility for opportunism exists even in (or perhaps especially in) services to previously excluded and devalued persons, as Edgerton (1975) has so clearly shown. Board and care facility operators are notorious for withholding information from residents about their rights to decide to leave or stay; keeping a full house is essential for maintaining a profit in those facilities licensed "for profit" rather than "not for profit." Edgerton found that most of the board and care facilities in his study were closed, ghettolike places. Individuals were walled off from access to community life: "The little institutions appear to be no better than the large ones from which they came, and some are manifestly worse" (p. 131).

The 1977 Comptroller General's report, *Returning the Mentally Retarded to the Community: Government Needs to Do More*, found that most of the individuals in their study were "deinstitutionalized" from institutions into nursing homes, where living conditions were worse than in the original institution. Most "treatment" consisted solely of medication, and readmission rates to the sponsoring institutions were high.

The community-placed clients in Collins and Hussain's (1977) study were overmedicated, suffered regressions in skill development, had no chance to participate in community activities, and were inappropriately placed into nursing homes. Incompetent staff held negative attitudes toward the clients. Severely retarded individuals were often placed in one chair or room for the entire day. Skarnulis (1976) found very shabby board and room situations for the retarded individuals he studied. They had much difficulty adjusting, and close proximity to other retarded clients led to inappropriate behaviors.

Birenbaum and Re (1977) found prosaic, boring, daily routines in boarding homes. Staff discouraged growth and independence. Residents had *less* participation in community activities than they had had while living in the institution, and many were extremely frustrated. Scheerenberger and Felsenthal (1977), in assessing the quality of community-based programs, reported that conformity, social isolation, and lack of transportation were critical deficiencies in many of these programs.

In researching another type of community residential facility, Browder, Ellis, and Neal (1974) found that half of 27 foster placements in 22 foster homes needed substantial improvement. The children were adversely affected by the health and emotional problems of the foster parents, by the large number of children present in the home, and by the unrealistic expectations of the foster parents. Both the children's in-home and out-of-home needs were deemed to be inadequately met, and frequent changes in placements were an additional burden on them.

In summarizing this morose situation, Scull (1977; as quoted by Ferleger, 1978) has charged that "The alternative to the institution has been to be herded into newly emerging 'deviant ghettoes,' sewers of human misery and what is conventionally defined as social pathology within which (largely hidden from outside inspection or even notice) society's refuse may be repressively tolerated'' (p. 41).

INCREASING READMISSIONS

Perhaps the most potent piece of evidence for charging that the deinstitutionalization movement is failing is the alarming trend of which Conroy (1977) warns: readmissions to institutions are increasing more rapidly than releases. (However, the absolute number of releases is still larger.) The pressure to empty institutions is outstripping the pressure to create adequate and sufficient normalizing alternatives, and it is becoming evident that much deinstitutionalization actually consists of interinstitutional relocation, rather than community placement. Individuals are being "deinstitutionalized," but not "integrated" into the community; or, as Galloway (1979) sees it, what is occurring is not *de*-institutionalization, but rather *trans*-institutionalization.

Scheerenberger (1977) notes that the *rate* of decline of total resident population in public residential facilities was less in 1976-1977 than it had been in the previous 3 years. The percent of decrease in the PRF population dropped from 4.3 percent in 1971 to 1.36 percent in 1976; the number of mentally retarded persons being returned to the community is decreasing and the number of readmissions is rising.

Sigelman and her associates (Sigelman, Bell, Schoenrock, Elias, & Danker-Brown, 1978) point to the mounting evidence against the quality of small residential facilities. The difficulties and problems encountered by small homes are numerous—low rates of reimbursement for house parents, lack of training for client rehabilitation, lack of support services, and lack of increase in clients' community living skills. The highest rates of reinstitutionalization are for clients placed in group homes and halfway houses. Sigelman et al. (1978), Gollay, Freedman, Wyngaarden, and Kurtz (1978), and Intagliata (1978) found that small group homes and foster homes are more normalized than large facilities, but are also less permanent. The lowest rates of return to the institution, among all the residential alternatives considered, were from natural homes and from independent living. Sigelman has concluded that the effectiveness of community residential facilities as habilitative settings has not been demonstrated, and notes that serious questions have been raised about "the state of the art" in deinstitutionalization.

Schalock (1978) has written of another current trend: that many facilities that are presumably "community-based" and "normalized" are, in essence, places without movement or future direction, dead-ends in themselves. When their ideology is not outward directed and forward moving, community facilities become imitative of the very institutions that they are supposed to be deinstitutionalizing. Schalock advocates more effective evaluation of the placements from and exits from community programs; a concerted effort needs to be made to integrate and mainstream beyond the present model of merely being "community"-based—another issue in the "state of the art" in community integration.

CONCLUSIONS

The deinstitutionalization movement is perhaps headed for serious crises and profoundly disturbing confrontations. The briefs filed in the *Wyatt v. Stickney* appeal in an Alabama deinstitutionalization case indicate one already disturbing disagreement and rift in the ranks of professional support for community integration. The "expert witnesses" who have filed this brief supporting the institution challenge the philosophical principles of "least restrictiveness" and the importance of individual habilitation. They assert that, in effect, deinstitutionalization is an unrealistic and unachievable goal for many severely and profoundly retarded individuals. In an age of high inflation and Proposition 13 conservatism, financial constraints seriously limit the possibilities for necessary high-quality training and high-intensity community support systems. As Rosenberg and Friedman (1979) analyzed this brief, professionals are becoming increasingly concerned that programming policy decisions are being taken out of their hands and transferred to the hands of lawyers and judges. Additionally, in almost none of the court-ordered class action decisions, whether regarding deinstitutionalization (*New York State Association for Retarded Citizens v. Rockefeller*, 1973; *Dixon v. Weinberger*, 1975) or education (*Mills v. Board of Education of the District of Columbia*, 1972; *Larry P. v. Riles*, 1972), have professionals and legislators rallied to fully implement the decisions and fully reform service systems as mandated.

As Biklen (1979) has noted, researchers, social planners, and decision makers have lodged serious complaints against deinstitutionalization: that it's merely a slogan with little empirical support; that some individuals cannot benefit from community placement and should receive only "enriched" custodial care in an institution; that the community will not accept severely and profoundly retarded individuals; that there is no evidence that disabled persons develop more in the community; that neither institutions nor community settings are inherently good or bad; that institutions are a more efficient way to provide services; and that current deinstitutionalization policy is but a temporary position of the historical, swinging pendulum of the community's treatment of "deviant" persons, and that soon institutions will become fashionable again, after the community thrust has run its course and failed.

Many possible avenues exist for developmentally disabled clients to fail after having been placed in the community: serious depressions and deaths among those who are emotionally vulnerable to any form of relocation, the dehumanizing and "institutional" conditions of some "community" facilities, and releases into the community without any preparatory training. There are also avenues available to the public to ensure failure of community placements, among them: resistance to the establishment of group homes, parental pressure to keep large institutions open, and the nonacceptance of those clients placed in the community, especially the ones who have not been trained to survive or to act "normal." In order for all individuals to be guaranteed their rights to maximum development, to life as close as possible to the normal, to dignity and well-being in the community, to life amid their fellow human beings, it is imperative that the deinstitutionalization movement succeed.

Parents must become comfortable with the concepts of "normalization" and "dignity of risk." The environmental factors that constitute "dumping" and that contribute to reinstitutionalization must be eliminated; it has been shown that these environmental factors, such as lack of adequate support systems and lack of training, rather than characteristics of handicapped individuals themselves, are responsible for the present failures of many community placements. Individuals who find it difficult to transfer into new living settings must be eased in with graduated transitions; the number of moves individuals are subjected to must be carefully limited. Multiple transfers between different group homes and different foster homes, for instance, contribute only to a loss of sense of home, sense of family, and ultimately sense of self.

Since every phenomenon in society has both positive and negative effects, the accumulation of visible negative effects of integrating developmentally disabled persons into the community must be diminished in order to prevent the rejection of the entire principle. Unless disabled individuals, their parents, facility staff, and the community are involved in more and better planning and preparation for deinstitutionalization, its few negative aspects will mass into a burdensome total weight that will bury the movement in public and professional consciousness.

Part V
CONCLUSIONS

Chapter 14
Implications for Direct Service Planning, Delivery, and Policy

James E. Martin and Thomas J. Laidlaw

This chapter summarizes the conceptual aspects of the previous chapters and draws implications from research findings and ideological principles for practice and policy relating to integration of developmentally disabled individuals into the community mainstream. Chapter citations are given (in parentheses) so that the reader can investigate a topic in more detail by referring to the fuller discussion in the chapter(s) so referenced. We hope that the conclusions that appear below will stimulate additional conceptualizing for planners and further action for practitioners.

JUSTIFICATION FOR COMMUNITY INTEGRATION

Empirical Support for Deinstitutionalization

Empirical evidence suggests that institutional life adversely affects human health, functioning, and ability (2). The earlier in their lives that children are admitted into an institution, the higher their mortality rate; these high mortality rates for very young children may result, in part, from the disease-prone, overcrowded conditions. Simultaneous maternal and environmental deprivation can result in severe mental retardation and psychological withdrawal in infants and toddlers (2). Subsequent environmental enrichment, however, can promote normal development, but, if the deprivation continues past 2 years of age, progressively greater permanent retardation may be the result. That is, the longer a preschool child is institutionalized, the lower his/her IQ will be. The effects of institutionalization on the development of older children and adults are less severe than those on infants and toddlers. Indeed, the changes that are measured and observed in older individuals seem to be due more to motivational factors than to cognitive changes per se (2). That is, institutionalized individuals are more interested in talking to the tester than they are in making a good score on a test. In terms of speech and language, individuals subjected to institutionalization have fewer language skills than those who are not. Also, mentally retarded individuals who are institutionalized develop poor self-concepts, and have large gaps between their real and ideal self-images. Despite the findings that institutionalization adversely affects social and intellectual functioning, there is little evidence that community integration becomes more difficult the longer an individual is institutionalized (2, 5).

Normalization and Egalitarianism

Integration of the developmentally disabled individual into the community is dependent on public support and political acknowledgment (1, 3, 7, 8, 11, 12). The current emphasis on normalization of the lives of disabled individuals is a result of the unravelling of complicated attitudes and values of our society (1, 3, 4, 7, 13, 15). The principle of normalization developed as the convergence of many values into the belief that means should be utilized that are as culturally normative as possible to establish and then maintain culturally normative behaviors (3, 4, 7, 10).

Normalization has fostered several tenets of applied practice: community-based programs should 1) be culturally normative; 2) develop expectations of participatory citizenship in the client population, and about the client population in the eyes of the community; 3) integrate facilities and activites into the community; 4) offer a continuum of independence and supervision; 5) separate services from one another; and 6) establish small housing arrangements (3, 4, 6, 8). Programs that are culturally normative are ones in which the roles, expectations, labels, and rhythms of daily life, work, and home environments of handicapped individuals are typical of those of the mainstream of society (4, 8). The establishment of expectations, both in handicapped individuals for themselves and in the eyes of others, is an important prelude to individual skill development, since willingness to grow and change one's role appears to be an important factor for successful community living (4, 7, 8). Developmentally disabled individuals should be integrated into the activities and generic functions of their communities, since segregation denies culturally normative opportunities (6, 7). Service components should be separate; the adult day-training classroom should be in a different location from the early childhood program; a domicile should be separate from a work environment or an environment where medical services are dispensed (4, 5, 6, 7). Community housing units should be small and similar to other types within a neighborhood (4, 5, 6, 7, 8).

Normalization as a humanistic ideology is a variation of the egalitarian tradition that has pervaded American history. It can be seen as regarding handicapped people as good and valuable, but weak. Their weakness is taken as justification for compensatory services to remediate initial frailty (3). The egalitarian position, as opposed to the principle of normalization, has slightly different implications for human services (3). Given the assertion that persons who have been labeled handicapped are simply manifesting individual differences that exist within the full, rich range of the human condition, the egalitarian position requires a continuum of generic services that can be utilized by every human being. Compensatory services that are provided as charity are seen to accentuate, segregate, and demean the very persons whom they are designed to help. The egalitarian alternative to compensatory charity is a guaranteed resource reservoir that *every* individual may, as a matter of right, draw on to purchase necessary services to facilitate his or her integration into the community at large.

Judicial and Legislative Directives

Numerous court decisions, legislative rules, and executive mandates have established a legal base for service delivery (11, 12, 13). The concept of the right to habilitation in the least restrictive environment is fundamental to this legal base. Habilitation for developmentally disabled citizens and its requisite corollary, quality training, have been mandated by courts and legislative bodies (1, 6, 8, 11, 12). Implementation of the principle of least restrictive environment requires that a continuum of residential settings and training modes must exist. For instance, a continuum ranging from quality skilled nursing homes to independent community apartments should be established statewide and nationally (4, 7, 8). In conjunction, an appropriate continuum of vocational services, ranging from sheltered to nonsheltered employment, will complement and perhaps precede the residential continuum because of the need for earned income (8).

The Rehabilitation Act of 1973 and its 1978 Amendments (11) synthesize previous judicial decisions and legislative advancements. The Act integrates vocational training and placement with community independent living training, so that developmentally disabled individuals can live independently to the greatest extent possible. It places top priority on vocational and residential training and placement and, in addition, provides funds to the states to facilitate the mandate. The legislative directives, for the most part, encourage novel training interventions, data-based training procedures, and control by the client or client's advocate. However, these directives have created many challenges, including the very intense opposition emerging in many neighborhoods across the country. Neighborhood control as manifested through zoning laws continues to constrain integration efforts (11, 12).

Service providers and local policy makers need to be concerned about the acceptance of handicapped individuals by the larger community (6, 7, 8, 13). Since our society stresses an individual's conformity to majority values, such as work and living standards, the disabled individuals who conform to the accepted work ethic and other values will be the most accepted (7). At the same time, the larger community must start reshaping its value systems to allow maximum acceptance of individual differences, to see differences as normal and acceptable variations of the human condition (3, 15).

In summary, judicial and legislative directives have established a framework for community service provisions. The emphases in this framework are: mandating treatment or training in the skills needed by the handicapped person to become integrated into the community, guaranteeing of rights, and assuring the maximum amount of independence in the least restrictive environment possible. Direct service providers need to establish high standards of program implementation in order to meet the intent of the various legal directives.

RECOMMENDED PRACTICES IN ESTABLISHING COMMUNITY RESIDENTIAL ALTERNATIVES

This section reviews the implications that relate to the practical issues in establishing community residential settings for developmentally disabled individuals. First, a brief account of typical community residential facilities is compared with a description of ideal community settings. This is followed by a review of various considerations in the establishment of a community residential facility, such as institutional release policies, economic concerns, training, coordination of support services, site and size selection, refocusing of state regulations, and staff training.

Characteristics of Community Residential Facilities (CRFs)

The most typical community living facility is a large (7 to 20 rooms) older house that is located in a medium-size metropolitan area in a residential or combined residential/small business area, with a large grocery store nearby (7). Many are in deteriorating neighborhoods in transitional urban zones (7). Most have been open for less than 5 years. Almost half of community facility residents report unavailable or inadequate transportation to be a major problem. About half of the people living in the facility come from their own (parents') homes and the other half come from institutions (1, 4, 5). Most facilities have some curfew or set bedtime, prohibit the consumption of alcohol, and restrict interactions with members of the opposite sex (7).

Physically, the ideal CRF should have the following characteristics: location in a pleasant and safe neighborhood, availability of public transportation, proximity to residents' places of employment, existence of specialized programs, and low cost (7). Research indicates that the best positive predictors of normalized living arrangements are: younger staff, highly educated staff, and recency of deinstitutionalization policies and programs (4). Another characteristic an ideal CRF should have, although it might seem to be of indirect benefit to the clients, is a sound evaluation technology. This technology should include measurement of a client's satisfaction with his/her placement; periodic determination of the client's level of functioning; assessment of others' satisfaction with the placement; analysis of residential climate; estimation of approximation to normalization; and measurement of the costs involved (10).

Establishment of a complete continuum of alternatives, with varying degrees of supervision and independence, is mandatory (4, 12); movement to the next level of independence, with its accompanying anticipation on the part of staff and residents, is also essential (5, 13). A description of a complete continuum of community residential alternatives is offered by the (Illinois) Governor's Planning Council on Developmental Disabilities (1977) (4). Types of residential settings suggested are: natural, adoptive, or foster homes; independent, supported, or supervised apartments; transitional, long-term, or specialized group homes; transitional, skilled nursing homes; and ranch/farm settings for a few severely emotionally disturbed individuals.

Release Policies and Client Characteristics

The methods used for the selection of individuals who are to be placed into the community, the characteristics of clients who are selected for placement, and the types of facilities selected all offer many implications for the establishment of successful CRFs. First, various factors relate to successful placement of clients. Personal appearance appears to be positively related to successful placement, as do high levels of functioning in vocational and in social skills. Individuals who are more active in sports are also more likely to be successful (5). Common sense would suggest that an individual's intellectual level would be a good predictor of successful community placement. However, IQ is related to some measures of community adjustment, but not to others. Individuals with higher IQs are more likely to be employed, are less likely to live at home, and are more active in programs and leisure activities. They are also more likely to be arrested than those individuals with lower IQs (5); but, in the authors' experience, there is a difference between being arrested and being caught in an illegal activity. If the culprit *appears* to be different in intellectual functioning from the rest of the local population, the legal authorities are less likely to press charges, especially involving misdemeanors.

As compared to the mildly retarded, severely retarded individuals have more support needs and are allowed less independence in their community residential alternatives. Yet, recent studies report that severely retarded persons are more likely to remain in the community and apparently have fewer unmet needs while living there (5). Possibly, environmental factors work to lessen the demands for independent functioning on those individuals labeled as severely retarded. Another reason for the inconsistent relationship between IQ and placement success is the higher prevalence of personality disorders among the less retarded. Therefore, IQ level should not be a major criterion for release (since severely retarded persons are able to succeed in the community with the appropriate support services); however, it should be considered in matching the client to the residential alternative so that the demands for independent functioning match the client's abilities. Environmental supports and client needs can be matched in order to maximize client-environment fit (5).

Possibly the most important factor in determining an individual's suitability for community placement is the desire the individual has for living in the community. Clients of any intellectual functioning level can live in the community as long as adequate supports are provided. Thus, individuals who have daily interactions with their caretakers are more successful in community living, and, conversely, more reinstitutionalization occurs when funds for support services decrease (6). Therefore, the primary consideration in selecting a client for release should be the match of his needs to the amount of support services the particular agency can afford to offer or can coordinate with other agencies.

Economic Considerations

Community service programs for developmentally disabled individuals are usually within the control of private corporations that are either "for profit" or "not for profit" (5, 13). The margin of profit is ordinarily drawn "off the top," directly from client and/or program funding; in contrast, the nonprofit model can presumably use all funds for client development. Unfortunately, client funding levels are often tied to the dependency of the client, providing an economic disincentive to client movement to more independent residential settings. Very likely, the absence of profit motive is a partial reason why individuals are more likely to progress to more independent settings if the residential programs are nonprofit (5). Thus, policy makers should consider establishing only nonprofit facilities and programs.

The majority of residents in the various studies reviewed in this volume work in sheltered workshops; only a small number are competitively employed (7). Since such a small number enjoy competitive employment, the income level of most CRF residents falls well below the U.S. median income, which directly affects clients' ability to afford independent living arrangements. However, with the combination of income transfer payments through various programs administered by the Social Security Administration and rent subsidies from county housing authority funds (HUD-Section 8), many developmentally disabled citizens are able to afford their own apartments (4, 11). Indeed, the public resources required to maintain the more able of these citizens in apartments are usually less than those required in other publicly supported settings (10).

Preparing Individuals for Community Integration

It appears evident that the majority of developmentally disabled individuals are able to reside in community living arrangements; however, a few will require extensive supervision in highly structured environments, both in transitional and more permanent arrangements (5, 8). Community placements alone will not provide the skills needed to live in a community setting; additional training is required for successful community integration.

The development of systematic programming of environmental antecedents and consequences of behavior have expanded our abilities to train community survival skills. Individual assessments are also needed in order to develop personalized training programs. Continued assessments, over time, can document client progress. The ability to travel independently, clean a house, prepare a meal, take medication, manage money, use a telephone, enjoy leisure time, and appropriately interact in social relationships are but some of the skills that have been acquired by developmentally disabled individuals (8). Acquisition of these community survival skills has facilitated successful community residential placement.

Successful integration will also depend, in part, on the acquisition of language communication skills (9). For instance, community living experiences will be enhanced by the ability to ask for information. The ability to follow simple and complex instructions must also be acquired and then generalized, since it is impossible to train an individual to respond to each and every instruction that could possibly be presented in a future community environment. Training retarded individuals to follow instructions seems to be within our current technology, in terms of our present understanding of such training procedures as instruction modification, prompt pacing, preinstructions, and verbal rehearsal. Expressive language is important for self-control of behavior and for engaging in conversation (9). Acquiring appropriate conversational abilities, with a particular focus on learning turn-taking and interaction skills, will facilitate interaction with nonhandicapped peers. In terms of both receptive and expressive communication, optimum training will depend on compilation of the minimum language and communication needs that the individual will have when s/he is integrated into the community. These needs dictate selection of language content for training. A careful analysis of the communication requirements of the community environment and a systematic application of training technology will result in successful and meaningful integrative social interactions.

In terms of preparing individuals for community integration, several researchers have also suggested methods for easing the transfer of individuals who might find it difficult to cope with the emotional stresses required in shifting to new living environments. These methods include: preparatory site visits to the new facility, involvement of the client in the actual move, involvement of the client's family, close concern by a personal advocate, and staff concentration on the affective as well as skill-training domains (13). Attention must be paid to gradual transitions and to limiting the number of moves an individual is subjected to in his/her life; multiple transfers contribute to a loss of sense of home, sense of family, and sense of self.

Support Services

Various support services are needed to integrate the developmentally disabled individual, as much as possible, into the mainstream of community life. The following services should be available: transportation, education and training, vocational habilitation, the opportunity for competitive employment, leisure and sports development, medical care, psychological counseling, and specialized therapies (1, 5, 6). A second group of services, which are of more indirect benefit to the clients, should also be available; these include home management (for parents), family/parental counseling, family education, homemaker services, and respite programs (1). Furthermore, relationships and friendships outside the facility, with identifiable "friends" and benefactors in the community, should be strongly encouraged, since these outside friendships correlate highly with success in remaining in the community (5, 7). An additional service, which must be provided by the agency sponsoring the residential alternative, is that of coordination of the various services mentioned above, so that the client population may receive optimum benefit from these services, especially from generic agencies. This coordination seems to be an absolute necessity if deinstitutionalization is to be successful.

The most active generic agency providing services to developmentally disabled persons on a voluntary basis is the church (6). Many other generic agencies offer a high level of services to handicapped individuals as a result of their funding; these include guidance and counseling centers, mental health clinics, family agencies, and sociorecreational centers. In principle, these agencies should be required to hire staff who are trained and interested in providing services to persons with developmental disabilities in order to receive funding.

Unfortunately, research indicates that in over half of the cases of readmissions to institutions, the primary cause of failure in community living is shortcomings in community services. The services provided by generic agencies are not available in sufficient quantity, are uncoordinated, have low visibility, are costly, and are delivered by agencies that are not used to dealing with developmentally disabled clients. Vocational training programs were reportedly difficult for a handicapped client to enter even when they could be located. Sociorecreational programs to assist clients in learning to use free time were lacking (6). Other reported deficits in community services include lack of trained professionals, inadequate transportation, inadequate distribution of services, lack of agency coordination, lack of any community services, and the unresponsive nature of generic agencies (1, 5, 6).

Facility Size

Size is an important factor to consider in the planning of a community residential facility; the building's relationship to the functioning levels of the prospective clients and the degree of autonomy it allows are inherent in its size. In matching a client's functioning level to a residential alternative, group homes should not be the only alternative considered for moderately and severely handicapped individuals, as opposed to independent or supervised apartments for mildly handicapped individuals. Other options for severely handicapped persons include apartments with additional support available; an example is a program in Omaha, Nebraska, that uses "live-in" friends as a support system for the disabled individual (7). Other options include 24-hour shifts for apartment staff, or staff accompanying the clients at all times except for sleeping and working hours.

If a group home is the most attractive choice for a residential alternative because of available funding sources and influential community groups, then size of the home should be given special attention. It has been found that group home size is negatively correlated with clients' autonomy and responsibilities within the group home, staff-to-resident ratio, and quality of work experience (5). There is evidence that small group homes are more normalized, but they are also less permanent options. Clients placed in foster homes, halfway houses, and small group homes have the highest rates of reinstitutionalization (5, 13). The lowest rates of return to institutions are from natural homes and independent living; this seems logical since these two alternatives are furthest from institutions on the continuum of residential alternatives for developmentally disabled individuals.

Site Selection

Besides size, site selection is an important concern in planning a CRF. The problems of choosing a site in an area that has easy accessibility to transportation and community services, has appropriate ordinances that allow unrelated persons to live in the same dwelling, and yet provides the possibility of a suitably normalized household environment were discussed in Chapters 1, 7, 11, and 12. Zoning codes vary from one community to another, but most communities treat family and group care facilities as special or conditional uses within the zoning district. This allows for the establishment of such facilities once it has been shown to the planning commission that the spirit of the ordinance is met by the proposed facility (11, 12).

It appears that most neighbors oppose facilities when they are proposed, but accept them once they are established (7). As a result of this initial opposition at the planning stage, many agencies attempt to establish a facility without informing the neighbors; an alternative approach is to select different methods for different settings. A recent study proposes that, in cases where a facility is planned in the suburbs or in a rural area, an informal canvass should be conducted to determine whether the community has recently fought the opening of a similar facility, to gauge the intensity of attitudes, to discover the existence of potentially antagonistic organizations, and to check the viewpoint of powerful people in the neighborhood. In heterogeneous neighborhoods in the inner city and in transitional zones, less care needs to be taken (7).

There is strong evidence that the closer individuals live to the institutions where they formerly resided, the more dependent they will remain on the institutional staff for their support services, and the more likely it is that they will eventually be reinstitutionalized (5, 6). Therefore, community facilities should be located at a reasonable distance from a client's former institution, and dependence for support services should be actively transferred to generic or specialized community agencies.

State Regulations

Other aspects in the establishment of a community residential facility are both compliance with and development of the various state regulations governing these facilities. The majority of these regulations concern the mundane details of physical plant specifications, dietary requirements, and medical requirements, rather than the more challenging aspects of structured and stimulating programming, staff requirements, and discharge and transfer policies (11). If the needs of the client population are to be met, this fixation with the custodial care model must be replaced with a focus on the developmental model. The 1977 Comptroller General's Report, *Returning the Mentally Retarded to the Community: Government Needs to Do More,* found that most of the individuals who were "deinstitutionalized" were placed in nursing homes where most "treatment" consisted of medication, and where the living conditions were worse than in the institutions (13).

Staff and Parent Training

Problems that have contributed to reinstitutionalization include: low rates of reinbursement for house parents, lack of training for clients, lack of increase in clients' community living skills, caretaker illness, and inadequacies in care provided. These staff-related factors, rather than any lack of client abilities, contribute substantially to the failure of community living (5). Several researchers have reported that staff training and development are the major problems cited by CRF administrators. In addition, parents of individuals returned to their natural homes have expressed disappointment and confusion over the lack of any training in handling their returned children (5). Parent counterreactions to the deinstitutionalization movement can also be seen as attributable to inadequacy of training in the ideological concepts of the principle of normalization and "the dignity of risk" (13). For the community placements of deinstitutionalized individuals to continue to succeed, continuous staff and parent training is mandatory (5, 13).

SUMMARY

This chapter summarized implications for direct service planning, delivery, and policy developments indicated by the research studies investigating community integration reported in earlier chapters. Ideological and empirical justifications for community integration were reviewed, as were judicial and legislative directives mandating deinstitutionalization and emphasizing the right to live in the least restrictive setting necessary. The range of living situations for individuals who have been "deinstitutionalized" was described, and the typical community living situation was compared with the ideal. Practices were recommended in response to such issues as: who should be released; how should individuals be prepared for integration; what support services need to be provided; how large should a community facility be and where should it be located; what state regulations need to be changed; what environmental factors contribute to successful placement; and other matters integral to the problems of how we can ensure that developmentally disabled individuals "make it" in the community.

Epilogue: A Perspective on the Present and Notes for New Directions

Angela R. Novak

> Now that you have broken through the wall with your head, what will you do in the neighboring cell?
> —S. J. Lee, *New Unkempt Thoughts*

The chapters in this book have centered on persons with developmental disabilities—their residences, services, rights, and training. However, additional commentary on their status and acceptance is necessary; "deinstitutionalization" needs to be put into the larger perspective of societal trends in currently dealing with those individuals perceived as and categorized as disabled and deviant. In these concluding statements about the field of "community integration," further suggestions must be made about our direction as a society. A step beyond our current practices needs to be taken.

It is seductively easy to list events and activities of recent years that could be viewed as outstanding achievements in this field: establishment of the constitutional right to treatment, court orders to close institutions, model systems and continua of living alternatives established, more training programs and training literature, the word "normalization" on everyone's lips, millions more in federal dollars available, the presence of dozens if not hundreds of formal advocacy organizations, and thousands of new buildings. Yet, what is the underlying implication of all of these "achievements"? Who has accomplished what? We, the professionals, have been doing and accomplishing all of these things *to* and *on* these handicapped persons, our clients. The accomplishments of persons with handicaps get buried under the accomplishments of professionals. Maybe we think things are better than they used to be, but it is still *us* doing it to *them;* and doing it *to* them under the guise of doing it *for* them. It is still the same old message being delivered: you are deficient, you have the problem. Even though you are living in a group home now rather than the institution (or are in an integrated school rather than a segregated one) the problem is still within you and your handicap. We, the trained professionals, are going to help you because you have your problem; we are going to help you learn in this special way and treat you in this special way because of your special handicap.

Our numbers are increasing and our roles are becoming more specialized. Special educators, vocational rehabilitation counselors, recreational therapists, program coordinators, group home managers, IPP coordinators, learning specialists, program specialists, feeding specialists, community living specialists... our numbers escalate, and consequently we seek out more and more clients to justify our numbers, to fill our work weeks, to get that training grant money, to build our new centers, to hire more staff, to justify the explosion in human services. As more people who deal with other people's needs get professional labels and get put on payrolls, more people in need come to them. More "clients" get more and more "needy." We have become a society of helpers helping helpees. Needs escalate, more money gets appropriated to fill them; but they are never salved, absolved, assuaged—they simply multiply. Hence our society of walking wounded, of dependent, unhappy, "needy" clients; and well-paid, middle-class, professionals who are equally "needy," who need more and more clients to justify their own existence.

As Farber and Lewis (1972) have noted, "We need the poor." We need the surplus population because they have become an industry. If the surplus population were suddenly removed, serious economic crises would result because of the large number of persons presently engaged in handling problems related to these surplus populations. We are suffering from the "necessity to manufacture needs in order to rationalize a service economy" (McKnight, 1977, p. 111). An economy based on service, such as ours, needs deficiency. The economic unit we need to keep our service economy booming is the individual; the maximal economic unit we need is an individual with multiple deficiencies and multiple problems. The circuit of manufacturing clients' needs to satisfy professionals' needs escalates, under the guise of caring for and helping people.

This overflow of needs in a service-based economy leads directly to two diseases. The first is Ryan's (1971) concept of "blaming the victim," analyzing social problems in terms of deficiencies that social victims have, and then developing programs that are aimed at correcting those victim deficiencies, rather than being aimed at changing the basic weaknesses and problems of society (such as racism, slum landlords, or the school system). In terms of helping those who are "not like us," Ryan describes what happens:

> The formula for action becomes extraordinarily simple: Change the victim. All of this happens so smoothly that it seems downright rational. First, identify a social problem. Second, study those affected by the problem and discover in what ways they are different from the rest of us as a consequence of deprivation and injustice. Third, define the differences as the cause of the social problem itself. Finally, of course, assign a government bureaucrat to invent a humanitarian action program to correct the differences. (p. 8)

In schools we focus on a child's failure to learn to read rather than on the school s/he attends or her/his teaching. We help poor, adolescent, unwed mothers adjust to impossible life circumstances of unemployment, welfare, housing projects, and single mothering, rather than trying to change the circumstances that created those conditions. The poor remain stubbornly unhealthy, and we blame their poverty, despite their living in a country with a health care system claimed to be one of the best in the world. With retarded or other developmentally disabled individuals, it is particularly easy to blame the handicap or "low functioning level" for how that individual is dressed, what kind of widgets s/he is putting together for 13¢ an hour, or for the fact that s/he is living with 12, or 60, or 1200 other people rather than with one or two, or three or four other people, like the rest of us.

It is easy to see the problem as lying within individuals (in their handicaps), and not in our perception of them or in the various aspects of society that create and continually increase their problems, including their contacts with, reliance on, and dependence on professionals to help them. Thus, it is easy to justify our model of treating, training, social-working, supervising disabled individuals with their individual problems in order to get them to "be productive members of society" and "fit in." It is so easy with handicapped persons to fall into the "we and they" trap (Wicker, 1975), since "they really do have a handicap"; it is easy to continue to believe that the "clients" must be diagnosed, taught, rehabilitated, or changed in some way in order to allow them to quietly accept their places in society. All of our training, educational, and residential models are geared to this end: spending as much money, effort, and training as possible under the guise of trying to make our clients (students, trainees, residents) "normalized," to make them look and act like us, to get them jobs, homes, and identities that are acceptable, contributiong to society, and non-noticeable. We say we want an individual to be just another worker, apartment resident, grocery store customer. We force the standard of normality down their throats, and continue to oppress them with our inability to accept human differences.

We continue to believe that it's possible to have enough time, money, energy, or people to really solve the problem. What we failed to do for Blacks (Head Start, integrated schools), for prisoners (rehabilitation programs, social work, counseling), and for the poor (the War on Poverty), we now think we can accomplish for the handicapped, with more money, programs, staff, and lawsuits. For a few years, devotion to "the cause" will be high, but, as it becomes known that expensive programs are not accomplishing what they claimed, interest will wane, it will seem that "it's not worth the price"—in an age when even programs for "normal" schoolchildren and "normal" adults seem to not be working, and in an age of high inflation and Proposition 13 conservativeness (Rosenberg & Friedman, 1979).

The belief that, given enough, it is possible to solve the problem means that the problem continues to be defined as: what we need to change is individual members of society rather than the "rules of the game" (Watzlawick, Weakland, & Fisch, 1974). In the helping services the myth that the problem is solveable, given enough time and money, is perpetuated by the emphasis on professionals helping people. This leads to the second disease: iatrogenesis, or doctor-created disease (McKnight, 1977). By our very presence as treaters of the problem (in the individual) we contradict our ethos of having him or her be normal. By our very presence as professionals needing clients to treat, we create more clients. We create new "diseases," such as learning disabilities and child abuse, to create more social programs and more professionals to treat them. We have more policemen and more lawyers and we have more crime; we have more social workers and we have more family collapse; we have more special education teachers and we have more special education students. Thus, we are caught in the trap of treating the disease we created.

We work for a system that tends, as every system does, to functionally maintain itself. We stay plugged in to our clients, conducting Child Find studies to locate more, reluctant to release individuals from our care, unwilling to (saying that "we can't") train them to total independence, unwilling to release them from agency lists (because that would confound our follow-up research), reluctant to rely on generic services, saying that they are unqualified to serve the handicapped, and instead creating more and more specialized services— everywhere wanting to advance the well-being of our own professions, and unwilling to face a decrease in our numbers.

As long as we continue to see the problem as resting within the individual client, only principles of individual change will be applied and what will be continued will be efforts to change performance only at the individual level. However, in addition, we need to begin to focus change efforts and energy at the organizational, institutional, community, and societal levels (Reiff, 1971). The more effort we put into perpetuating change only at the individual client level, the more change there will be within a system that itself stays invariant. (The more things change, the more they remain the same.) We will be suffering from Farber and Lewis's (1972) concept of "progressive status quoism," where a symbolic attack on a problem without an attempt to deal with its genuine root fosters the illusion that *something* is being done (we are making progress) when actually very little is being accomplished (the status quo is being maintained).

Many professionals currently believe that their challenge is to help handicapped persons "fit in," be culturally normative, integrate into our community, and "be productive members of society," but perceiving the challenge in that way still implies: there is something wrong with you. The principle of normalization implies and panders to the belief: we will not rest until you have a "normal" life at least as good as that of the average citizen. The focus of normalization is minimizing the projection of deviancy by an individual, rather than working toward changing the perceptions and values of the perceivers—those who create the deviancy in the first place. The focus of normalization is enhancing currently devalued individuals, rather than changing the process of what is valued and what is devalued. We try to fit people into already existing structures, rather than evaluating what is wrong with a social system that does not accept an individual as s/he is. The problem remains the clients and what to do with them. Many members of the helping professions, including community integrationists, are simply agents of the status quo.

This volume could end with a plea for better and more research, for better and more services, for better and more training, so that more individuals could "make it" in the community, but the ethic of pouring "more" into "half-empty vessels" won't change the basic operating principle, the modus operandi, the status quo, or the "rules of the game" (Watzlawick et al., 1974). As McKnight has written, "The basic function of modernized professionalism is to legitimize human beings whose capacity is to see their neighbors as half-empty" (Galloway, 1979, p. 7). The real challenge to our profession and our society is the revolution in consciousness that is necessary. We must refocus our present attempts to assimilate individuals into closed settings, and instead focus on accommodating and accepting individual differences. We must, as representatives of society, accept the pluralism, cultural diversity, and cultural relativism of a healthy society where ecologically appropriate settings maximize person-environment fit (Rappaport, 1977). A "celebration of deviance" (Illich, 1971; Laing, 1967, 1969) is a starting point on this path toward open systems and "new environments" (Sarason, 1972). Wolfensberger's (1972) "interpretive level" on the "dimension of social systems" is another starting point: "shaping cultural values, attitudes, and stereotypes so as to elicit maximal feasible cultural acceptance of differences" (p. 32).

We must begin to employ a psychology of social change that differs from one based on fitting people into existing structures. Work must begin and continue toward an egalitarian, pluralistic society that values equal access to resources (see Chapter 3 of this volume). The conversion of citizens to "clients" must stop. The people now perceived as "socially marginal" must be provided with the resources, the power, and the control over their own lives that is "necessary for a society of diversity, rather than of conformity" (Rappaport, 1977). Nicholas Kittrie (1971) in *The Right to be Different,* summarizes the issue:

> A realistic and pluralistic society must recognize, furthermore, that unless it is willing to pay the price for total conformity, it must learn to tolerate its deviants. (p. 295)

In terms of application to practice, as a minimum beginning, residential, vocational, and educational services must be integrated. "Handicapped" persons must live, work, shop, exist where all persons do. The community must accept the "deviant" neighbor or the "disabled" employee with equanimity, with the perception of his/her value rather than his/her difference. "Professionals" must apply the principle that what is okay for *me* is the only thing okay for "them." Instead of focusing on what alternatives must be constructed for those individuals who have disabilities, we must ask, "How much do we have to *compromise* on the most natural and valued living, educational, and vocational arrangements to increase this person's opportunity and ability to participate as a valued member of our community?" (Galloway, 1979, p. 6). Rather than a legitmate set of alternatives, our services should be perceived as a set of compromises on the possible best. We will then, with humility, work toward reducing the degrees of compromise.

We must switch from models of pity, resistance, or "helping," to ones of respect and dignity. We must tear down the curtain between "client" and "professional," between "handicapped" and "nonhandicapped," between "special" and "normal." We are all handicapped; we are all normal. "We and they" must give way to a celebration and quiet acceptance of the multitudinous, varied "we."

> The way out is through the door. Why is it that no one will use this exit?
> —Confucius

References

Abramson, E. E., & Wunderlich, R. A. Dental hygiene training for retardates: An application of behavioral techniques. *Mental Retardation*, 1972, *10*, 6-8.

Achenbach, T., & Zigler, E. Cue learning and problem learning strategies in normal and retarded children. *Child Development*, 1968, *3*, 827-848.

Adams, M. E. Foster care for mentally retarded children: How does child welfare meet this challenge. *Child Welfare*, 1970, *49*, 260-269.

Adams, M. *Mental retardation and its social dimensions*. New York: Columbia, 1971.

Adams, M. Foster family care for the intellectually disadvantaged child: The current state of practice and some research perspectives. In M. J. Begab & S. A. Richardson (Eds.) *The mentally retarded and society: A social science perspective*. Baltimore: University Park Press, 1975.

Aldrich, C., & Mendkoff, E. Relocation of the aged and disabled: A mortality study. *Journal of the American Geriatric Society*, 1963, *11*, 185-195.

Ames, T. R., & Levy, J. M. The hostel: Plans and purposes. *Journal of Rehabilitation*, 1973, *39* (3), 28-30.

Aninger, M. & Bolinsky, K. Levels of independent functioning of retarded adults in apartments. *Mental Retardation*, 1977, *15* (4), 12-13.

Aninger, M., Growick, B., & Bolinsky, K. *Individual community placement of deinstitutionalized retarded adults: Some personal concerns*. Paper presented at the annual convention of the American Association on Mental Deficiency, Denver, May, 1978.

APA Monitor. NIMH eyes new support systems: Seeking the missing rungs in the service ladder. 1977, *8*, 1-11.

Arnold, I., & Goodman, L. Homemaker services to families with young retarded children. *Children*, 1966, *13*, 149-152.

Azrin, N. H., & Foxx, R. M. A rapid method of toilet training the institutionalized retarded. *Journal of Applied Behavior Analysis*, 1971, *4*, 89-99.

Azrin, N. H., Schaeffer, R. M., & Wesolowski, M. D. A rapid method of teaching profoundly retarded persons to dress by a reinforcement-guidance method. *Mental Retardation*, 1976, *14*, 29-34.

Baer, D. M., Wolf, M., & Risley, T. R. Some current dimensions of applied behavior analysis. *Journal of Applied Behavior Analysis*. 1968, *1*, 91-98.

Baker, B. L., Seltzer, G. B., & Seltzer, M. *As close as possible*. Cambridge, MA: Behavioral Education Projects (Harvard Univ.) 1974.

Baker, B., Seltzer, G., & Seltzer, M. *As close as possible*. Boston: Little, Brown, and Co., 1977.

Baker, F., & Schulberg, H. C. The development of a community mental health ideology scale. *Community Mental Health Journal*, 1967, *3*, 216-225.

Ball, T. S., Seric, K., & Payne, L. E. Long-term retention of self-help skill training in the profoundly retarded. *American Journal of Mental Deficiency*, 1971, *76*, 378-382.

Balla, D. Relationship of institution size to quality of care: A review of the literature. *American Journal of Mental Deficiency,* 1976, *81* (2), 117-124.

Balla, D., Butterfield, E. C., & Zigler, E. Effects of institutionalization on retarded children: A longitudinal cross-institutional investigation. *American Journal of Mental Deficiency,* 1974, *78,* 530-549.

Balthazar, E. E. *Balthazar scales of adaptive behavior. Section II: Scales of social adaptation.* Palo Alto, CA: Consulting Psychologists Press, 1973.

Balthazar, E. E. *Balthazar Scales of adaptive behavior. Section I: Scales of functional independence.* Palo Alto, CA: Consulting Psychologists Press, 1976.

Bank-Mikkelsen, N. Metropolitan area in Denmark-Copenhagen. In R. B. Kugel & W. Wolfensberger (Eds.), *Changing patterns in residential services for the mentally retarded.* Washington, D.C.: President's Committee on Mental Retardation, 1969.

Baroff, G. *On "size" and quality of institutional care: Another interpretation.* Paper presented at the 102nd annual meeting of the American Association on Mental Deficiency, Denver, May, 1978.

Barrett, B. Behavior analysis. In J. Wortis (Ed.), *Mental retardation and development disabilities,* Vol. 9. New York: Brunner-Mazel, 1977.

Bassett, J. E., & Blanchard, E. B. The effect of the absence of close supervision on the use of response cost in a prison token economy. *Journal of Applied Behavior Analysis,* 1977, *10,* 375-380.

Bassuk, E. L., & Gerson, S. Deinstitutionalization and mental health services. *Scientific American,* 1978, *238,* 46-53.

Bates, E. *Language and context: The acquisition of pragmatics.* New York: Academic Press, 1976. (a)

Bates, E. Pragmatics and sociolinguistics in child language. In D. M. Morehead and A. E. Morehead (Eds.), *Normal and deficient child language.* Baltimore: University Park Press, 1976. (b)

Bates, E., Benigni, L., Bretherton, I., Camaioni, L., & Volterra, V. From gesture to first word: On cognitive and social prerequisites. In M. Lewis & L. A. Rosenblum (Eds.), *Interaction, conversation and the development of language.* New York: John Wiley, 1977.

Bates, P. Community transition: A behavioral approach with the severely/profoundly retarded and their families. *AAESPH Review,* 1977, *2,* 217-223.

Bauman, K. E., & Iwata, B. A. Maintenance of independent housekeeping skills using scheduling plus self-recording procedures. *Behavior Therapy,* 1977, *8,* 554-560.

Beck, H. L. Casework with parents of mentally retarded children. *American Journal of Orthopsychiatry,* 1962, *32,* 870-877.

Becker, W., Engelmann, S., & Thomas, D. *Teaching 2: Cognitive learning and instruction.* Chicago: Science Research Associates, 1975.

Bedrosian, J. L., & Prutting, C. A. Communicative performance of mentally retarded adults in four conversational settings. *Journal of Speech and Hearing Research,* 1978, *21,* 79-95.

Bell, N. IQ as a factor in community lifestyle of previously institutionalized retardates. *Mental Retardation,* 1976, *14* (3), 29-33.

Bellak, L. *Community psychiatry and community mental health.* New York: Grune, 1964.

Bellamy, G. T. *Habitation of severely and profoundly retarded adults.* Research and Training Center in Mental Retardation, University of Oregon, 1976.

Bellamy, T., & Buttars, K. L. Teaching trainable level retarded students to count money: Toward personal independence through academic instruction. *Education and Training of the Mentally Retarded,* 1975, *10,* 18-26.

Bellamy, G. T., Horner, R. H., & Inman, D. P. *Vocational Habilitation of Severely Retarded Adults.* Baltimore: University Park Press, 1979.

Bellamy, G. T., Peterson, L., & Close, D. Habilitation of the severely and profoundly retarded: Illustrations of competence. *Education and Training of the Mentally Retarded*, 1975, *10*, 174–187.

Bender, M., & Vallettuti, P. *Teaching the moderately and severely handicapped: Curriculum objectives, strategies, and activities*, (Vol. I). Baltimore: University Park Press, 1976.

Berdiansky, H., & Parker, R. Establishing a group home for the adult mentally retarded in North Carolina. *Mental Retardation*, 1977, *15* (4), 8–11.

Bernard, J. Cost benefit analysis and mental retardation center funding. *Mental Retardation*, 1979, *17*, 156–157.

Bernstein, C. Advantages of colony care of mental defectives. *Psychiatric Quarterly*, 1927, *1*, 419–425.

Berry, P. B., Andrews, R. J., & Elkins, J. *An evaluative study of educational, vocational, and residential programs for the moderately to severely mentally handicapped in three states*. St. Lucia, Queensland, Australia: Fred & Eleanor Schonell Educational Research Centre, University of Queensland, 1977.

Biklen, D. *The community imperative: A refutation of all arguments in support of institutionalizing anybody because of mental retardation*. Center on Human Policy, Syracuse University, 1979.

Birenbaum, A., & Re, M. A. Resettling mentally retarded adults in the community—almost four years later. *American Journal of Mental Deficiency*, 1979, *83*, 323–329.

Birenbaum, A., & Seiffer, S. *Resettling retarded adults in a managed community*. New York: Praeger, 1976.

Birnbrauer, J. S. Mental retardation. In H. Leitenberg (Ed.), *The handbook of behavior modification and behavior therapy*. Englewood Cliffs, N.J.: Prentice Hall, 1976.

Bishop, E. B. Family care: The patients. *American Journal of Mental Deficiency*, 1957, *61*, 583–591.

Bishop, E. B. Family care: Boarding homes. *American Journal of Mental Deficiency*, 1959, *63*, 703–706.

Bjaanes, A. T., & Butler, E. W. Environmental variation in community care facilities for mentally retarded persons. *American Journal of Mental Deficiency*, 1974, *78* (4), 429–439.

Blatt, B., & Kaplan, F. *Christmas in Purgatory: A photographic essay in mental retardation*. Boston: Allyn and Bacon, 1966.

Bloom, B. L. *Community mental health: A general introduction*. Monterey, CA: Brooks/Cole, 1977.

Bock, W. M., & Weatherman, R. F. *Minnesota developmental programming system*. Revised edition. Minneapolis: University of Minnesota, 1976.

Boggs, E. Legal aspects of mental retardation. In I. Phillips (Ed.), *Prevention and treatment of mental retardation*. New York: Basic Books, 1966.

Boggs, E. M. Chronicle. In J. Wortis (Ed.), *Mental Retardation: An Annual Review, III*. New York: Grune & Stratton, 1971. (a)

Boggs, E. M. Federal legislation: 1955–1965. In J. Wortis (Ed.), *Mental Retardation: An Annual Review, III*. New York: Grune & Stratton, 1971. (b)

Boggs, E. M. Federal legislation: 1966–1971. In J. Wortis (Ed.), *Mental Retardation: An Annual Review, IV*. New York: Grune & Stratton, 1972.

Bourestrom, N., & Tars, S. Alterations in life patterns following nursing home relocation. *The Gerontologist*, 1974, *14*, 506–510.

Bowlby, J. *Maternal care and mental health*. World Health Organization, 1951.

Bradley, V. J. *Deinstitutionalization of developmentally disabled persons*. Baltimore: University Park Press, 1978.

Brickey, M. A behavioral procedure for teaching self-medication. *Mental Retardation,* 1978, *16,* 29-32.

Bronfenbrenner, U. Early deprivation in monkey and man. In U. Bronfenbrenner (Ed.), *Influences on human development.* Hinsdale, IL: Dryden Press, 1972.

Browder, J., Ellis, L., & Neal, J. Foster homes: Alternatives to institutions? *Mental Retardation,* 1974, *12,* 33-36.

Brown, J. S., & Guard, K. A. The treatment environment for retarded persons in nursing homes. *Mental Retardation,* 1979, *17* (2), 77-82.

Brown, L., Bellamy, T., & Sontag, E. *The development and implementation of a public school prevocational training program for trainable retarded and severely emotionally disturbed children.* Madison, Wisconsin: Madison Public Schools, 1971.

Brown, L., Nietupski, J., & Hamre-Nietupski, S. The criterion of ultimate functioning. In M. A. Thomas (Ed.), *Hey, don't forget about me!* Reston, Virginia: The Council for Exceptional Children, 1976.

Browning, R. M., & Stover, D. O. *Behavior modification in child treatment.* New York: Atherton, 1971.

Bruininks, R. H., Hauber, F. A., & Kudla, M. J. *National survey of community residential facilities: A profile of facilities and residents in 1977.* Minneapolis, MN: University of Minnesota, Department of Psychoeducational Studies, 1979. Also available in *American Journal of Mental Deficiency,* 1980, *84,* (5), 470-478.

Bruininks, R. H., Kidla, M. J., Wieck, C. A., & Hauber, F. A. *Management problems in community residential facilities.* Unpublished manuscript. 1979.

Bruininks, R. H., Rynders, J. E., & Gross, J. C. Social acceptance of mildly retarded pupils in resource rooms and regular classes. *American Journal of Mental Deficiency,* 1974, *78* (4), 377-383.

Bruner, J. S. The ontogenesis of speech acts. *Journal of Child Language,* 1975, *2,* 1-19.

Budoff, M., & Gottlieb, J. Special-class EMR children mainstreamed: A study of an aptitude (learning potential) treatment interaction. *American Journal of Mental Deficiency,* 1976, *81* (1), 1-11.

Bundschuh, E. L., Williams, W., Hollingworth, J., Gooch, S., & Shirer, C. Teaching the retarded to swim. *Mental Retardation,* 1972, *10,* 14-17.

Burgdorf, R. L. *The legal rights of handicapped persons.* Baltimore: Paul H. Brookes Publishers, 1980.

Burmeister, J. G. Leisure services and the cultural arts as therapy for the mentally retarded individual. *Therapeutic Recreation,* 1976, *10,* 139-142.

Burton, T. Mental health clinic services to the retarded. *Mental Retardation,* 1971, *9* (3), 38-41.

Butler, E. W., & Bjaanes, A. T. Activities and the use of time by retarded persons in community care facilities. In G. P. Sackett (Ed.), *Observing behavior: Theory and applications in mental retardation.* Baltimore: University Park Press, 1978.

Butterfield, E. A provocative case of over-achievement by a mongoloid. *American Journal of Mental Deficiency,* 1961, *66,* 444-448.

Butterfield, E. Some basic changes in residential facilities. In R. B. Kugel & A. Shearer (Eds.), *Changing patterns in residential services for the mentally retarded.* Washington, D.C.: President's Committee on Mental Retardation, 1976.

Butterfield, E. C. Institutionalization and its alternatives for mentally retarded people in the United States. *International Journal of Mental Health,* 1977, *6,* 21-34.

Cain, L. F., Levine, S., & Elzey, F. F. *Manual for the Cain-Levine Social Competency Scale.* Palo Alto, CA: Consulting Psychologists Press, 1963.

Carhill, K. G., Rader, L. C., & Schonfeld, H. Level of retardation as a factor in the successful family care placement of mentally retarded children. *Psychiatric Social Work Review,* 1967, *1* (9).

Chandler, J., & Ross, S. Zoning restrictions and the right to live in the community. In M. Kindred, J. Cohen, D. Penrod, & T. Shaffer (Eds.), *The mentally retarded citizen and the law.* New York: The Free Press, 1976.

Chapanis, A., & Williams, W. C. Results of a mental survey with the Kuhlmann-Anderson intelligence tests in Williamson County, Tennessee. *Journal of Genetic Psychology,* 1945, *67*, 27-55.

City of White Plains v. Ferraioli, 34 N. Y. 2d 300, 313 N. E. 2d, 375 N.Y.S. 2d 449, 1974.

Clarke, A. B. D., & Clarke, A. M. How constant is the IQ? *Lancet,* 1953, *265*, 877-880.

Clarke, A. D. B., & Clarke, A. M. Cognitive changes in the feebleminded. *British Journal of Psychology,* 1954, *45*, 173-179.

Clarke, A. D. B., Clarke, A. M., & Reiman, S. Cognitive and social changes in the feebleminded: Three further studies. *British Journal of Psychology,* 1958, *49*, 144-157.

Clarke, A. M., & Clarke, A. D. B. *Early experience: Myth and evidence.* London: Open Books, 1976.

Close, D. W. Community living for severely and profoundly retarded adults: A group home study. *Education and Training of the Mentally Retarded,* 1977, *3*, 256-262.

Cobb, H. V. *The forecast of fulfillment.* New York: Teachers College Press, 1972.

Cochran, W., Sran, P., & Varano, G. The relocation syndrome in mentally retarded individuals. *Mental Retardation,* 1977, *15* (2), 10-12.

Coffman, T. L., & Harris, M. C. *Transition shock and the deinstitutionalization of the mentally retarded citizen.* Paper presented at the annual meeting of the American Association on Mental Deficiency, Denver, May, 1978.

Cohen, H. J. Obstacles to developing community services for the mentally retarded. In M. J. Begab & S. A. Richardson (Eds.), *The mentally retarded and society: A social science perspective.* Baltimore: University Park Press, 1975.

Cohen, H., Conroy, J., Frazer, D., Snelbecker, G. E., & Sprent, S. Behavioral effects on interinstitutional relocation of mentally retarded residents. *American Journal of Mental Deficiency,* 1977, *82* (1), 12-18.

Cohen, J. S., Butter, I., Deline, S., & Nutter, R. E. *Benefit-cost analysis for mental retardation programs.* Ann Arbor, MI: Institute for the Study of Mental Retardation and Related Developmental Disabilities, undated (c1971).

Collins, S. H., & Hussain, S. B. *Can communities provide all services to the retarded? Maybe: An institution's efforts to work with communities.* Paper presented at the annual meeting of the American Association on Mental Deficiency, New Orleans, May, 1977.

Comptroller General. *Returning the mentally disabled to the community: Government needs to do more.* Washington, D. C.: United States General Accounting Office, 1977.

Conley, R. W. *The economics of mental retardation.* Baltimore: Johns Hopkins University Press, 1973.

Connecticut Association for Retarded Citizens v. Mansfield Training School. Civil Action No. H-78-653, D. Conn., 1979.

Conroy, J. W. Trends in deinstitutionalization of the mentally retarded. *Mental Retardation,* 1977, *15* (4), 44-46.

Cortazzo, A., & Sansone, R. Travel training. *Teaching Exceptional Children,* 1969, *3*, 67-82.

Cotten v. Evangelist Temple Homes. Civil No. J. 78-0045 U.S. District Ct. for Southern Dist. of Miss., 1974.

Cotter, V. Effects of music on performance of manual tasks by retarded adolescent females. *American Journal on Mental Deficiency,* 1971, *76*, 242-248.

Council for Exceptional Children: Handicapped Children in Head Start Series. *Utilizing resources in the handicapped services field: A directory of Head Start personnel.* Reston, VA: Council on Exceptional Children, 1974.

Crissey, O. L. The mental development of children of the same IQ in differing institutional environments. *Child Development,* 1937, *8,* 217-220.

Crnic, K. A., & Pym, H. A. Training mentally retarded adults in independent living skills. *Mental Retardation,* 1979, *17* (1), 13-16.

Crosby, K. G. Attention and distractibility in mentally retarded and intellectually average children. *American Journal of Mental Deficiency,* 1972, *77,* 46-53.

Crosson, J. E. A technique for programming sheltered workshop environments for training severely retarded workers. *American Journal of Mental Deficiency,* 1969, *73,* 814-818.

Cuvo, A. J., Leaf, R. B., & Burakove, L. S. Teaching janitorial skills to the mentally retarded: Acquisition, generalization and maintenance. *Journal of Applied Behavior Analysis,* 1978, *11,* 345-355.

Danker-Brown, P., Sigelman, C., & Bensberg, G. J., Jr. Advocate-protege: Pairings and activities in three citizen advocacy programs. *Mental Retardation,* 1979, *17* (3), 137-141.

Datel, W. E., & Murphy, J. G. A service-integrating model for deinstitutionalization. *Administration in Mental Health,* 1975, Spring, 35-45.

Davidson, P., Clark, F., & Hamerlynck, G. *Evaluation of behavioral programs in community, residential and school settings.* Champaign, IL: Research Press, 1974.

Davies, S. P. *The mentally retarded in society.* New York: Columbia, 1959.

Davis, K. Final note on a case of extreme isolation. *American Journal of Sociology,* 1947, *52,* 432-437.

Dayton, N. A. Mortality in mental deficiency over a fourteen year period: Analysis of 8976 cases and 878 deaths in Massachusetts. *Journal of Psycho-Asthenics,* 1931, *36,* 127-212.

Dayton, N., Doering, C. R., Hilferty, M. M., Maher, H. C., & Dolan, H. H. Mortality and expectation of life in mental deficiency in Massachusetts: Analysis of the fourteen-year period 1917-1930. *New England Journal of Medicine,* 1932, *206,* 555-570 and 616-631.

Demaine, G., Wilson, S., Silverstein, A., & Mayeda, T. *Facility ratings based on a tested organizational nomenclature and a validated PASS 3.* Paper presented at the annual meeting of the American Association on Mental Deficiency, Denver, May, 1978.

Dennis, W. Causes of retardation among institutional children. *Journal of Genetic Psychology,* 1960, *96,* 47-59.

Dennis, W. *Children of the Crèche.* New York: Appleton-Century-Crofts, 1973.

Dennis, W., & Najarian, P. Infant development under environmental handicap. *Psychological Monographs,* 1957, *71,* No. 7.

Dennis, W., & Sayegh, Y. The effect of supplementary experiences upon the behavioral development of infants in institutions. *Child Development,* 1965, *36,* 81-90.

Department of Health, Education, and Welfare. *A summary of selected legislation relating to the handicapped, 1963-1967.* Washington, D. C.: United States Government Printing Office, 1968.

De Silva, R., & Faflak, P. From institution to community—a new process? *Mental Retardation,* 1976, *14* (6), 25-28.

Dixon v. Weinberger. 405 F. Supp. 974 (D.D.C. 1975).

Dokecki, P. R., Strain, B., Bernal, J., Brown, C., & Robinson, M. E. Low-income and minority group children and families. In N. R. Hobbs (Ed.), *Issues in the classification of children: A sourcebook on categories, labels and their consequences.* San Francisco: Jossey-Bass, 1975.

Doll, E. A. *The measurement of social competence.* Educational Test Bureau, 1953.

Doll, E. A historical survey of research and management of mental retardation in the United States. In E. P. Trapp & P. Himelstein (Eds.), *Readings on the exceptional child.* New York: Appleton, 1962.

Doll, E. A. *Vineland Social Maturity Scale: Condensed manual of directions.* 1965 edition. Circle Pines, MN: American Guidance Service, Inc., 1965.

Driscoll v. Goldberg. No. 72-C1 1258 (Mahoning Co. Ct. of Comm. Pleas), 1970. 73 C. A. (Ohio Ct. of Appeals, 7th D.) 1974.

Eagle, E. Prognosis and outcome of community placement of institutionalized retardates. *American Journal of Mental Deficiency,* 1967, *72,* 232-243.

Edgerton, R. B. *The cloak of competence: Stigma in the lives of the mentally retarded.* Berkeley: University of California Press, 1967.

Edgerton, R. B. Issues relating to the quality of life among mentally retarded persons. In M. J. Begab & S. A. Richardson (Eds.), *The mentally retarded and society: A social science perspective.* Baltimore: University Park Press, 1975.

Edgerton, R. B., & Bercovici, S. The cloak of competence: Years later. *American Journal of Mental Deficiency,* 1976, *80* (5), 485-497.

Edwards, A. L. *Techniques of attitude scale construction.* New York: Appleton-Century-Crofts, Inc., 1957.

Eichenbaum, B., & Bednarek, N. Square dancing and social adjustment. *Mental Retardation,* 1964, *2,* 105-109.

Ellis, N., Moore, S., Taylor, J., & Bostick, G. *A follow-up of severely and profoundly retarded children after short-term institutionalization.* Unpublished manuscript, University of Alabama, February, 1978.

English, R. W. Correlates of stigma towards physically disabled persons. *Rehabilitation Research and Practice Review,* 1971, *2* (4), 1-18.

Erikson, K. T. *Wayward Puritans: A study in the sociology of deviance.* New York: Wiley, 1966.

Eyman, R., & Call, T. Maladaptive behavior and community placement of mentally retarded persons. *American Journal of Mental Deficiency,* 1977, *82* (2), 137-144.

Eyman, R. K., Demaine, G. C., & Lei, T. Relationship between community environments and resident changes in adaptive behavior: A path model. *American Journal of Mental Deficiency,* 1979, *83,* 330-338.

Eyman, R. K., O'Connor, G., Tarjan, G., & Justice, R. S. Factors determining residential placement of mentally retarded children. *American Journal of Mental Deficiency,* 1972, *76,* 692-698.

Eyman, R. K., Silverstein, A. B., McLain, R., & Miller, C. Effects of residential settings on development. In P. Mittler & J. M. deJong (Eds.), *Research to practice in mental retardation: Vol. 1, Care and prevention.* Baltimore: University Park Press, 1977.

Fanning, F. Coordinating community services. *Mental Retardation,* 1973, *11* (6), 46-47.

Fanshel, D. *Toward more understanding of foster parents.* Unpublished doctoral dissertation, New York School of Social Work, Columbia University, 1960.

Fanshel, D. Specializations within the foster care role: A research report. Part II: Foster parents caring for the "acting out" and the handicapped child. *Child Welfare,* 1961, *40* (4), 19-23.

Farber, B., & Lewis, M. Compensatory education and social justice. *Peabody Journal of Education,* 1972, *49,* 85-95.

Ferleger, D. The future of institutions for retarded citizens: The promise of the Pennhurst case. *Mental Retardation and the Law,* July, 1978. Washington, D. C.: President's Commission on Mental Retardation. (DHEW publication No. (OHD) 78-21012.)

Ferrara, D. S. Attitudes of parents of mentally retarded children toward normalization activities. *American Journal of Mental Deficiency,* 1979, *84* (2), 145-151.

Festinger, T. B. The impact of the New York court review of children in foster care: A followup report. *Child Welfare*, 1976, *55*, 515-544.

Fiorelli, J. S., & Thurman, S. K. Client behavior in more and less normalized residential settings. *Education and Training of the Mentally Retarded*, 1979, *14* (2), 85-94.

Fisher, M. A., & Zeaman, D. Growth and decline of retardate intelligence. In N. R. Ellis (Ed.), *International review of research in mental retardation*. Vol. 4, New York: Academic Press, 1970.

Floor, L., Rosen, M., Baxter, D., Horowitz, J., & Weber, C. Socio-sexual problems in mentally handicapped females. *Training School Bulletin*, 1971, *68*, 106-112.

Flynn, R. J. *Assessing human service quality with PASS 2: An empirical analysis of 102 service program evaluations*. Toronto: National Institute on Mental Retardation, 1975.

Flynn, R. J. Normalization, PASS, and service quality assessment: How normalizing are current human services. In R. J. Flynn & K. E. Nitsch (Eds.), *Normalization, social integration, and community services*. Baltimore: University Park Press, 1980.

Flynn, R. J., & Heal, L. W. *Psychometric properties of Wolfensberger and Glenn's PASS 3 and other measures of the cost-effectiveness analysis of residential alternatives for developmentally disabled citizens*. Paper presented at the Gatlinburg conference on Research in Mental Retardation/Developmental Disabilities, Gatlinburg, TN, March, 1980.

Foster, R. W. *Camelot Behavioral Checklist Manual*. Parsons, Kansas: Camelot Behavioral Systems, 1974.

Fredericks, H. D., Baldwin, V. L., Heyer, M., Alrick, B., Bunse, C., & Samples, B. *Teaching research curriculum for severely handicapped adolescents and adults*. Monmouth, Oregon: Instructional Development Corporation, in press.

Freedman, R. Approaches to defining and measuring the community adjustment of mentally retarded persons: A review of the literature. Vol. I of *A study of the community adjustment of deinstitutionalized mentally retarded persons*. Contract No. OEC-0-74-9183, U. S. Office of Education. Cambridge, MA: Abt Associates, Inc., 1976.

Friedenburg, W. P., & Martin, A. S. Prevocational training of the severely retarded using task analysis. *Mental Retardation*, 1977, *15*, 16-20.

Frisch, S. A., & Schumaker, J. B. Training generalized receptive prepositions in retarded children. *Journal of Applied Behavior Analysis*, 1974, *7*, 611-621.

Galloway, C. Hearing: Impact of continuum of services on people with disabilities. Testimony to the California Senate Subcommittee on the Disabled. Sacramento, Oct. 29, 1979.

Garber, H., & Heber, F. R. The Milwaukee Project: indications of the effectiveness of early intervention in preventing mental retardation. In P. Mittler (Ed.), *Research to practice in mental retardation: Care and intervention*. Vol. 1. Baltimore: University Park Press, 1977.

Gardner, J. M. Community residential alternatives for the developmentally disabled. *Mental Retardation*, 1977, *15* (6), 3-8.

Garrett, B. Foster family services for mentally retarded children. *Children*, 1970, *17*, 228-233.

Gelman, S. A system of services. In C. Cherington & G. Dybwad (Eds.), *New neighbors: The retarded citizen in quest of a home*. Washington, D. C.: U. S. Government Printing Office, 1974.

General Accounting Office. GAO urges greater effort on community care. Washington, D.C.: Report to the Congress, Department of Health, Education, and Welfare, January, 1977.

Gilhool, R. K. Notes for PARC Executive Committee and chapters on the Court of Appeals opinion in the *Pennhurst* case. Public Interest Law Center of Philadelphia, December 20, 1979.

Gilhool, R. K. Notes for PARC Executive Committee and chapters on the Court of Appeals opinion in the *Pennhurst* case. December 20, 1979.
Goffman, E. *Asylums*. Garden City, N. Y.: Anchor Books, 1961.
Gold, M. Stimulus factors in skill training of the retarded on a complex assembly task: Acquisition, transfer, and retention. *American Journal of Mental Deficiency*, 1972, *76*, 517–526.
Gold, M. Task analysis of a complex assembly task by the retarded blind. *Exceptional Children*, 1976, *43*, 78–84.
Goldfarb, W. The effects of early institutional care on adolescent personality. *Journal of Experimental Education*, 1943, *12*, 106–129.
Goldfarb, W. Effects of psychological deprivation in infancy and subsequent stimulation. *American Journal of Psychiatry*, 1945, *102*, 18–33.
Goldfarb, W. Variations in adolescent adjustment of institutionally reared children. *American Journal of Orthopsychiatry*, 1947, *17*, 449–457.
Goldfried, M., & Davison, G. *Clinical behavior therapy*. New York: Holt, Rinehart, and Winston, 1976.
Goldstein, H. Social and occupational adjustment. In H. A. Stevens & R. Heber (Eds.), *Mental Retardation*. Chicago: University of Chicago Press, 1964.
Gollay, E. *An analysis of factors associated with community adjustment*. Vol. V. of *A study of the community adjustment of deinstitutionalized mentally retarded persons*. Contract No. OEC-0-74-9183, U. S. Office of Education, Cambridge, MA: Abt Associates, Inc., 1976.
Gollay, E., Freedman, R., Wyngaarden, M., & Kurtz, N. R. *Coming back*. Cambridge, Mass.: Abt Books, 1978.
Goroff, N. N. Research on community placement—An exploratory approach. *Mental Retardation*, 1967, *5*, 17–19.
Gottesfeld, H. Alternatives to psychiatric hospitalization. *Community Mental Health Review*, 1976, *1*, 1–10.
Gottlieb, J. Public, peer, and professional attitudes toward mentally retarded persons. In M. J. Begab & S. A. Richardson (Eds.), *The mentally retarded and society: A social science perspective*. Baltimore: University Park Press, 1975.
Gottlieb, J., & Corman, L. Public attitudes toward mentally retarded children. *American Journal of Mental Deficiency*, 1975, *80*, 72–80.
Gottwald, H. *Public awareness about mental retardation*. Arlington, VA: Council on Exceptional Children, 1970.
Governor's Planning Council on Developmental Disabilities. *Community living alternatives for persons with developmental disabilities. Vol. I: The model system*. Springfield, IL: GPCDD, 1977.
Green, C., & Zigler, E. Social deprivation and the performance of retarded and normal children on a satiation type task. *Child Development*, 1962, *33*, 499–508.
Grice, H. P. Logic and conversation. In P. Cole & J. L. Morgan (Eds.), *Syntax and semantics, Vol. 3: Speech acts*. New York: Academic Press, 1975.
Grossman, H. J. (Ed.) *Manual on terminology and classification in mental retardation*. Washington, D.C.: American Association on Mental Deficiency, 1973.
Grunewald, K. A rural county in Sweden: Malmöhus county. In R. B. Kugel & W. Wolfensberger (Eds.), *Changing patterns in residential services for the mentally retarded*. Washington, D.C.: President's Committee on Mental Retardation, 1969.
Guess, D., Keogh, W., & Sailor, W. Generalization of speech and language behavior: Measurement and training tactics. In R. L. Schiefelbusch (Ed.), *Bases of language intervention*. Baltimore: University Park Press, 1978.
Guess, D., Sailor, W., & Baer, D. M. *Functional speech and language training for the severely handicapped. Parts 1 and 2*. Lawrence, KS: H & H Enterprises, 1976.

Guess, D., Sailor, W., & Baer, D. M. A behavioral-remedial approach to language training for the severely handicapped. In E. Sontag, J. Smith, & N. Certo (Eds.), *Educational programming for the severely and profoundly handicapped.* Reston, VA: Division on Mental Retardation, Council for Exceptional Children, 1977.

Guess, D., Sailor, W., & Baer, D. M. *Functional speech and language training for the severely handicapped. Parts 3 and 4.* Lawrence, KS: H & H Enterprises, 1978.

Gunzburg, H. C. *Progress Assessment Chart of social and personal development: Manual.* 3rd edition. Birmingham, England: SEFA (Publications) LTD, 1974.

Halderman et al. v. Pennhurst State School et al. Civil Action No. 74-1345, U. S. District Court, Eastern District of Pennsylvania, 1978.

Hamilton, J., Allen, P., Stephens, L., & Davall, E. Training mentally retarded females to use sanitary napkins. *Mental Retardation,* 1969, *7,* 40–43.

Hamre, S. An approximation of an instructional model for developing home living skills in severely handicapped students. In L. Brown, W. Williams, & T. Crowner (Eds.), *A collection of papers and programs related to public school instruction for severely handicapped students. Vol. IV.* Madison, WI: Madison Public Schools, 1974.

Hamre-Nietupski, S., & Williams, W. W. Implementation of selected sex education and social skills to severely handicapped students. *Education and Training of the Mentally Retarded,* 1977, *12,* 364–372.

Hanson, M. Evaluations of training procedures used in a parent implemented intervention program for Down's syndrome infants. *AAESPH Review,* 1976, *1,* 36–52.

Harasymiw, S., Horne, M., & Lewis, S. A longitudinal study of disability group acceptance. *Rehabilitative Literature,* 1976, *37* (4), 98–102.

Harlow, H. F., Schiltz, K. A., & Harlow, M. K. The effects of social isolation on the learning performance of rhesus monkeys. In C. R. Carpenter (Ed.), *Proceedings of the second international congress of primatology.* Vol. 1. New York: Karger, 1969.

Harrelson, L. E. *A Guttman facet analysis of attitudes toward the mentally retarded in the Federal Republic of Germany: Content, structure, and determinants.* Unpublished doctoral dissertation, Michigan State University, 1970.

Harris, J. M., Veit, S. W., Allen, G. J., & Chinsky, J. M. Aide-resident ratio and ward population density as mediators of social interaction. *American Journal of Mental Deficiency,* 1974, *79,* 320–326.

Harris, S. L. Teaching language to nonverbal children: With emphasis on problems of generalization. *Psychological Bulletin,* 1975, *82,* 565–580.

Harris-Vanderheiden, D., & Vanderheiden, G. C. Basic considerations in the development of communicative and interactive skills for non-vocal severely handicapped children. In E. Sontag, J. Smith & N. Certo (Eds.), *Educational programming for the severely and profoundly handicapped.* Reston, VA: Division on Mental Retardation, Council on Exceptional Children, 1977.

Harter, S. Mental age, IQ, and motivation factors in the discrimination learning set performance of normal and retarded children. *Journal of Experimental Child Psychology,* 1967, *5,* 123–141.

Harter, S., Brown, L., & Zigler, E. Discrimination learning in retarded and nonretarded children as a function of task difficulty and social reinforcement. *American Journal of Mental Deficiency,* 1971, *76,* 275–283.

Harth, R. Attitudes and mental retardation: Review of the literature. *Training School Bulletin,* 1973, *69,* 150–164.

Hartzler, E. A follow-up study of girls discharged from the Laurelton State Village. *American Journal of Mental Deficiency,* 1951, *55,* 612–618.

Hartzler, E. A ten-year survey of girls discharged from the Laurelton State Village. *American Journal of Mental Deficiency,* 1953, *57,* 512–518.

Hauber, F., Kudla, M., Wieck, C., & Anderson, D. 1977 Survey completed: Community residential findings summarized. *Developmental Disabilities Project on Residential Services and Community Adjustment, 1* (2), December, 1978.

Hauber, F., Kudla, M., Wieck, C., Masiee, E., & Kirwin, D. 1977 National survey between public and community residential findings. *Developmental Disabilities Project on Residential Services and Community Adjustment, 1*(3), March, 1979.

Heal, L. W., & Daniels, B. S. *A cost-effectiveness analysis of residential alternatives for selected developmentally disabled citizens of three northern Wisconsin counties.* Paper presented at the annual meeting of the American Association on Mental Deficiency, Denver, May, 1978.

Heal, L. W., Sigelman, C. K., & Switzky, H. N. Research on community residential alternatives for the mentally retarded. In N. R. Ellis (Ed.), *International review of research in mental retardation*, Vol. 9. New York: Academic Press, 1978.

Henshel, A. *The forgotten ones. A sociological study of Anglo and Chicano retardates.* Austin: University of Texas Press, 1972.

Hersh, A, & Brown, G. Preparation of mental health personnel for the delivery of mental retardation services. *Community Mental Health Journal,* 1977, *13* (1), 13-23.

Hill, B., & Bruininks, R. H. *Assessment of behavioral characteristics of people who are mentally retarded.* Minneapolis: University of Minnesota Department of Psychoeducational Studies, 1977.

Hill, B. K., Sather, L. B., Kudla, M. J., & Bruininks, R. H. *A survey of the types of residential programs for mentally retarded people in the United States in 1978.* Unpublished report, Dept. of Psychoeducational Studies, University of Minnesota, Minneapolis, 1978.

Hirsch, N. D. M. An experimental study of the east Kentucky mountaineers. *Genetic Psychology Monographs,* 1928, *3,* 183-244.

Hobbs, M. A comparison of institutionalized and non-institutionalized mentally retarded. *American Journal of Mental Deficiency,* 1964, *69,* 206-210.

Hobbs, N. *The futures of children.* San Francisco: Jossey-Bass, 1975.

Holmes, R. F. Characteristics of five community living arrangements serving mentally retarded adults in southwestern urban Pennsylvania. *Mental Retardation,* 1979, *17* (3), 181-183.

Holowinsky, I. IQ constancy in a group of institutionalized mental defectives over a period of three decades. *Training School Bulletin,* 1962, *59,* 15-17.

Holt, K. S. Home care of retarded children. In J. J. Dempsey (Ed.), *Community services for retarded children: The consumer-provider relationship.* Baltimore: University Park Press, 1975.

Hopperton, R. *Zoning for community homes: Handbook for local legislative change.* Columbus, OH: Law Reform Project, Ohio State University, Nov., 1975. (a)

Hopperton, R. *Zoning for community homes: A handbook for municipal officials.* Columbus, OH: The Law Reform Project, Ohio State University, Dec., 1975. (b)

Horejsi, C. R. *Deinstitutionalization and the development of community based services for the mentally retarded: An overview of concepts and issues.* Washington, D. C.: Educational Resources Information Center (ERIC), 1975.

Humm-Delgado, D. *Community living for mentally retarded persons: Community residences for adults in Massachusetts.* Paper presented at the annual convention of the American Association on Mental Deficiency, Denver, May, 1978.

Humm-Delgado, D. Opinions of community residence staff about their work responsibilities. *Mental Retardation,* 1979, *17* (5), 250-251.

Hunter, J., & Bellamy, T. Cable harness construction for severely retarded adults: A demonstration of a training technique. *AAESPH Review,* 1976, *1,* 2-13.

Huttenlocher, J. The origins of language comprehension. In R. L. Solso (Ed.), *Theories in cognitive psychology: The Loyola symposium*. Potomac, Md.: Lawrence Earlbaum Associates, 1974.

Hynes, J., & Young, J. Adolescent group for mentally retarded persons. *Education and Training of the Mentally Retarded*, 1976, *11*, 226-231.

Illich, I. *Celebration of awareness*. New York: Doubleday, 1971.

Intagliata, J. *Use of family care homes as a community placement for mentally retarded persons in New York State*. Paper presented at the annual convention of the American Association on Mental Deficiency, Denver, May, 1978.

Intagliata, J. C., Willer, B. S., & Cooley, F. B. Cost comparison of institutional and community-based alternatives for mentally retarded persons. *Mental Retardation*, 1979, *17*, 134-136.

Intagliata, J., Willer, B., & Wicks, N. *Factors related to the quality of community adjustment in family care homes*. Paper presented at the Conference on Community Adjustment, Minneapolis, March, 1979. Conference proceedings, *American Association on Mental Deficiency*, Monograph No. 4, in press.

Irvin, L. K. General utility of easy to hard discrimination training procedures with the severely retarded. *Education and Training of the Mentally Retarded*, 1976, *11*, 247-250.

Israel, A. C. Some thoughts on correspondence between saying and doing. *Journal of Applied Behavior Analysis*, 1978, *11*, 271-276.

Israel, A. C., & O'Leary, K. D. Developing correspondence between children's words and deeds. *Child Development*, 1973, *44*, 575-581.

Jackson, J. Factors of the treatment environment. *Archives of General Psychiatry*, 1969, *21*, 39-45.

Jaslow, R. *A modern plan for modern services to the mentally retarded*. Washington, D.C.: U.S. Government Printing Office, 1967.

Jens, K., & Shores, R. Behavioral graphs as reinforcers for work behavior of mentally retarded adolescents. *Education and Training of the Mentally Retarded*, 1969, *4*, 21-26.

Johnson, J. L., & Mithaug, D. E. A replication of sheltered workshop entry requirements. *AAESPH Review*, 1978, *3*, 116-122.

Joint Commission on Mental Illness and Health. Action for Mental Health. Summarized in Comptroller General, *Returning the mentally disabled to the community: Government needs to do more*. Washington, D. C.: United States General Accounting Office, 1977.

Jones, K. J., & Jones, P. P. *The measurement of community placement success and its associated costs. Interim Report 2*. Medford, MA: Florence Heller School for Advanced Studies in Social Welfare, Brandeis University, 1976. (a)

Jones, P. P., & Jones, K. J. *Costs of ideal services to the developmentally disabled under varying levels of adequacy. Interim Report Number 4*. HEW Contract OS-74-278. Medford, MA: Florence Heller School, Brandeis University, 1976. (b)

Justice, R., Bradley, J., & O'Connor, G. Foster family care for the retarded: Management concerns for the caretaker. *Mental Retardation*, 1971, *9* (4), 12-15.

Kadushin, A. *Child welfare services*. New York: Macmillan, 1967.

Kagan, J. Resilience and continuity in psychological development. In A. M. Clarke & A. D. B. Clarke (Eds.), *Early experience: Myth and evidence*. London: Open Books, 1976.

Kaplan, O. L. Mental decline in older morons. *American Journal of Mental Deficiency*, 1943, *47*, 277-285.

Karan, O. C., Wehman, P., Renzaglia, A., & Schutz, R. *Habilitation practices with the severely developmentally disabled.* Rehabilitation Research and Training Center, University of Wisconsin, 1976.

Karlan, G. R., & Rusch, F. R. *Some "additional" thoughts on correspondence between saying and doing.* Unpublished manuscript, University of Illinois, 1980.

Karlan, G. R., Rusch, F. R., & Menchetti, B. M. Social and communication survival skills for employment. In F. R. Rusch (Ed.), *Vocational Habilitation of the Mentally Retarded Adult in Nonsheltered Settings: Research Report 1978-1980.* University of Illinois at Urbana, 1980.

Kastner, L. S., Reppucci, N. D., & Pezzoli, J. J. Assessing community attitudes toward mentally retarded persons. *American Journal of Mental Deficiency,* 1979, *84* (2), 137-144.

Kaufman, M. E. The formation of a learning set in institutionalized and non-institutionalized mental defectives. *American Journal of Mental Deficiency,* 1963, *67,* 601-605.

Kazdin, A. E. Assessing the clinical or applied importance of behavior change through social validation. *Behavior Modification,* 1977, *1,* 427-457.

Keating, R. The war against the mentally retarded. *New York,* September 17, 1979.

Kelly, N., & Menolascino, F. Physicians' awareness and attitudes toward the retarded. *Mental Retardation,* 1975, *13* (6), 10-13.

Kenowitz, L., & Edgar, E. Intra-community action networks: The ICAN system. *Mental Retardation,* 1977, *15* (3), 13-16.

Kephart, N. C., & Strauss, A. A. A clinical factor influencing variations in IQ. *American Journal of Orthopsychiatry,* 1940, *10,* 343-351.

Keys, V., Boroskin, A., & Ross, R. The revolving door in a MR hospital: A study of returns from leave. *Mental Retardation,* 1973, *11* (1), 55-56.

Kindred, M., Cohen, J., Penrod, D., & Shaffer, T. (Eds.) *The mentally retarded citizen and the law.* New York: The Free Press, 1976.

King, R. D., & Raynes, N. V. An operational measure of inmate management in residential institutions. *Social Science and Medicine,* 1968, *2,* 41-53. (a)

King, R. D., & Raynes, N. C. Patterns of institutional care for the severely subnormal. *American Journal of Mental Deficiency,* 1968, *72,* 700-709. (b)

King, R. D., Raynes, N. V., & Tizard, J. *Patterns of residential care: Sociological studies in institutions for handicapped citizens.* London: Routledge & Kegan Paul, 1971.

Kirk, S. A., & Therrien, M. E. Community mental health myths and the fate of former hospitalized patients. *Psychiatry,* 1975, *38,* 209-217.

Kittrie, N. *The right to be different: Deviance and enforced therapy.* Baltimore: The Johns Hopkins Press, 1971.

Klaber, M. M. The retarded and institutions for the retarded: A preliminary research report. In S. B. Sarason & J. Doris (Eds.), *Psychological problems in mental deficiency.* New York: Harper & Row, 1969.

Koluchova, J. Severe deprivations in twins: A case study. *Journal of Child Psychology and Psychiatry,* 1972, *13,* 107-114.

Koluchova, J. A report on the further development of twins after severe and prolonged deprivation. In A. M. Clarke & A. D. B. Clarke (Eds.), *Early Experience: Myth and evidence.* London: Open Books, 1976.

Kramer, M., Person, P. H., Tarjan, G., Morgan, R., & Wright, S. W. A method for determination of probabilities of stay, release, and death, for patients admitted to a hospital for the mentally deficient: The experience of Pacific State Hospital during the period 1948-1952. *American Journal of Mental Deficiency,* 1957, *62,* 481-495.

Kraus, J. Supervised living in the community and residential and employment stability of mental retarded male juveniles. *American Journal of Mental Deficiency,* 1972, *77,* 283–290.

Krishef, C. H. The influence of rural-urban environment upon the adjustment of dischargees from the Owatonna State School. *American Journal of Mental Deficiency,* 1959, *63,* 860–865.

Krishef, C. H., Reynolds, M. C., & Stunkard, C. L. A study of factors related to rating post-institutional adjustment. *Minnesota Welfare,* 1959, *11,* 5–15.

Kurtz, R. A. Advocacy for the mentally retarded: The development of a new social role. In M. J. Begab & S. A. Richardson (Eds.), *The mentally retarded and society: A social science perspective.* Baltimore: University Park Press, 1975.

Kurtz, R. A., & Wolfensberger, W. Separation experiences of residents in an institution for the mentally retarded: 1910–1959. *American Journal of Mental Deficiency,* 1969, *74,* 389–396.

Laing, R. *The politics of experience.* New York: Pantheon, 1967.

Laing, R. *The divided self.* New York: Pantheon, 1969.

Lambert, C. *Typologies of adaptive behaviors in community settings.* Paper presented at the annual meeting of the American Association of Mental Deficiency, Toronto, June, 1974.

Langworthy, R., Anderson, C., Bryne, K., Hathaway, P., Holum, B., & Swenson, R. *Program procedures manual.* Boulder, Montana: Boulder River School and Hospital, 1974.

Larry P. v. Riles. Civil No. C-71-2270, N.D. CA, 343 F. Supp. 1306, 1972.

Lauber, D., & Bangs, F. S. *Zoning for family and group care facilities.* Planning Advisory Service Report No. 300. Chicago: American Society of Planning Officials, 1974.

Layard, R. *Cost benefit analysis.* Baltimore: Penguin Books, 1972.

Leff, R. B. Teaching the TMR to dial the telephone. *Mental Retardation,* 1974, *12,* 12–13.

Lent, J. R. Mimosa cottage: Experiment in hope. *Psychology Today,* 1968, *2,* 51–58.

Lent, J. R., Holvoet, J. F., Ferneti, C. L., Keilitz, I., & Tucker, D. J. Direction-following of retarded and non-retarded adolescents. *American Journal of Mental Deficiency,* 1973, *78,* 316–322.

Lessard v. Schmidt. Civil Action No. 71-C-602. U. S. District Court, Eastern District of Wisconsin, 1972.

Levin, H. M. Cost-effectiveness analysis in evaluation research. In M. Guttentag & E. L. Struening (Eds.), *Handbook of evaluation research.* Beverly Hills, CA: Sage Foundation, 1975.

Lewis, J. F. The community and the retarded: A study in social ambivalence. In G. Tarjan, R. K. Eyman, & C. E. Meyers (Eds.), *Sociobehavioral studies in mental retardation. Papers in honor of Harvey F. Dingman.* Monograph No. 1. Washington, D. C.: American Association on Mental Deficiency, 1973.

Lind, E. B., & Kirman, B. H. Imbecile children. *British Medical Journal,* 1958, *2,* 743–751.

Lippincott, M. K. A sanctuary for people: Strategies for overcoming zoning restrictions on community homes for retarded persons. *Stanford Law Review,* 1979, *31* (4), 767–783.

Little Neck Community Association v. Working Organization for Retarded Children. N.Y. Sup. Ct. App. Div., 2nd Dept., May 3, 1976.

Lovaas, O. I., & Bucher, B. (Eds.) *Perspectives in behavior modification with deviant children.* Englewood Cliffs, N. J.: Prentice-Hall, 1974.

Lowe, M., & Cuvo, A. Teaching coin summation to the mentally retarded. *Journal of Applied Behavior Analysis,* 1976, *9,* 483–489.

Luria, A. R. *The role of speech in the regulation of normal and abnormal behavior.* New York: Liveright, 1961.
MacMillan, D. *Mental retardation in school and society.* Boston: Little, 1977.
MacMillan, M. B. Adjustment and process: A neglected feature of follow-up studies of retarded people. *American Journal of Mental Deficiency,* 1963, *68,* 345-353.
Madison, H. L. Work placement success for the mentally retarded. *American Journal of Mental Deficiency,* 1964, *69,* 50-53.
Mamula, R. The use of developmental plans for mentally retarded children in foster family care. *Children,* 1971, *18,* 65-68.
Mamula, R. A., & Newman, N. *Community placement of the mentally retarded: A handbook for community agencies and social work practitioners.* Springfield, Ill.: Charles C Thomas, 1973.
Marholin, D., Touchette, P., Berger, P., & Doyle, D. I'll have a Big Mac, large fries, large coke, and an apple pie—or teaching adaptive community skills. *Behavior Therapy,* 1979, *10,* 236-248.
Martin, A. S., & Flexer, R. W. *Three studies on training work skills and work adjustment with the severely retarded.* Research and Training Center in Mental Retardation, Texas Tech. University, 1975.
Martin, G. L. The future for the severely and profoundly retarded: Kin Kare? Foster homes? *The Canadian Psychologist,* 1974, *15,* 188-241.
Martin, G. L., Kehoe, B., Bird, E., Jensen, V., & Darbyshire, M. Operant conditioning in dressing behavior of severely retarded girls. *Mental Retardation,* 1971, *9,* 27-31.
Mayeda, T., & Wai, F. *The cost of long-term developmental disabilities care.* Pomona, CA: UCLA Research Group at Pacific State Hospital, 1975.
Maynard, M. The value of creative arts for the developmentally disabled child: Implications for recreation therapists in community day service programs. *Therapeutic Recreation Journal,* 1976, *10,* 10-13.
McCarver, R. B., & Craig, E. M. Placement of the retarded in the community: Prognosis and outcome. In N. R. Ellis (Ed.), *International Review of Research in Mental Retardation,* Vol. 7. New York: Academic Press, 1974.
McCormick, M., Balla, D., & Zigler, E. Resident care practices in institutions for retarded persons: A cross-institutional, cross-cultural study. *American Journal of Mental Deficiency,* 1975, *80,* 1-17.
McDaniel, C. O. Extra-curricular activities as a factor in social acceptance among EMR students. *Mental Retardation,* 1971, *10,* 26-28.
McGunigle, D. Speech performance of mentally retarded as related to selected aspects of hospitalization. *American Journal of Mental Deficiency,* 1967, *71,* 558-560.
McKnight, J. The professional service business. *Social Policy,* 1977, *8* (3), 110-116.
Meichenbaum, D. H. Cognitive factors in behavior modification: Modifying what clients say to themselves. In R. D. Rubin, J. P. Brady, & J. D. Henderson (Eds.), *Advances in behavior therapy,* Vol. 4. New York: Academic Press, 1973.
Mental Disability Law Reporter. *Zoning for community residences.* Sept.-Dec. 1977, 315-327.
Mercer, J. R. Patterns of family crisis related to reacceptance of the retardate. *American Journal of Mental Deficiency,* 1966, *71,* 19-32.
Meyer, G. A. Twelve years of family care at Belchertown State School. *American Journal of Mental Deficiency,* 1951, *55,* 414-417.
Miller, C. R. Deinstitutionalization and mortality trends for the profoundly retarded. In C. Cleland & L. Talkington (Eds.), *Research with profoundly retarded: Conference proceedings.* Austin, Texas: Western Research Conference, 1975.
Miller, D., & Lieberman, M. A. The relationship of affect state and adaptive capacity to relations to stress. *Journal of Gerontology,* 1965, *20,* 492-497.

Mills v. Board of Education of the District of Columbia. United States District Court for the District of Columbia, 348 F. Supp. 866, 1972.

Mithaug, D. E. Case studies in the management of inappropriate behaviors during prevocational training. *AAESPH Review*, 1978, *3*, 132-144. (a)

Mithaug, D. E. Case study in training generalized instruction-following responses to preposition-noun combinations in a severely retarded young adult. *AAESPH Review*, 1978, *3*, 230-245. (b)

Mithaug, D. E., & Hagmeier, L. D. The development of procedures to assess prevocational competencies of severely handicapped young adults. *AAESPH Review*, 1978, *3*, 94-115.

Moos, R. H. A situational analysis of a therapeutic community milieu. *Journal of Abnormal Psychology*, 1968, *73*, 49-61.

Moos, R. H. Sources of variance in responses to questionnaires and in behavior. *Journal of Abnormal Psychology*, 1969, *74*, 405-412.

Moos, R. H. *Evaluating treatment environments*. Toronto: John Wiley & Sons, 1974.

Moos, R. H. *Evaluating correctional and community settings*. New York: John Wiley & Sons, 1975.

Moos, R. H., & Moos, B. S. A typology of family social environments. *Family Process*, 1976, *15*, 357-371.

Morrissey, J. R. Status of family-care programs. *Mental Retardation*, 1966, *4* (5), 8-11.

Murphy, H. B. Foster home variables and adult outcomes. *Mental Hygiene*, 1964, *48*, 587-599.

Murphy, H., Renee, B., & Luchins, D. Foster homes: The new back wards? *Canada's Mental Health*, Monograph Supplement No. 71, 1972.

Murphy, J. G., & Datel, W. E. A cost-benefit analysis of community versus institutional living. *Hospital and Community Psychiatry*, 1976, *27*, 165-176.

National Association for Retarded Citiznes. *National Forum on Residential Services*. Arlington, TX: National Association for Retarded Citizens, 1976.

National Association of Superintendents of Public Residential Facilities for the Mentally Retarded. *Residential programming: Position statements*. Washington, D. C.: President's Committee on Mental Retardation, 1974.

National Center for Law and the Handicapped. *Community living: Zoning obstacles and legal remedies*. South Bend, IN: Legal Monograph, December, 1977.

New York State Association for Retarded Children v. Rockefeller, E.D.N.Y., 357 F. Supp. 752, 762-763, 1973.

Nietupski, J., & Williams, W. Teaching severely handicapped students to use the telephone to initiate selected recreational activities and to respond appropriately to telephone requests to engage in selected recreational activities. In L. Brown, T. Crowner, W. Williams & R. York (Eds.), *A collection of papers and programs related to public school services for severely handicapped students*. Madison, WI: Madison Public School System, 1974.

Nihira, K. Dimensions of adaptive behavior in institutionalized mentally retarded children and adults: Developmental perspective. *American Journal of Mental Deficiency*, 1976, *81*, 215-226.

Nihira, K., Foster, R., Shellhaas, M., & Leland, H. *American Association on Mental Deficiency Adaptive Behavior Scale*. Washington, D.C.: American Association on Mental Deficiency, 1974.

Nihira, L., & Nihira, K. Jeopardy in community placement. *American Journal of Mental Deficiency*, 1975, *79*, 538-544. (a)

Nihira, L., & Nihira, K. Normalized behavior in community placement. *Mental Retardation*, 1975, *13* (2), 9-13. (b)

Nirje, B. The normalization principle and its human management implications. In R. Kugel & W. Wolfensberger (Eds.), *Changing patterns in residential services for the mentally retarded*. Washington, D. C.: President's Committee on Mental Retardation, 1969.

Novak, A. R., Heal, L. W., Pilewski, M. E., & Laidlaw, T. *Independent apartment settings for developmentally disabled adults: An empirical analysis*. Paper presented at the annual meeting of the American Association on Mental Deficiency, San Francisco, May, 1980.

O'Connor, G. *Home is a place: A national perspective of community residential facilities for developmentally disabled persons*. Washington, D. C.: American Association on Mental Deficiency, Monograph No. 2, 1976.

Olshansky, S., Johnson, G., & Sternfeld, L. Attitudes of some pediatricians toward the institutionalization of mentally retarded children. *Training School Bulletin*, 1962, *59*, 67–73.

Orr, G. J. Money management in life situations. *Education and Training of the Mentally Retarded*, 1977, *12*, 65–67.

Osgood, C. E., May, W. H., & Miron, M. S. *Cross-cultural universals of affective meaning*. Urbana, IL: University of Illinois Press, 1975.

Page, T. L., Iwata, B. A., & Neef, N. A. Teaching pedestrian skills to retarded persons: Generalization from the classroom to the natural environment. *Journal of Applied Behavior Analysis*, 1976, *9*, 433–444.

Palo Alto Tenants Union v. Morgan: 321 F. Supp. 908, U. S. Dist. Ct., 1970.

Parkes, M. Psycho-social transitions: A field for study. *Social Science and Medicine*, 1971, *5* (2), 101–115.

Payne, J. The deinstitutional backlash. *Mental Retardation*, 1976, *14* (3), 43–45.

Peat, Marwick, Mitchell, & Company. *Community living alternatives for persons with developmental disabilities. Vol. 2: Financial Requirements*. Springfield, IL: Governor's Planning Council on Developmental Disabilities, 1977.

Peniston, E. *An evaluation of the Portage project*. Cooperative Educational Service Agency No. 12, Portage, Wisconsin, 1972.

Penniman, T. L. Initial screening and identification of predictors for possible use in selecting foster mothers for the mentally retarded. *Dissertation Abstracts International*, 1974, *35* (6-A), 3879.

Pense, A. W., Patton, R. E., Camp, J. L., & Kebalo, C. A cohort study of institutionalized young mentally retarded children. *American Journal of Mental Deficiency*, 1961, *66*, 18–22.

Perry, M. A., & Cerreto, M. C. Structured learning training of social skills. *Mental Retardation*, 1977, *15*, 31–34.

Perske, R., & Marquiss, J. Learning to live in an apartment: Retarded adults from institutions and dedicated citizens. *Mental Retardation*, 1973, *11* (5), 18.

Phillips, E. L. Achievement place: Token reinforcement procedures in a home-style rehabilitation setting for "pre-delinquent" boys. *Journal of Applied Behavior Analysis*, 1968, *1*, 213–223.

Phillips, L. *Human adaptation and its failures*. New York: Academic Press, 1968.

Pinneau, S. R. The infantile disorders of hospitalism and anaclitic depression. *Psychological Bulletin*, 1955, *52*, 429–452. (a)

Pinneau, S. R. Reply to Dr. Spitz. *Psychological Bulletin*, 1955, *52*, 459–462. (b)

Planning and Zoning Commission of the Town of Westport v. Synanon Foundation, Inc. 153 Conn. 305, Jan. 1966.

Polivka, C. H., Marvin, W. E., Brown, J. L., & Polivka, L. J. Selected characteristics, services, and movement of group home residents. *Mental Retardation*, 1979, *17* (5), 227–230.

Pollock, H. M. Family care of mental defectives in Scotland. *American Journal of Mental Deficiency,* 1936, *20,* 414-423.

President's Committee on Mental Retardation. *President's Committee on Mental Retardation Gallup pool shows attitudes on mental retardation improving.* Washington, D. C.: President's Committee on Mental Retardation Message, April, 1975.

President's Committee on Mental Retardation. *A plan for deinstitutionalization of mentally retarded persons.* Washington, D. C.: President's Committee on Mental Retardation, 1976.

President's Panel on Mental Retardation. *A proposed program for national action to combat mental retardation.* Washington, D. C.: U. S. Superintendent of Documents, 1962.

Public Law 93-112, Rehabilitation Act of 1973, as amended by P. L. 93-516. Federal Register, Vol. 42, No. 86, Part IV, PP. 22675-22702, May 4, 1977.

Rago, Jr., W. V. On the transfer of the PMR. *Mental Retardation,* 1976, *14* (2), 27.

Rainwater, L. Neutralizing the disinherited: Some psychological aspects of understanding the poor. In V. L. Allen (Ed.), *Psychological factors in poverty.* Chicago: Markham, 1970.

Rappaport, J. *Community psychology: Values, research, and action.* New York: Holt, Rinehart, and Winston, 1977.

Raush, H., Dittmann, A., & Taylor, T. Person, setting, and change in social interaction. *Human Relations,* 1959, *12,* 361-378.

Rees, N. S. Pragmatics of language: Applications to normal and disordered language development. In R. L. Schiefelbusch (Ed.), *Bases of language intervention.* Baltimore: University Park Press, 1978.

Reiff, R. R. From swampcott to swamp. *Division of Community Psychology Newsletter,* 1971, *4,* 1-3.

Retherford, R. Selected characteristics of foster parents and acceptance of the postinstitutional retardate into the family structure. *Dissertation Abstracts International,* 1975, *35* (7-A), 4289.

Rich, M. Foster homes for retarded children. *Child Welfare,* 1965, *44,* 392-394.

Risley, T., & Hart, B. Developing correspondence between verbal and nonverbal behavior of preschool children. *Journal of Applied Behavior Analysis,* 1968, *1,* 267-281.

Robinson-Wilson, M. A. Picture recipe cards: An approach to teaching severely and profoundly retarded adults to cook. *Education and Training of the Mentally Retarded,* 1977, *12,* 69-73.

Rogers-Warren, A. R., & Baer, D. M. Correspondence between saying and doing: Teaching children to share and praise. *Journal of Applied Behavior Analysis,* 1976, *9,* 335-354.

Rosen, M., Clark, G., & Kivitz, M. *The history of mental retardation: Collected papers.* Baltimore: University Park Press, 1976.

Rosen, M., Diggory, J. C., & Werlinsky, B. E. Goal-setting and expectancy of success in institutionalized and noninstitutionalized mental subnormals. *American Journal of Mental Deficiency,* 1966, *71,* 249-255.

Rosen, M., & Kivitz, M. S. Beyond normalization: Psychological adjustment. *British Journal of Mental Subnormality,* 1973, *19,* 64-70.

Rosenberg, N. S., & Friedman, P. R. Developmental disability law: A look into the future. *Stanford Law Review,* 1979, *13* (4), 817-829.

Rothbart, M. Perceiving social injustice: Observations on the relationship between liberal attitudes and proximity to social problems. *Journal of Applied Social Psychology,* 1973, *3,* 291-302.

Rusch, F. R. A functional analysis of the relationship between attending and producing in a vocational training program. *Journal of Special Education,* 1979, *13,* 399-411. (a)

Rusch, F. R. Toward the validation of social-vocational survival skills. *Mental Retardation,* 1979, *17,* 143-149. (b)

Rusch, F. R., Connis, R. T., & Sowers, J. The modification and maintenance of time spent attending using social reinforcement and response cost in an applied restaurant setting. *Journal of Special Education Technology,* 1979, *2,* 18-26.

Rusch, F. R., & Mithaug, D. E. *Vocational training for mentally retarded adults: A behavior analytic approach.* Champaign, IL: Research Press, 1980.

Rusch, F. R., Schutz, R. P., & Heal, L. W. The impact of setting on non-sheltered work behavior: A recommendation. In M. J. Begab, R. B. Edgerton, & K. Kernan (Eds.), *The impact of specific settings on the development and behavior of retarded persons.* Baltimore: University Park Press, in press.

Rusch, F. R., Schutz, R. P., Lamson, D. S., & Menchetti, B. M. *Vocational training and employment program: Interim report.* Department of Special Education, University of Illinois, Urbana, Illinois, 1979.

Rusch, F. R., Weithers, J. A., Menchetti, B. M., & Schutz, R. P. Social validation of a program to reduce topic repetition in a non-sheltered setting. *Education and Training of the Mentally Retarded,* in press.

Rutman, I. D., & Piasecki, J. R. *A national survey of community-based residential facilities.* Philadelphia, PA: Horizon House Institute, 1976.

Ryan, W. *Blaming the victim.* New York: Random House, 1971.

Sarason, S. B. *The creation of settings and the future societies.* San Francisco: Jossey-Bass, 1972.

Savino, M., Sterns, P., Merwin, E., & Kennedy, R. The lack of service to the retarded through community mental health programs. *Community Mental Health Journal,* 1973, *9,* 158-168.

Schalock, R. L. Can we train for and predict successful community living? Paper presented at the annual meeting of the American Association for the Education of the Severely/Profoundly Handicapped, Baltimore, October, 1978.

Schalock, R. L. *Independent living screening test standardization manual.* Hastings, NB: Mid-Nebraska Mental Retardation Services, 1979. (a)

Schalock, R. L. A systems analysis approach to client and program evaluation. In R. L. Schalock (Ed.), *A model comprehensive service delivery system for persons with developmental disabilities.* Springfield, Illinois: Governor's Planning Council on Developmental Disabilities, 1979. (b)

Schalock, R. L., & Harper, R. S. Three-track approach to programming in a rural community-based mental retardation program. In P. Mittler (Ed.), *Research to practice in mental retardation.* Baltimore: University Park Press, 1977.

Schalock, R. L., & Harper, R. S. Placement from community-based MR programs: How well do clients do? *American Journal of Mental Deficiency,* 1978, *83* (3), 240-247.

Scheerenberger, R. Generic services for the mentally retarded and their families. *Mental Retardation,* 1970, *8* (6), 10-16.

Scheerenberger, R. C. A model for deinstitutionalization. *Mental Retardation,* 1974, *12,* 3-7.

Scheerenberger, R. *Current trends and status of public residential services for the mentally retarded: 1974.* Madison, WI: National Association of Superintendents of Public Residential Facilities for the Mentally Retarded, Central Wisconsin Center for the Developmentally Disabled, 1975.

Scheerenberger, R. C. *Deinstitutionalization and institutional reform.* Springfield, IL: Charles C Thomas, 1976. (a)

Scheerenberger, R. C. *Public residential services for the mentally retarded.* Madison, WI: National Association of Superintendents of Public Residential Facilities for the Mentally Retarded, Central Wisconsin Center for the Developmentally Disabled, 1976. (b) Also available in N. R. Ellis (Ed.), *International Review of Research in Mental Retardation,* Vol. 9. New York: Academic Press, 1978.

Scheerenberger, R. C. Deinstitutionalization in perspective. In J. Paul, D. Stedman & G. Neufeld (Eds.), *Deinstitutionalization: Program and policy development*. Syracuse, NY: Syracuse University Press, 1977.

Scheerenberger, R. C. *Public residential services for the mentally retarded*. Madison, WI: National Association of Superintendents of Public Residential Facilities for the Mentally Retarded, Central Wisconsin Center for the Developmentally Disabled, 1978.

Scheerenberger, R. C., & Felsenthal, D. Community settings for mentally retarded persons: Satisfaction and activities. *Mental Retardation*, 1977, *15* (4), 3-7.

Schlanger, B. Speech examination of a group of institutionalized mentally handicapped children. *Journal of Speech and Hearing Disorders*, 1953, *18*, 339-349.

Schroeder, S. Parametric effects of reinforcement frequency, amount of reinforcement, and required response force on sheltered workshop behavior. *Journal of Applied Behavioral Analysis*, 1972, *5*, 431-441.

Schutz, R. P., Keller, K. F., Rusch, F. R., & Lamson, D. S. *The use of contingent pre-instruction and social validation in the acquisition, generalization, and maintenance of sweeping and mopping responses*. Unpublished manuscript, 1979.

Schutz, R. P., Rusch, F. R., & Lamson, D. S. Evaluation of an employee's procedure to eliminate unacceptable behavior on the job. *Community Services Forum*, 1979, *1*, 4-5.

Schutz, R., Wehman, P., Renzaglia, A., & Karan, O. Efficacy of contingent social disapproval on inappropriate verbalizations of two severely retarded males. *Behavior Therapy*, 1978, *9*, 657-662.

Schwindler, W. *Court and constitution of the 20th century*. New York: Bobbs, 1974.

Seaman, J. A. Right up their alley. *Teaching Exceptional Children*, 1973, *5*, 196-198.

Seevers, C. J. An evaluation of the effects of group home living. *REAP*, 1975, *1* (1-2), 51-65.

Segal, R. Trends in services for the aged mentally retarded. *Mental Retardation*, 1977, *15*, 25-27.

Segal, R., & Aviram, U. Community based sheltered care for the mentally ill: A viable alternative to chronic hospital care. In P. Ahmed & S. Plog (Eds.), *State mental hospitals: What happens when they close*. New York: Plenum, 1976.

Sells, C. J., & West, M. A. Interdisciplinary clinics for the developmentally disabled. *Mental Retardation*, 1976, *14* (5), 19-21.

Shafter, A. J. Criteria for selecting institutionalized mental defectives for vocational placement. *American Journal of Mental Deficiency*, 1957, *61*, 599-616.

Shearer, M. S., & Shearer, D. E. The Portage Project: A model for early childhood education. *Exceptional Children*, 1972, *36*, 217-220.

Shelton v. Tucker. 364 U. S. 479, 488, 1960.

Sievers, D., & Essa, S. Language development in institutionalized and community mentally retarded children. *American Journal of Mental Deficiency*, 1961, *66*, 413-420.

Sigelman, C. K. A Machiavelli for planners: Community attitudes and selection of a group home site. *Mental Retardation*, 1976, *14* (1), 26-29.

Sigelman, C., & Bell, N. *The role of the social environment in community adjustment*. Paper presented at the annual meeting of the American Association on Mental Deficiency, Portland, Oregon, May, 1975.

Sigelman, C., Bell, N., Schoenrock, C., Elias, S., & Danker-Brown, P. *Alternative community placements and outcomes*. Paper presented at the annual meeting of the American Association on Mental Deficiency, Denver, May, 1978.

Sigelman, C. K., Schoenrock, C. J., Spanhel, C. L., Hromas, S. G., Winer, J. L., Budd, E. C., & Martin, P. W. Surveying mentally retarded persons: Responsiveness and response validity in three samples. *American Journal of Mental Deficiency*, 1980, *84* (5), 479-486.

Sinclair, N. Cross country skiing for the mentally retarded. *Challenge*, 1975, *5*, 33-35.

Sipe, N. W. *Accounting system for groups for developmentally disabled persons.* (Working Paper No. 97) Eugene, OR: University of Oregon Research and Training Center in Mental Retardation, 1976.

Sirkin, J., & Lyons, W. F. A study of speech defects in mental deficiency. *American Journal of Mental Deficiency,* 1941, *46,* 74-80.

Sitkei, E. G. *A two year follow-up on mobility rates for a sample of group homes for developmentally disabled persons, or after group home living—what alternatives?* Paper presented at the annual meeting of the American Association on Mental Deficiency, Chicago, June, 1976.

Sitton, M. *Housekeeping management assistant manual for training of the mentally retarded.* Lubbock, TX: Texas Tech University, 1972.

Skarnulis, L. Less restrictive alternatives in residential services. *AAESPH Review,* 1976, *3* (1), 42-84.

Skeels, H. M. Adult status of children with contrasting early life experiences. *Monographs of the Society for Research in Child Development,* 1966, *31* (3), 1-65.

Skeels, H. M., & Dye, H. B. A study of the effects of differential stimulation on mentally retarded children. *Proceedings and Addresses of the American Association on Mental Deficiency,* 1939, *44,* 114-136.

Skinner, B. F. *Verbal behavior,* New York: Appleton, Century, Crofts, 1957.

Skodak, M., & Skeels, H. M. A follow-up study of children in adoptive homes. *Journal of Genetic Psychology,* 1945, *66,* 21-58.

Sloan, W., & Harmon, H. H. Constancy of IQ in mental defectives. *Journal of Genetic Psychology,* 1947, *71,* 177-185.

Sloop, E. W., & Kennedy, W. A. Institutionalized retarded nocturnal enuretics treated by a conditioning technique. *American Journal of Mental Deficiency,* 1973, *77,* 717-721.

Smith, M., & Meyers, A. Telephone-skills training for retarded adults: Group and individual demonstrations with and without verbal instruction. *American Journal of Mental Deficiency,* 1979, *83,* 581-587.

Snyder, L. K., Lovitt, T. C., & Smith, J. O. Language training for the severely retarded: Five years of behavior analysis research. *Exceptional Children,* 1975, *42,* 7-15.

Soforenko, A. Z., & Macy, T. W. *A study of the characteristics and life status of persons discharged from a large state institution for the mentally retarded during the years 1969-1977.* Orient, Ohio: Orient State Institute, 1977.

Soforenko, A. Z., & Macy, T. W. Living arrangements of MR/DD persons discharged from an institutional setting. *Mental Retardation,* 1978, *16* (3), 269-270.

Soloyanis, G. Chronicle. In J. Wortis (Ed.), *Mental retardation: An annual review, IV.* New York: Grune & Stratton, 1972.

Soloyanis, G., & Yoder, S. Chronicle: 1972. In J. Wortis (Ed.), *Mental retardation and developmental disabilities: An annual review, V.* New York: Brunner/Mazel, 1973.

Soloyanis, G., & Yoder, S. Chronicle: 1973-1974. In J. Wortis (Ed.), *Mental retardation and developmental disabilities: An annual review, VII.* New York: Brunner/Mazel, 1975.

Song, A. Y., & Song, R. H. Prediction of job efficiency of institutionalized retardates in the community. *American Journal of Mental Deficiency,* 1969, *73,* 567-571.

Southeastern Community College v. Davis. No. 78-711, U.S. Supreme Court, June 11, 1979.

Sowers, J., Rusch, F. R., Connis, R. T., & Cummings, L. E. Teaching mentally retarded adults to time manage in a vocational setting. *Journal of Applied Behavior Analysis,* 1980, *13,* 119-128.

Sowers, J., Rusch, F. R., & Hudson, C. Training a severely retarded young adult to ride the city bus to and from work. *AAESPH Review,* 1979, *4,* 15-23.

Sowers, J., Thompson, L. E., & Connis, R. T. The food service vocational training program: A model for training and placement of the mentally retarded. In G. T. Bellamy, G. O'Connor & O. C. Karan (Eds.), *Vocational rehabilitation of severely handicapped persons*. Baltimore: University Park Press, 1979.

Spitz, R. A. Hospitalization: An inquiry into the genesis of psychiatric conditions in early childhood. In O. Fenichel *et al.* (Eds.), *The psychoanalytic study of the child, Vol. 1*. New York: International Universities Press, 1945.

Spitz, R. A. Hospitalism: A follow-up report on investigation described in Vol. 1, 1945. In O. Fenichel *et al.* (Eds.), *The psychoanalytic study of the child, Vol. 2* New York: International Universities Press, 1946.

Stedman, D. J. Introduction. In J. L. Paul, D. J. Stedman & G. R. Neufeld (Eds.), *Deinstitutionalization: Program and policy development*. Syracuse, NY: Syracuse University Press, 1977.

Stedman, D. J., & Eichorn, D. H. A comparison of the growth and development of institutionalized and home-reared monogoloids during infancy and early childhood. *American Journal of Mental Deficiency*, 1964, *69*, 391-401.

Sternlicht, M. Variables affecting foster care placement of institutionalized retarded residents. *Mental Retardation*, 1978, *16* (1), 25-27.

Stremel-Campbell, K., Cantrell, D., & Halle, J. Manual signing as a language system and as a speech initiator for the nonverbal severely handicapped student. In E. Sontag, J. Smith, & N. Certo (Eds.), *Educational programming for the severely and profoundly handicapped*. Reston, VA: Division on Mental Retardation, Council on Exceptional Children, 1977.

Striefel, S., Bryan, K. S., & Atkins, D. S. Transfer of stimulus control from motor to verbal stimuli. *Journal of Applied Behavior Analysis*, 1974, *7*, 123-135.

Striefel, S., & Wetherby, B. Instruction-following behavior of a retarded child and its controlling stimuli. *Journal of Applied Behavior Analysis*, 1973, *6*, 663-670.

Striefel, S., Wetherby, B., & Karlan, G. R. Establishing generative verb-noun instruction-following skills in retarded children. *Journal of Experimental Child Psychology*, 1976, *22*, 247-260.

Striefel, S., Wetherby, B., & Karlan, G. R. Developing generalized instruction-following behavior in the severely retarded. In C. E. Meyers (Ed.), *Quality of life in profoundly and severely retarded persons: Research foundation for improvement*. (American Association on Mental Deficiency Monograph Series No. 3.) Washington, D. C.: American Association on Mental Deficiency, 1978.

Tarjan, B. Mental retardation and the organization of services. *Psychiatric Annals*, 1976, *6* (7).

Tarjan, G., Wright, S. W., Eyman, R. K., & Keeran, C. V. Natural history of mental retardation: Some aspects of epidemiology. *American Journal of Mental Deficiency*, 1973, *77* (4), 369-379.

Tavris, E. An attempt to distinguish between "successful" and unsuccessful separation groups in a hospital for mentally retarded patients. *Training School Bulletin*, 1964, *60*, 184-191.

Terman, L. M., & Merrill, M. A. *Stanford-Binet Intelligence Scale: Manual for the Third Revision, Form L-M*. Boston: Houghton Mifflin, 1973.

Throne, J. M. Normalization through the normalization principle: Right ends, wrong means. *Mental Retardation*, 1975, *13*, 23-25.

Tinsley, D. J., O'Connor, G., & Halpern, A. S. *The identification of problem areas in the establishment and maintenance of community residential facilities for the developmentally disabled*. Eugene, OR: Rehabilitation and Training Center on Mental Retardation. Working paper No. 64, 1973.

Tizard, B., & Rees, J. The development of children whose first two years of life were spent in institutional care. *Child Development*, 1974, *45*, 92-99.

Tizard, J., & Grad, J. *The mentally handicapped and their families.* London: Oxford University Press, 1961.

Townsend, P. W., & Flanagan, J. Experimental preadmission program to encourage home care for severely and profoundly retarded children. *American Journal of Mental Deficiency,* 1976, *80,* 562–569.

Trace, M. W., Cuvo, A. J., & Criswell, J. L. Teaching coin equivalence to the mentally retarded. *Journal of Applied Behavior Analysis,* 1977, *10,* 85–92.

Treffry, D., Martin, G., Samels, J., & Watson, C. Operant conditioning of grooming behavior of severely retarded girls. *Mental Retardation,* 1970, *8,* 29–33.

Turnbull, H. R., & Turnbull, A. *Free appropriate public education: Law and implementation.* Denver, Colo.: Love Publishing Co., 1978.

Village of Belle Terre v. Borras. 416 U. S. 1, 39 L. Ed. 2d 797, 94 S. Ct. 1536 (1974).

Vogelsberg, R. T., Anderson, J., Berger, P., Haselden, T., Mitwell, S., Schmidt, C., Skowron, A., Ulett, D., & Wilcox, B. Selecting, setting up, and surviving in an independent living situation: An inventory and instructional approach for handicapped individuals. *AAESPH Review,* 1980, *5* (1), 38–54.

Vogelsberg, R. T., & Rusch, F. R. Training severely handicapped students to cross partially controlled intersections. *AAESPH Review,* 1979, *4,* 264–273.

Vurdelja-Maglajlic, D., & Jordan, J. E. Attitude-behaviors toward retardation of mothers of retarded and non-retarded in four nations. *Training School Bulletin,* 1974, *71,* 17–29.

Vygotsky, L. S. *Thought and language.* Cambridge, Mass.: M.I.T. Press, 1962.

Watzlawick, P., Weakland, J. H., & Fisch, R. *Change: Principles of problem formation and problem resolution.* New York: Norton, 1974.

Wechsler, D. *The measurement and appraisal of adult intelligence.* 4th ed. Baltimore: Williams & Wilkins, 1958.

Wehbring, K., & Ogren, C. *Community residences for mentally retarded people.* Arlington, TX: National Association for Retarded Citizens, 1975.

Wehman, P. Effects of token reinforcement on monitoring oral hygiene skills in geriatric retarded women. *Training School Bulletin,* 1974, *71,* 39–40.

Wehman, P. Research on leisure time and the severely developmentally disabled. *Rehabilitation Literature,* 1977, *38,* 98–105.

Wehman, P. Effects of different environmental conditions on leisure time activity of the severely and profoundly handicapped. *Journal of Special Education,* 1978, *12,* 183–193.

Wehman, P., & Marchant, J. A. Developing gross motor recreational skills in children with severe behavioral handicaps. *Therapeutic Recreation Journal,* 1977, *11,* 48–54.

Wehman, P., Renzaglia, A., Berry, G., Schutz, R., & Karan, O. Developing a leisure skill repertoire in severely and profoundly handicapped persons. *AAESPH Review,* 1978, *3,* 162–172.

Welsch v. Likens, 344 F. Supp. 487, D. Minn., 1974, Aff'd. in part, remanded in part on other grounds, 550 F. 2d 1122, 8th cir., 1977.

Wheeler, L. R. The intelligence of East Tennessee mountain children. *Journal of Educational Psychology,* 1932, *23,* 351–370.

Whitman, T. L., Zakaras, M., & Chardos, S. Effects of reinforcement and guidance procedures on instruction-following behavior of severely retarded children. *Journal of Applied Behavior Analysis,* 1971, *4,* 283–290.

Wicker, T. *A time to die.* New York: Quadrangle, 1975.

Wiegerink, R., & Pelosi, J. W. *Developmental disabilities: The DD movement.* Baltimore: Paul H. Brookes Publishers, 1979.

Willer, B. *Post-institutional adjustment of the retarded returned to the natural families.* Paper presented at the annual convention of the American Association on Mental Deficiency, Denver, May, 1978.

Willer, B. S., Atkinson, A. C., & Intagliata, J. C. *The crisis of deinstitutionalization for families of the mentally retarded.* Paper presented at the annual meeting of the American Psychological Association, San Francisco, 1977.

Willer, B., & Intagliata, J. Deinstitutionalization of mentally retarded persons in New York State: Final report. Buffalo, N.Y.: State University, Division of Community Psychiatry, 1980.

Windle, C. Prognosis of mental subnormals. *American Journal of Mental Deficiency,* 1962, *66,* Monograph Supplement.

Windle, C., Stewart, E., & Brown, E. Reasons for community failure of released patients. *American Journal of Mental Deficiency,* 1961, *66,* 213–217.

Winer, B. J. *Statistical principles in experimental design.* 2nd ed. New York: McGraw Hill Book Co., 1971.

Wolf, M. M. Social validity: The case for subjective measurement or how applied behavior analysis is finding its heart. *Journal of Applied Behavior Analysis,* 1978, *11,* 203–214.

Wolfensberger, W. A new approach to decision making in human management services. In R. B. Kugel & W. Wolfensberger (Eds.), *Changing patterns in residential services for the mentally retarded.* Washington, D. C.: President's Committee on Mental Retardation, 1969.

Wolfensberger, W. The principle of normalization and its implications to psychiatric services. *American Journal of Psychiatry,* 1970, *127,* 291–297.

Wolfensberger, W. Will there always be an institution? II: The impact of new service models. *Mental Retardation,* 1971, *9,* 31–38.

Wolfensberger, W. *The principle of normalization in human services.* Toronto: National Institute on Mental Retardation, 1972.

Wolfensberger, W. The origin and nature of our institutional models. In R. B. Kugel & A. Shearer (Eds.), *Changing patterns in residential services for the mentally retarded* (Rev. ed.) (040-000-003-65-7, President's Committee on Mental Retardation). Washington, D. C.: U. S. Government Printing Office, 1976.

Wolfensberger, W. Definition of normalization—update, problems, disagreements, and misunderstandings. In R. J. Flynn & K. E. Nitsch (Eds.), *Normalization, social integration, and community services.* Baltimore: University Park Press, 1980.

Wolfensberger, W., & Glenn, L. *PASS 3. Program analysis of service systems field manual.* Toronto: National Institute on Mental Retardation, 1975. (a)

Wolfensberger, W., & Glenn, L. *PASS 3. Program analysis of service systems handbook.* Toronto: National Institute on Mental Retardation, 1975. (b)

Wolfensberger, W., & Menolascino, F. Reflections on recent mental retardation developments in Nebraska: A new plan. *Mental Retardation,* 1970, *8,* 20–27.

Wolfson, I. Follow-up studies of 92 male and 131 female patients who were discharged from the Newark State School in 1946. *American Journal of Mental Deficiency,* 1956, *61,* 224–238.

Wolins, M. Licensing and recent developments in foster care. *Child Welfare,* 1968, *47,* 570–583.

Wolpert, J. *Group homes for the mentally retarded: An investigation of neighborhood property impacts.* Study prepared for the New York State Office of Mental Retardation and Developmental Disabilities, August, 1978.

Wyatt v. Hardin. No. 3195-N (M. D. Ala., Feb. 28, 1975, modified July 1, 1975).

Wyatt v. Stickney, 344 F. Supp. 373, 344 F. Supp. 387 (M. D. Ala. 1972), aff'd sub nom. *Wyatt v. Aderholt,* 503 F. 2d. 1305 (5th Cir. 1974).

Wyngaarden, M., Freedman, R., & Gollay, E. *Descriptive data on the community experiences of deinstitutionalized mentally retarded persons.* Vol. IV of *A study of the community adjustment of deinstitutionalized mentally retarded persons.* Contract No. OEC-0-74-9183, U. S. Office of Education. Cambridge, MA: Abt Associates, Inc., 1976.

Wyngaarden, M., & Gollay, E. *Profiles of national deinstitutionalization patterns 1972-1974*. Vol. II of *A study of the community adjustment of deinstitutionalized mentally retarded persons*. Cambridge, Mass.: Abt Associates, 1976.

Yaron, A. *Final report: A project to evaluate the effectiveness of resocialization for mentally retarded discharged from institutions and other segregated environments; July, 1971-June, 1974*. Denver, CO: State of Colorado Division of Developmental Disabilities, 1974.

Zigler, E., & Balla, D. Developmental course of responsiveness to social reinforcement in normal children and institutionalized retarded children. *Developmental Psychology*, 1972, *6*, 66-73.

Zigler, E., & Balla, D. *Motivation and the retarded person*. Paper presented at the Gatlinburg Conference on Mental Retardation, Gatlinburg, Tennessee, March, 1978.

Zigler, E., Balla, D., & Butterfield, E. C. A longitudinal investigation of the relationship between preinstitutional social deprivation and social motivation in institutionalized retardates. *Journal of Personality and Social Psychology*, 1968, *10*, 437-445.

Zigler, E., Balla, D., & Watson, N. Developmental and experiential determinants of self-image disparity in institutionalized and noninstitutionalized retarded and normal children. *Journal of Personality and Social Psychology*, 1972, 23, 81-87.

Zigler, E., Butterfield, E. C., & Capobianco, F. Institutionalization and the effectiveness of social reinforcement: A five- and eight-year follow-up study. *Developmental Psychology*, 1970, *3*, 255-263.

Zigler, E., Butterfield, E. E., & Goff, G. A measure of preinstitutional social deprivation for institutionalized retardates. *American Journal of Mental Deficiency*, 1966, *70*, 873-885.

Zigler, E., & Williams, J. Institutionalization and the effectiveness of social reinforcement: A three-year follow-up study. *Journal of Abnormal Social Psychology*, 1963, *66*, 197-205.

Zimmerman, J., Overpeck, C., Eisenberg, J., & Garlick, B. Operant conditioning in a sheltered workshop. *Rehabilitation Literature*, 1969, *30*, 326-334.

Zusman, J., & Lamb, R. In defense of community mental health. *American Journal of Psychiatry*, 1977, *134*, 887-890.

Index

Adaptive Behavior Scale, in evaluation of individual skill and social competence, 145
Adaptive skills and training, for community placement, 108-116
Adjustment, of developmentally disabled individuals to community living
  and age at admission, 33
  and characteristics of community environment, 66
  and characteristics of residential service system, 69-71
  and generic services, 83-88
  and interaction between individual and setting, 71-73
  and prerelease training, 63-65
  and role of benefactors, 66-69
  factors correlating with success, 59-63
  success in relation to IQ, 59
Age at admission, and placement success, 33
Alternative placement, 11-16
Attention measures, in environmentally deprived subjects, 30
Attitude research, 97
Attitudes, of community toward residential alternatives, 97-102
Average costs, in determining true cost of CRF, 159

Benefactors, role in community adjustment of individual, 66-69
Boarding homes, definition, 50
Building types, of CRFs, 53

Camelot Behavioral Checklist for evaluation of individual skill and social competence, 146
Caretakers, of CRFs, characteristics of, 54
Case law, as foundation for community integration, 173-175

City of White Plains v. Ferraioli and zoning barriers to deinsitutionalization, 178
Client satisfaction, in evaluation of community placement, 147-149
Community adjustment (*see* Adjustment, of developmentally disabled individuals to community living)
Community integration (*see* Integration)
Community mental health novement, compared to deinstitutionalization, 3-6
Community reaction, in community care facilities, 15
Community residential facilities (CRFs)
  as alternative placement, 14-15
  building types, 53
  characteristics of, 196-197
  characteristics of caretakers, 54
  characteristics of ideal site, 92
  characteristics of residents, 51-52
  classification system, 48-51
  cost comparison with PRF, 157-162
  major difficulties, 15
  release policies and client characteristics, 197
  role in normalization, 54-56
  state licensing regulations, 166-170
  success rate, 14
  summary of state requirements (table), 167
Community support services, 17-19
Connecticut Association for Retarded Citizens v. Mansfield Training School, and parental backlash reaction to deinstitutionalization, 183
Convalescent home, definition, 48
Cost accounting, in determining true costs of CRFs, 155-157
Cost-effective analysis, for CFFs, 159-162
Costs
  comparison between PRFs and CRFs, 157-162
  of services, evaluation of, 151-162

235

236 / INDEX

Cost studies, for residential alternatives, 152-155
Cotton v. Evangelist Temple Homes Inc., and discrimination in public housing, 179
County home, definition, 550

Deinstitutionalization
  and community mental health movement, 3-6
  backlash reaction to, 181-189
  empirical support for, 193-196
  litigation and legal action, 6-9
  studies of (table), 46-47
Deinstitutionalized individuals, characteristics of, 58-59
Deprivation, persistent, effects of, 26
Developmental delays, and environmental deprivation, 22-34
Discrimination, and public housing, litigation, 179-180
Domestic skills, as adaptive training for community placement, 110
Domiciliary costs, economic value in determining true cost of CRF, 158
Domiciliary funds, 157
Driscoll v. Goldberg, and zoning barriers to deinstitutionalization, 178
"Dumping," and backlash reaction to deinstitutionalization, 185-187

Education, of CRF residents within community, 96
Egalitarianism, as alternative to normalization, 41
Employment, of CRF residents within community, 96
Eligibility, for residential admissions, legal restrictions, 7-9
Environment, community, and relation to placement success, 66-71
Environmental enrichment, role in prevention of mental retardation, 25
Environmental deprivation, and developmental delays, 22-34
  and irreversible retardation, 26
  and learning differences between institutionalized and noninstitutionalized individuals, 30
  and self-image, 32
  and social responsiveness, 33
  methodology for study, 27

  motivation and attention, 30
  speech and language development, 32
Evaluation of individual skill and social competence, 145-147
Evaluation tools (*see* Measurement devices)
Expressive language training, implications for community integration, 132

Facility size, and service planning, 200
Family Care, as alternative placement, 11-13
  factors predictive of success, 12
  locating providers, 13
Federal legislation, history, 163-165
Foster home, definition, 48
Friendships, of CRF residents within community, 95
Friend's home, definition, 48

Generalization, in instruction-following training, 125
Generic services
  and degree of community adjustment, 83-88
  current status, 76
  summary of (table), 79
  type of (table), 80, 86, 87
Gifts, value in estimating true cost of CRF, 158
"Good neighbor" profile, 98-99
Group home, definition, 48

Halderman v. Pennhurst State School and Hospital
  and parental backlash reaction to deinstitutionalization, 183
  and restrictions on eligibility for residential admissions, 8
  as case law foundation for community integration, 174

Ideologies, classification, 35-40
Independent living, definition, 48
Independent Living Screening Test, for evaluation of individual skill and social competence, 146
Independent living skills inventory, 115
Individual skill and social competence, measures of, 145-147

Infants, effects of environmental deprivation, 22
Inferential instructions, in instruction-following training, 128
IQ
  and relation to success in community placement, 59
  correlation with environmental deprivation, 28
Institutional climate, parameters for classification, 34
Institutionalized individuals, characteristics of, 51
Instruction-following training, as receptive language task, 122-130
Integration
  of developmentally disabled individuals into community
    and expressive language training, 132
    case law foundation for, 173-175
    legal barriers to, 175-179
    preparation for, 198
    social, 93-97
  of CRF into community, 91-97
Intellectual development, in environmentally deprived infants, 22
Intermediate care facility (ICF), definition, 48

Language behaviors, 121-137
Learning differences, between institutionalized and noninstitutionalized individuals, 30
Least restrictive alternative, as a legal concept, 174
Legislation, and direct service planning, 195
Legal barriers, to deinstitutionalization, 175-179
Leisure skills and social activities, as adaptive training for community placement, 112
Lessard v. Schmidt, and restrictions on eligibility for residential admissions, 7
Licensing regulations, state, for CRFs, 166-170
Litigation
  and deinstitutionalization, 6-9
  and discrimination in public housing, 179-180
Little Neck Community Association v. Working Organization for Retarded Children (WORC), and zoning barriers to deinstitutionalization, 178
Local zoning ordinances
  and challenging litigation, 178
  and deinstitutionalization, 170-172
Location, of CRFs, 91-93

Marble-in-the-hole task, and environmental deprivation, 29
Marginal costs, in determining true cost of CRF, 159
Measurement devices
  for evaluation of individual skill and social competence, 145-147
  for measuring normalization of facility, 141-144
Mental hospital, definition, 50
Mental health movement, compared to deinstitutionalization, 3-6
Milwaukee Project, in evaluating environmental enrichment, 25
Mobility skills, as adaptive training for community placement, 108-109
Money management skills, as adaptive training for community placement, 111
Mortality, in environmentally deprived infants, 22
Motivation, measures of, in environmentally deprived subjects, 30
Multiple instructions, in instruction-following training, 129

Natural home
  as alternative placement, 15-16
  definition, 48
Neighborhood opposition, 100-102
Normalization
  and direct service planning, 194
  and PASS 3 score, 141
  as an ideology, 38
  as egalitarian alternative, 194
  role in CRFs, 54-56
Nursing home, definition, 50

Operating costs, of CRFs, 157
Opportunism, and backlash reaction to deinstitutionalization movement, 186
Opposition, neighborhood, to CRFs, 100-102

Other relative's home, definition, 48
Others' satisfaction, in evaluation of community placement, 149

Palo Alto Tenants Union v. Morgan, as legal zoning barrier to deinstitutionalization, 177
Parents, and backlash reaction to relocation of handicapped offspring, 183–185
PASS 3
  factor-analytic studies, 143
  as operational definition of normalization, 141
  Short Form, 144
Payment, of natural parents in natural home placement, 16
Placement, alternative, 11–16
Placement success, variables in, 59–63
  and age at admission, 33
  and prerelease training, 63–65
  relation to IQ, 59
Preference, in instruction-following training, 123
Preparation for community living
  programs for, 116
  skills and training, 108–116
Prerelease training, and successful community placement, 63–65
Prevention, of depressed infant development, 23–27
Private residential facility, definition, 50
Program Analysis of Service Systems (*see* PASS 3)
Programs, to prepare for community living, 116
Progress Assessment Charts (PAC) for evaluation of individual skill and social competence, 146
Public housing, and discrimination, litigation, 179–180
Public residential facility (PRF)
  cost comparison with CRF, 157–162
  definition, 50

Readmissions, increase in, and backlash reaction to deinstitutionalization movement, 187
Receptive language training (*see* Instruction-following training)
Redundancy, in instruction-following training, 123

Reform, residential or institutional, 9–11
Release policies, and client characteristics, 197
Relocation, and backlash reaction to deinstitutionalization movement, 181–185
"Relocation syndrome," as reaction to deinstitutionalization, 182
Residential alternatives
  and community attitude, 97–102
  cost studies, 152–155
Residential climate, classification of, 150–151
Residential reform, 9–11
Resident's labor, value in estimating true cost of CRF, 158
Resident's satisfaction, in evaluation of community placement, 147–149
Residents of CRFs, characteristics of, 51, 197
Restrictions, legal, on eligibility for residential admissions, 7–9
Retardation, irreversible, in environmental deprivation, 26
Reversibility, of depressed infant development, 23–27

Selection, of CRF residents, and client characteristics, 197
Self-care skills, as adaptive training for community placement, 110
Self-image, in environmentally deprived subjects, 32
Self-instruction, in expressive language training, 131
Service planning, 193–201
Services
  community support, 17–19
  evaluation of costs, 151–162, 198
  role in community adjustment of individual, 69–71
  use, in assessment of community support services, 18
Services, generic (*see* Generic services)
Shelton v. Tucker, as case law foundation, for community integration, 174
Site selection, and service planning, 201
Size of facility, and service planning, 200
Social activities, of CRF residents within community, 94
Social responsiveness, and environmentally deprived subjects, 33

Southeastern Community College v. Davis, discrimination in public housing, 179
Speech and language development, in environmentally deprived subjects, 32
Staff and parent training, and service planning, 202
State regulations
 and deinstitutionalization, 165–170
 and service planning, 201
Stress, as reaction to relocation, 182
Support services (*see* Services)

Taxonomy, for community residential facilities, 48
Tests (*see* Measurement devices and individual tests)
Telephone skills, as adaptive training for community placement, 112
Training, staff and parents, and service planning, 202
Travel skills, as adaptive training for community placement, 108–109
True cost of services, estimating, 157–162

Uniform functional cost accounting, in human services, 155–157

Village of Belle Terre v. Borras, as legal zoning barrier to deinstitutionalization, 177

Vineland Social Maturity Scale, in evaluation of individual skill and social competence, 145
Vocational skills, as adaptive training for community placement, 113
Volunteer labor, value in estimating true cost of CRF, 158

Welsch v. Likens
 and restrictions on eligibility for residential admissions, 7
 as case law foundation for community integration, 175
Wyatt v. Stickney
 and residential reform, 8, 9
 and restrictions on eligibility for residential admissions, 7
 as case law foundation for community integration, 173, 174
Work placement, definition, 50

Zigler, motivational interpretation of IQ test results in institutional subjects, 29
Zoning
 as legal barrier to deinstitutionalization, 175–179
 local ordinances, and deinstitutionalization, 170–172
 working definition, 175